Walking
Village London

Walking
Village London

ANDREW DUNCAN

ORIGINAL WALKS THROUGH
25 LONDON VILLAGES

NEW
HOLLAND

First published in 1997 by
New Holland Publishers (UK) Ltd
London • Cape Town • Sydney • Auckland

24 Nutford Place
London W1H 6DQ
United Kingdom

80 McKenzie Street
Cape Town 8001
South Africa

14 Aquatic Drive
Frenchs Forest, NSW 2086
Australia

ISBN 1 85974 271 8

Commissioning editor: Jo Hemmings
Editor: Helen Varley
Assistant editor: Sophie Bessemer
Copy editor: Geraldine Christy
Designer (colour section and jacket): Alan Marshall, Wilderness Design
Design consultant (text): Penny Mills
Cartographer: ML Design
Indexer: Alex Corrin

Reproduction by Dot Gradation
Printed and bound in Singapore by Kyodo Printing Co (Singapore) Pte Ltd

Photographic Acknowledgments
All photographs by the author with the exception of the following:
Martin Charles/Dulwich Picture Gallery: Plate 26; English Heritage Photographic Library:
Plate 4; Oliver Lim: Plates 5, 7, 8, 11, 19, 21, 22, 23; Norman Plastow: Plate 35;
The William Morris Gallery: Plate 18.

Front cover: Golden Square, Hampstead, photographed by Oliver Lim.

Contents

Preface 6
Introduction 7
   Choosing villages to visit 9
Key to Route Maps 11
Map of London Villages 12–13

Villages North of the River Thames

Brentford 15
Chipping Barnet and Monken Hadley 20
Chiswick 27
Enfield 33
Hampstead 39
Harrow-on-the-Hill 45
Highgate 50
Isleworth 56
Kensington 62
Pinner 68
Walthamstow 74

Villages South of the River Thames

Barnes 80
Bexley 86
Blackheath 92
Carshalton 98
Dulwich 104
Greenwich 111
Ham and Petersham 117
Kew 124
Mitcham 129
Rotherhithe and Bermondsey 135
Wimbledon 142

Further Information 148
   Opening times 148
   Libraries 154
Bibliography 156
Index 157

Preface

Village London? Sounds like a contradiction in terms, but outside its historic centre of City, Westminster and West End, London is, in fact, a collection of villages, gobbled up when the capital expanded on the backs of the railways in the 19th century.

Many of these once quiet country villages were wiped out by the advancing tide of bricks and mortar. But for various reasons – a powerful preservation society perhaps, or a local shift in the centre of commercial and administrative activity – many also survived. While the surrounding countryside was transformed into a featureless landscape of suburbia, they managed to hang on to their visual identity and historical distinctness.

Were London's villages still to be in the traditional rural setting they once enjoyed, many of them would feature in guide books, and draw hordes of trippers at weekends in search of a good pub lunch and a stroll in the fresh air. But engulfed in London as they are, their charms are overlooked, their delights ignored and the good things they have to offer are left to the locals to appreciate and enjoy.

In a bid to bring their attractions to a wider audience, *Village London* explores 25 of the best of them – I won't say *the* best because there is an element of subjectivity in the choice. Six of the villages are paired with neighbours so there are 22 entries in all. A glance at the map of London villages on pages 12–13 will show that they cover the whole city, north, south, east and west, extending from Kensington and Rotherhithe close to the city centre to Monken Hadley and Carshalton right out on its fringes.

The central London villages – hilly Hampstead with its heath and winding lanes and alleys, Chiswick with its beautiful Mall, Kew with its perfectly preserved 18th-century green – are inevitably slightly less unknown than some of the outer London ones. But anyone who makes a trip out to Carshalton with its ponds forming the source of the Wandle, to Pinner with its wonderful High Street and half-timbered farmhouses, to Mitcham with its historic cricket green, to Petersham with its farm selling eggs and honey, and to Bexley with its beautiful riverside mansion, is in for a whole succession of extremely pleasant surprises.

I have thoroughly enjoyed writing this book, and I hope you get just as much pleasure out of reading and using it. 'Using' is the operative word for the only way to see London is on foot. So get out those trainers and hit the trail: you've only got 25 villages and 65¾ miles to go!

Andrew Duncan
Kensal Green

Introduction

About the book

Each village entry contains two main features: an historical introduction giving a brief account of the origins and development of the village up to the time when it was absorbed into the greater London conurbation – usually sometime in the mid to late 19th century – and a guided walk. The walk explores the old village centre and points out not just the features that survive but also the location of such things as rectories and manor houses that have long since disappeared.

Each entry also has its own essential information listing and a detailed map. The information listing covers distance from central London, rail and Underground connections, main sights, local events, and details of where to eat and drink. The map shows, in addition to the route of the walk and the main sights, the location of public toilets. The maps are detailed enough to make an A–Z atlas of London unnecessary, but it is always a good idea to have one along, if only to identify any places mentioned in the text which are not included in the walks.

Choosing a walk

During the writing of this book I have often pondered on how people will use it. Will they start with the first village and then work through to the end? Will they visit villages close to where they happen to live? Or will they choose those that are easiest to get to? Maybe some museum or historic house will be the deciding factor. And what about visitors to London who do not know the city at all? How will they make their choice?

To help all readers – whether they are capital residents or visitors – I have produced on pages 9 and 10 a set of lists which group villages according to certain categories, for example riverside villages and villages with cricket clubs (a match on a weekend afternoon in summer provides an excellent focal point for a walk in the same way that a museum or historic house does). Using these lists, even the most undecided village explorer should be able to choose which place to visit without too much difficulty.

Further information

At the back of the book further information is provided for the walks. The opening times section starting on page 148 gives addresses, telephone numbers and opening times for places included in the walks which are open to the public. You will know when to consult this section because all the places which have entries in it are highlighted in the body of the book – both in the text and on the maps – in **bold type**. Tourist information centres also appear in the opening times section. These and local libraries have free leaflets on local places of interest, booklets for sale, and collections of books, photographs and other material on local history. In addition, local councils and local history societies often display information about parks, gardens, cemeteries and places of historical interest on notice boards at the entrance. Libraries are listed village by village starting on page 154.

Walking in London

All the walks start and finish at Underground or rail stations for maximum travel convenience. I urge all walkers to use this form of transport. Not only is it much better for the city, but with a bit of planning it is also much easier than going by car, and it adds to the element of adventure in the outing. I have not included bus information because I have found from experience that it soon goes out of date. For the latest information and full advice on routes the easiest thing to do is ring London Transport's 24-hour information service on 0171 222 1234.

The walks range in length from just under 2 miles (3 kilometres) to just over 4 miles (7 kilometres). The average is roughly 3 miles (about 4.8 kilometres). A list of walks in order of length appears on the next page. I find that a 3-mile (4.8-kilometre) walk takes approximately two hours at a gentle pace, not including stops. But of course different people walk at different speeds. Mine is quite quick so slower walkers might find they need more time. Either way, there's never any point in rushing a walk. You never know when you will want to stop and linger, or for how long. My advice is to turn each walk into a day trip, or in summer a long afternoon/early evening excursion. That way you'll really be able to savour the outing and make it an event to remember.

The walks can be done on any day of the week, but bear in mind that the villages will be liveliest on weekdays when all the shops will be open, and that the recreational areas – parks, gardens, commons and other open spaces – will be busiest at weekends, especially in summer.

Walking in London is not like walking in the country. The endless traffic and hordes of people (except in the quietest sections, of which there are fortunately many in the book) are surprisingly tiring, and of course tarmac is a lot harder on the feet than turf. So again, my advice, especially for those not as young as they were, is to take things easy and have frequent stops for rest and refreshment (the refreshment listings at the beginning of each village entry should help here).

On many of the walks you will see coloured wall plaques commemorating people, places and events. The most common are the circular blue plaques first put up by the old Greater London Council and now by English Heritage. Other plaque-providing organizations include local councils and history societies. A surprising amount can be learned from these plaques, some of which are pointed out on the walks.

Choosing villages to visit

Villages by distance from central London (miles/kilometres from Charing Cross)

mi	km	
3	4.8	Kensington
3¾	6	Rotherhithe and Bermondsey
4½	7.2	Hampstead
5	8	Dulwich
5½	8.8	Barnes
5½	8.8	Chiswick
5½	8.8	Greenwich
5½	8.8	Highgate
6½	10.4	Blackheath
7½	12	Kew
7½	12	Walthamstow
7½	12	Wimbledon
8	12.8	Brentford
8½	13.6	Mitcham
9	14.4	Ham and Petersham
10	16	Carshalton
10	16	Isleworth
10½	14.2	Harrow-on-the-Hill
11	17.6	Chipping Barnet and Monken Hadley
11	17.6	Enfield
12½	20	Bexley
13	20.8	Pinner

Villages by length of walk (in miles/kilometres)

mi	km	
1¾	2.8	Hampstead
1¾	2.8	Harrow-on-the-Hill
2	3.2	Kew
2¼	3.6	Kensington
2½	4	Chiswick
2¾	4.4	Carshalton
2¾	4.4	Ham and Petersham (5¾ miles/9.2 kilometres if you walk to and from Richmond)
2¾	4.4	Pinner
2¾	4.4	Walthamstow
3	4.8	Blackheath
3	4.8	Enfield
3	4.8	Isleworth
3	4.8	Mitcham
3	4.8	Barnes
3¼	5.2	Bexley
3½	5.6	Brentford
3½	5.6	Greenwich
3½	5.6	Highgate
3½	5.6	Rotherhithe and Bermondsey
3¾	6	Wimbledon
4	6.4	Chipping Barnet and Monken Hadley
4¼	6.8	Dulwich

Villages beside the River Thames

Barnes
Brentford
Chiswick
Greenwich
Ham and Petersham
Isleworth
Kew
Rotherhithe and Bermondsey

Villages with views

Chipping Barnet and Monken Hadley
Dulwich
Greenwich
Hampstead
Harrow-on-the-Hill
Highgate
Wimbledon

Villages with cricket clubs

Bexley
Kew
Mitcham

Villages beside heaths and commons

Barnes
Blackheath
Chipping Barnet and Monken Hadley
Dulwich
Greenwich
Ham and Petersham
Hampstead
Highgate
Mitcham
Wimbledon

Villages by Underground line/railway station/steamer pier

Underground		**Rail**	
Circle Line	Kensington	Cannon Street	Greenwich
District Line	Chiswick	Charing Cross	Bexley
	Ham and		Blackheath
	Petersham		Greenwich
	Kensington	Kings Cross	Enfield
	Kew	Liverpool Street	Enfield
	Wimbledon		Walthamstow
Docklands Light		London Bridge	Dulwich
Railway	Greenwich		Wimbledon
East London Line	Rotherhithe and	Marylebone	Harrow-on-
	Bermondsey		the-Hill
Metropolitan Line	Harrow-on-	Moorgate	Enfield
	the-Hill	North London Line	Ham and
	Pinner		Petersham
Northern Line	Chipping Barnet		Hampstead
	and Monken		Kew
	Hadley	North London Line	Walthamstow
	Rotherhithe and	Victoria	Carshalton
	Bermondsey		Dulwich
	Hampstead		Mitcham
	Highgate	Waterloo	Barnes
Piccadilly Line	Brentford		Brentford
	Chiswick		Ham and
Victoria Line	Walthamstow		Petersham
			Isleworth
			Kew
Steamer			Mitcham
Charing Cross Pier	Greenwich		Wimbledon
Wesminster Pier	Kew		

Key to Route Maps

Each of the walks in this book is accompanied by a detailed map on which the route of the walk is shown in green. Places of interest along the walks – such as historic houses, museums and churches – are clearly identified. Those that are open to the public appear in **bold type** (as in the text). Opening times are listed village by village at the back of the book, starting on page 148.

The following is a key to symbols and abbreviations used on the maps:

Symbols

- route of walk
- footpath
- railway line
- railway station
- Underground station
- major building
- † church
- public toilets
- viewpoint
- wood

Abbreviations

APP	Approach	PH	Public
AVE	Avenue		House
CLO	Close		(Pub)
COTTS	Cottages	PK	Park
CT	Court	PL	Place
DLR	Docklands	RD	Road
	Light Railway	S	South
DRI	Drive	SQ	Square
E	East	ST	Saint
GDNS	Gardens	ST	Street
GRN	Green	STN	Station
GRO	Grove	TER	Terrace
HO	House	UPR	Upper
LA	Lane	VW	View
LWR	Lower	W	West
MS	Mews	WD	Wood
MT	Mount	WHF	Wharf
N	North	WLK	Walk
PAS	Passage	WY	Way
PDE	Parade		

Map of London Villages

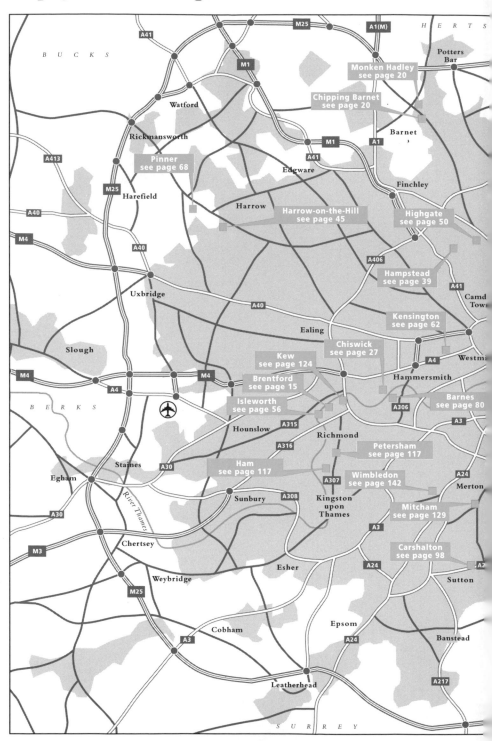

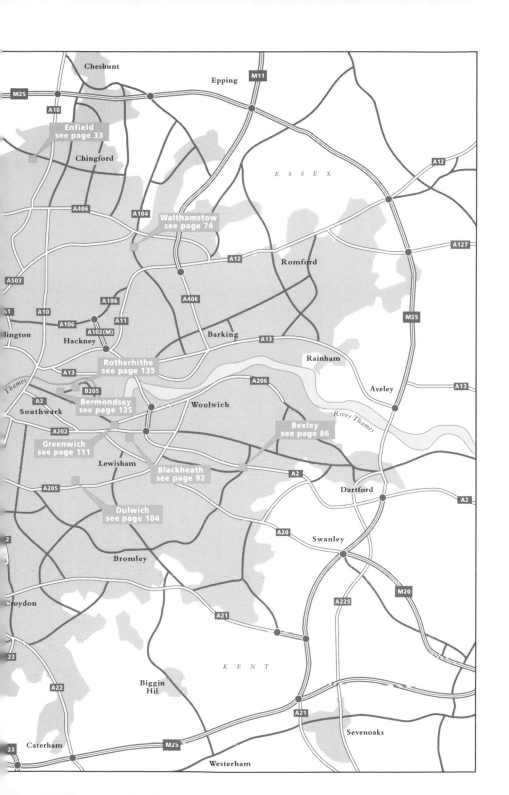

Villages North of the River Thames

Brentford

Location	8 miles (12.8 kilometres) west of Charing Cross.
Transport	Boston Manor Underground Station (Piccadilly Line). Brentford Station (overground trains from Waterloo) can be used if more convenient: it is on the walk and being closer to the village centre cuts out the longish walk between Boston Manor Station and Boston Manor House.
Features	**Boston Manor House**; The Butts estate of late 17th-century town houses; the Grand Union Canal; the wharves and working waterfront and the remains of Brentford Dock; views of the River Thames.
Refreshments	*High Street* cafés, pubs, fish and chip shop, pizza restaurant, bakery; *overlooking the marina* (on the walk) bar/restaurant; *wharf area* (on the walk) Brewery Tap pub; *near The Butts* (on the walk) White Horse (with a riverside garden). *St Paul's Church* (see map page 17 for location) morning coffee and cheap hot lunches.

Standing at the confluence of the rivers Brent and Thames, Brentford – or more properly New Brentford to distinguish it from nearby Old Brentford – clearly takes its name from a ford over the Brent, but some people think it also refers to a ford over the Thames. The Thames ford is supposed to have been the the lowest on the river and may well have been the one used by Julius Caesar during his invasion of England in 54BC. Later it was the scene of two battles: one in 1016 between Edmund Ironside and King Canute; and another during the Civil War in 1642, when the Royalists defeated the Roundheads.

Despite its strategic importance as a fording place, Brentford was not a particularly populous place and in the Middle Ages was therefore not a parish in its own right but an outlying settlement of the parish of Hanwell. Hanwell church was two miles away, however, so from an early date Brentford had its own church, which was dedicated to St Lawrence. Brentford at last became a parish in 1749. Fifteen years later, when the radical political writer Horne Tooke was parson, the bulk of the church was rebuilt in brick next to the original 15th-century stone tower. Rationalization during this century led to its closure in 1961. Plans to convert it into a theatre in the 1980s fell through and now the building stands redundant beside the busy High Street.

Boston Manor

Although the village was not a parish in the Middle Ages, it was a manor; but it was known as Bordestone and later Boston, rather than Brentford. The manor belonged to the priory of St Helen Bishopsgate in the City of London. After the dissolution of the monasteries it passed into secular hands. The Reade family rebuilt the manor house, which lay about three-quarters of a mile (1.2 kilometres) to the north of the village on the east bank of the Brent, in 1623. Half a century later James Clitherow, the fourth son of Sir Christopher Clitherow of Pinner, bought it and remodelled it following a fire. James's descendants owned the Boston Manor estate right down to 1924 when the advent of the Great West Road induced them to sell up. **Boston Manor House** was bought by the council and is now (partially) open to the public, together with its gardens and surrounding parkland.

About the time the Clitherows moved to Brentford, the village – or town, rather – was beginning to develop as a commercial and industrial centre. Inns and shops lined the High Street, serving travellers on the original Great West Road out of London. Corn and garden produce from orchards and market gardens were traded in the market place. To the south, industry (including several breweries and distilleries) crammed into the narrow space between the High Street and the waterfront, and the waterfront was lined with wharves. Here also lived Brentford's working population. Meanwhile, the increasingly prosperous middle classes migrated north to The Butts, an enclave of handsome new houses built in the late 1600s and early 1700s. The Butts survives more or less unspoilt today and features in the walk.

The canal

From the 1790s the construction of the Grand Union Canal between Brentford and Braunston in Northamptonshire linked London with the industrializing Midlands via the Thames This inevitably increased the economic significance of Brentford dramatically. So did the arrival of the railways, especially when the famous engineer Isambard Kingdom Brunel built a large dock at Brentford and connected it to his Great Western Railway by a branch line leading north to Southall. Brentford Dock has now been closed for over 30 years, but the canal and busy waterfront remain and the land between the High Street and the waterfront is still packed with boat-building firms and many other small businesses. The walk explores this area, as well as the manor house and grounds, The Butts and the old village centre.

THE BRENTFORD WALK

Start and finish Boston Manor Station.
Distance 3½ miles (5.6 kilometres).

Come out of the station and turn right down Boston Manor Lane. After about 200 yards (180 metres) you come to the gates of Boston Manor House. Turn in here and make your way round to the left of the house to the garden front with its stately old cedars. Today the view is of the M4 flyover, but originally the house looked over parkland to the River Brent and, beyond, to Osterley Park, former home of the Child banking family. Before the area was built up Brentford was surrounded

BRENTFORD

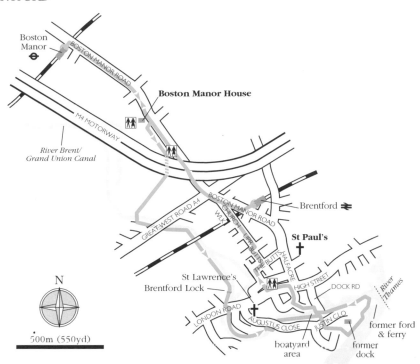

by a whole string of country mansions: Syon House, Osterley Park, Boston Manor House, Gunnersbury House (home of the Rothschild family) and, south of the river, Kew Palace. Remarkably, all survive today and all are open to the public.

Turn left down the broad tarmac walk, aiming for the tall office blocks. At the bottom by the toilets and the little car park, turn right and walk down the gently sloping hill towards the canal at the bottom. Here, in fact, the canal is no more than the canalized River Brent. At Hanwell, about 1 mile (1.6 kilometres) north of here, the river and canal diverge. The canal heads off east towards Uxbridge, while the river makes its way northwest to its source near Barnet. Cross over the footbridge and turn left, heading in the direction of the Samsung tower and the Great West Road bridge. Beyond the bridge you go round a corner and under a railway bridge before passing through a covered dock. Now you can see, ahead left, the old village centre on the far bank of the Brent with the spire of **St Paul's Church** rising up behind. The wide loop of the Brent here was cut off by the canal partly as a short cut and partly to create a backwater basin.

St Lawrence's Church and Brentford Lock
Carrying on, St Lawrence's Church comes into view straight ahead through the trees and beyond the Brentford Lock. Looking back just after you pass the lock, you

get a good view of The Butts area of the old village, laid out on high ground to protect it from flooding. The poorer areas were not so lucky: serious inundations were not infrequent in the days before the development of water management techniques. Turn left over the bridge on the site of the original Brent ford and then immediately right and down the steps to continue the towpath walk (signposted). Having flowed south until now, the canalized river here turns sharply east as it nears the Thames. Over on the far side, the trees denote the grounds of the Duke of Northumberland's Syon House. On this side new houses and offices are being built among the small factories and workshops that crowd what is called The Ham – a former piece of riverside common. When you reach the bridge that once carried the railway to Brunel's dock, you have to turn left onto the road to pass underneath it. A flight of shallow up-and-down steps brings you back onto the towpath and into the main waterfront and boatyard area.

Brentford Dock

Cross the footbridge and once you are on the other side do not go back down to the towpath but continue along the riverside, keeping to the tarmac (and do not go up the ramp). Good views of the basins and boatyards open up to the left. When you reach the lock, turn right on Dock Road and go under the arch by the dock management office. Carry on over the road and up the steps, now walking on red tarmac with flats to your left and a little car park on the right. You are now in the former dock, built on an islanded spit of land called Old England. The dock basin could accommodate boats up to 300 tons and all around were loading bays, warehouses and railway sidings. Like London docks downriver, Brentford Dock closed in the 1960s and was subsequently redeveloped with flats, houses and a marina for pleasure boats.

Turn left at the small fountain. Go under the walkway into a garden area and then up the steps ahead onto the terrace of the marina bar and restaurant. Cross the terrace diagonally to the right, go down the bank and turn left along the gravel walk by the river. Kew Gardens is surprisingly close on the right. Ahead, in Old Brentford, rises the graceful campanile of Kew Bridge Steam Museum, formerly the Grand Junction Waterworks Company.

Cross the entrance to the dock basin and follow the path round to the right, up the steps and back onto the red tarmac. From the viewpoint here you can see, away to the right, George III's Kew Palace, and near to the left, the entrance to the ferry basin. The King's ferry operated between here and the Surrey bank of the river, carrying horses and carriages as well as people, from at least the mid-17th century.

Soap and starch

To the left of the ferry basin there used to be a large soap factory which, as early as the 1820s was the biggest hard soap factory in the southeast of England. Production at the works – which, apart from the dock, was the largest enterprise in Brentford – ceased in 1961. Turn sharp left back along the entrance to the canal, which strictly speaking starts at the lock crossed by Dock Road. Cross the lock on the blue-painted footbridge and walk back along the canal. First you cross a weir and then a pair of disused floodgates called Dr Johnson's Lock after Dr William Johnson, the propri-etor of a starch mill in Catherine Wheel Yard in the 18th century. Turn right by the Brewery Tap pub and walk up Catherine Wheel Road (the Catherine Wheel was an inn). When you reach the High Street turn left and cross at the lights into the Market Place. Both the High Street and the Market Place have been dramati-cally altered in the 20th century to allow the main road to be widened and to pro-vide more up-to-date shopping facilities. The market was forced to move in the 1850s when the new courthouse was built. It went first to Old Brentford and then, in 1974, to Heston.

Pass to the right of the courthouse. To the left of the White Horse, the artist J.M.W. Turner spent four years as a boy living with his uncle, a local butcher, before going on to study at the Royal Academy. The White Horse has been here since at least 1603, though it has, of course, been rebuilt since then. Beyond the White Horse you come to The Butts.

The Butts

Originally common land used since at least the 16th century for compulsory archery practice (a butt is a target, hence the name). The Butts was enclosed and sold off for building in 1664. Most of the houses around the square date from soon after that time. Throughout the 18th century, and for much of the 19th, the elections for Middlesex's two MPs were held here. Local traders benefited enormously from what was effectively a two-week jamboree, but the reputation of the town suffered badly from the concomitant bribery, brawling, drunkenness, and even violence.

Make your way across to the far right-hand corner of the square. Here there is a wide avenue leading from the square to Half Acre. The houses on either side are rather later in date than those in the square. On the left side at least, this is because until well into the 19th century this was the site of Ronald's Nursery, one of the largest in the area and a supplier to Kew when the botanical garden was being developed. St Raphael's Convent takes up most of the avenue's right-hand side.

Exit the square via Upper Butts. At the end turn right into Somerset Road and then left into the continuation of Upper Butts. Go straight on down to the end (now Church Walk) and cross the bridge over the railway line, constructed through Barnes in 1849. When you reach the road you can either turn left, cross the Great West Road and continue up Boston Manor Road to Boston Manor Station, or turn right for Brentford Station (entrance over bridge) for trains to Waterloo.

Chipping Barnet and Monken Hadley

Location	11 miles (17.7 kilometres) north of Charing Cross.
Transport	High Barnet Underground Station (Northern Line).
Features	**St John's Church**; **St Mary's Church**; six almshouses; Elizabethan grammar school; Georgian mansions; Hadley Green and Common; **Barnet Museum**.
Refreshments	*Barnet High Street* variety of cafés, pubs, restaurants and fast-food outlets; *Hadley Highstone* (furthest extremity of the walk) Windmill pub; *Wood Street* (see map page 22) Black Horse pub.

Chipping Barnet and Monken Hadley sit on top of a 400-foot (122-metre)-high hill overlooking the valley of the Pymmes Brook to the east. South of Monken Hadley, Chipping Barnet also looks south over the valley of the Dollis Brook. On clear days there are therefore good views from the walk in both directions.

East Barnet, down in the valley of the Pymmes Brook, was the original Barnet village and remained for centuries the centre of the parish. Chipping Barnet grew up to the west of the village at a point where the Great North Road breasted its first major hill on the way out of London to York. Being a natural place for travellers to stop and change horses, it developed in the 18th century as a great coaching centre, with fine large inns and fleets of horses standing ready for the harness. By the end of the century at least 150 mail and stage coaches were passing through the village daily, not to mention post-chaises, private carriages, carts and wagons.

The old pre-suburban village of Chipping Barnet consisted of little more than the High Street and Wood Street, with the local church at their intersection. No new roads were added till the 1830s, by which time the growth of the coaching trade had generated some pressure for development. Woods, commons and fields lay all around. To the north was Hadley Green, and to the west was Barnet Common, stretching all the way from the Black Horse inn to the village of Arkley. Hadley Green, as you will see on the walk, is still open space, but Barnet Common has all disappeared save for a patch of manicured park in Wood Street.

Barnet horse fair

In the Middle Ages Chipping Barnet belonged to St Albans Abbey. The Abbey was granted the right to hold a market in 1199, hence the village's name ('chipping' means market). Four hundred years later in 1588, by which time the manor had passed into lay hands, Elizabeth I gave permission for two fairs a year to be held. One – the September horse fair – acquired an international reputation as dealers came from all over Europe to buy and sell. Horse-racing naturally developed as an offshoot of the fair, and for a time racing at Chipping Barnet rivalled the great Newmarket meeting. But the races, which were held first on the common and then, after the common was enclosed, in fields southeast of the village, ceased when High Barnet Station was built in 1871. The September horse fair is still held, however, usually in a council-owned farm in Mays Lane, but it is inevitably a shadow of its former self. The market survives, too. It is held in St Albans Road every Wednesday and Saturday.

The Wars of the Roses

The biggest event that has ever taken place in Chipping Barnet is the battle in 1471 between the Yorkists and the Lancastrians during the Wars of the Roses. After being deposed and forced into exile by Warwick the Kingmaker, Edward IV returned to England in March 1471, captured Henry VI and then defeated and killed Warwick at Barnet one foggy day in April, though backed by only 2,000 men. This victory, plus another one at Tewkesbury shortly after, established him securely on his throne for the rest of his life.

High place in a wood

Unlike Chipping Barnet, Monken Hadley, half a mile (0.8 kilometres) to the north has preserved its identity as a pretty country village with a church, a manor house, a rectory and cottages. The village was originally a clearing in a vast tract of woodland, hence the name Hadley, which means 'high place cleared in a wood'. In the 1130s Geoffrey de Mandeville, Earl of Essex, founded a hermitage in the village and gave it to the Monastery of Walden in Essex. The Monastery owned the village all through the Middle Ages and so it acquired its prefix of Monken, a corruption of 'monachorum' meaning 'of (i.e. belonging to) the monks'.

After the dissolution of the monasteries, Monken Hadley passed into lay hands, but like Chipping Barnet, no one family owned it for long enough to establish a squirearchical dynasty. The village developed as a retreat for wealthy merchants and professional men from London, however, and so besides the manor house, Monken Hadley has as fine a collection of gentlemen's residences as you will find anywhere in the Greater London area. In fact, Monken Hadley is one of those villages, like Petersham near Richmond, where the grand houses of the rich outnumber the humbler homes of the poor. And, as at Petersham, they stand in a fine rural setting, provided by the green on one side of the village and the common on the other.

THE CHIPPING BARNET AND MONKEN HADLEY WALK

Start and finish High Barnet Station.
Distance 4 miles (6.4 kilometres).

Turn right out of High Barnet Station and walk up the hill to the High Street. Turn right here and carry on up the hill. Crossing Meadway you can see down into the valley of the Pymmes Brook. The first railway in the area was built in the valley in 1850, 20 years before High Barnet Station was opened. Meadway was originally the

CHIPPING BARNET AND MONKEN HADLEY

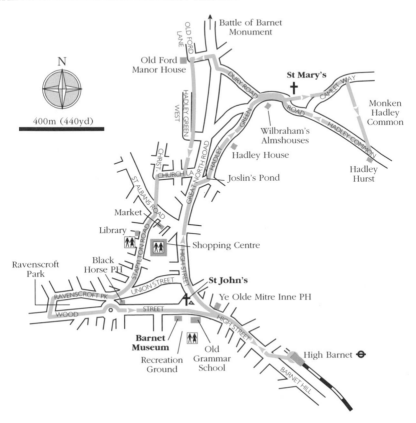

footpath made to link Chipping Barnet with that first station. Further up the High Street on the left, the Dandy Lion pub occupies part of the site of the Red Lion, probably the biggest and grandest of the old coaching inns in Chipping Barnet. The fine inn sign protruding way out over the street is a relic of the original inn. A few doors up on the right you come to Ye Olde Mitre Inne, dating from the century before the Red Lion and obviously more typical of an earlier age. It is the oldest pub in Barnet and one of the few 17th-century buildings to survive in the village.

Follow the High Street round to the right as it passes between **St John's Church** and the shops through a bottleneck called The Squeeze. Round the corner the street is much wider. The market was once held here, though it has now moved to its own site on the far side of The Spires shopping centre.

The Battle of Barnet
Walk all the way up the right-hand side of the street until you come to Hadley Green and open country. The 24-acre (10-hectare) Green, an ancient tract of common, is reputed to be the site of the Battle of Barnet in 1471, though whether it

took place exactly here or somewhere nearby is now impossible to say. Bear right by the garage, cross East View and continue between Joslin's Pond and Ossulstone House. By the time this house was built in the 1760s (by John Horton, a sugar refiner) Chipping Barnet was connected to Monken Hadley by a row of houses of this type, reflecting the area's popularity with wealthy businessmen from London.

Thackeray's grandfather

Beyond Ossulstone House and The Cottage there is now a gap in this row. Here, formerly, stood an old house that once belonged to the grandfather of the novelist William Thackeray. Thackeray knew Hadley quite well because his cousin was rector here. By that time his grandfather was dead and the house had passed into other hands. Between 1829 and 1934 Hadley's lords of the manor lived in the house. The last lord of the manor, Miss Rhoda Wyburn, gave the fields behind the house to the public and after her death in 1935 the house was demolished to provide access to the new open space. The former fields are now crossed by a bridle path connecting Hadley Green with East Barnet.

Dr Livingstone

After World War II the gap in the row was a lot bigger because three of the houses on the far side (The Elms, Mercers and Thackeray House) were destroyed by bombs. Since then, however, they have been rebuilt exactly as they were before and now it is almost impossible to tell from looking at them that they are not genuine. Beyond the new-old houses you come to Hadley House, the grandest house in the row and the original manor house of Monken Hadley. Beyond the manor house are Fairholt and Monkenholt, both dating from the mid-18th century, and then Monken Cottage followed by Livingstone Cottage. The latter was the residence of the famous explorer, Dr David Livingstone, in 1857–8. He had just come back to England from Africa for the first time and it was here that he wrote *Missionary Travels and Researches in South Africa*. Although the time he spent here was very short, it was nevertheless one of the happiest periods of his life for he had his family with him all the time, a rare occurrence in the great traveller's life. The plaque was put up by his daughter in 1913 on the centenary of his birth.

Trollope's sister

After Livingstone Cottage, keep right. Beyond Hollybush House, Grandon has connections with another great novelist of the 19th century, Anthony Trollope. In January 1836 Trollope's consumptive sister, Emily, moved here hoping that the healthy situation would help cure her condition. It did not, however, and before February was out she was dead. Go past Sir Roger Wilbraham's almshouses, which were founded in 1612, and follow the road round to the right into the centre of Monken Hadley village. When you get to White Lodge, cross the road and enter **St Mary's** churchyard, where Emily Trollope and Thackeray's grandparents, among many others, are buried.

Above the west door of the the medieval church the date 1494 denotes when it was substantially rebuilt. The coats of arms close by, put up when the west door was renovated in 1956, represent the Archbishop of Canterbury and the Bishop of London and their respective provinces at the time. In the church there are various brasses and old monuments, the most striking of which is the portrait of Sir Roger Wilbraham and his wife Mary, carved by the well-known Jacobean sculptor, Nicholas Stone.

Monken Hadley Common

Pass between the church and the flint-faced Pagitt's almshouses on the right. Justinian Pagitt founded this almshouse in 1678: the plaque was put up on 3rd October, 1978, to mark its tercentenary. The path through the churchyard brings you out on Monken Hadley Common with Hadley Wood ahead down in a dip. Monken Hadley grew up on the western edge of a huge medieval hunting park called Enfield Chase. When the Chase was split up and enclosed in 1779, the village received the land that is now called Monken Hadley Common as compensation for loss of grazing and other rights in the old Chase. Today the Common covers 190 acres (77 hectares) and stretches east nearly 2 miles (3 kilometres) as far as Cockfosters.

Hadley Hurst

Turn left along the road. At the entrance to the Church of England primary school, the original village school founded in 1832, turn right across the road and head across the Common, bearing slightly left along a path leading towards a red-brick house on the extreme left with two superb cedars in front. This is just one of many fine houses on the south side of the common and approaching them from this direction is the best way of admiring them. When you reach the red-brick house – Hadley Hurst, built around 1705 – turn right along the path worn in the broad verge. The white house called Hurst Cottage is a slightly earlier and slightly less grand house than Hadley Hurst. Attached to it on the left is a small house rather more recognizable as a cottage. This one was built in the 16th century and is prob-ably the oldest building in the village, apart from the church.

Further on along the row, Gladsmuir was the home of the Quilter family from 1736 until early this century. More recently it belonged to the novelist Kingsley Amis and it was during his tenure that the poet Cecil Day Lewis died in the house in 1972. Carry on back towards the village, passing the rectory on the right and then going through the Common gates. Retrace your steps through the centre of the village, this time on the right-hand side of the road and passing the 17th-century Pagitt's Almshouses. Beyond St Mary's Church you pass two large neo-Georgian houses set well back from the road in their own grounds. These were built in the early 1960s and replaced the so-called Hadley Priory, the largest house in the road leading from Hadley Green to the church. Although the house was built in the 16th century it was never a priory, but it was made to look like one around 1800 when the owner attached a sham Gothic front to it and gave it its religious-sounding name. The Priory was demolished in the 1950s.

When you reach the Green, again turn right along Dury Road, named after a family that lived in the vicinity in the 18th century. There are more Georgian houses here, but there are many more Victorian cottages, reflecting the expansion of the

Plate 1: *Boston Manor House, Brentford: the west front (see page 16).*

Plate 2: *Hurst Cottage and pond on Monken Hadley Common (see page 24).*

Plate 3: *Monken Hadley's 17th-century Wilbrahams almshouses (see page 23).*

Plate 4: The Gallery in Chiswick House, one of several sumptuously decorated rooms in this early Palladian mansion (see page 30).

Plate 5: The riverside terrace at Strand on the Green between Kew and Chiswick is a popular place for a stroll and a drink on a summer's day (see page 128).

Plate 6: A shady stretch of Gentlemans Row, Enfield (see page 36).

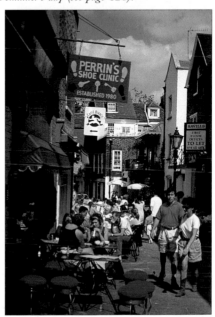

Plate 7: Perrin's Court, one of several narrow side streets off Hampstead High Street (see page 40).

Plate 8: The Keats House museum in Hampstead was once the home of Romantic poet John Keats (see page 43).

Plate 9: Harrow-on-the-Hill's winding High Street (see page 48).

Plate 10: Harrow School tuck shop just off the High Street (see page 48).

population at that time – and also the presence of Hadley Brewery. From at least 1770 this stood by the larger of the two ponds (the one with the wall along one side). Beer was brewed here until 1938. After World War II the old brewery became a distribution centre – latterly for Whitbread's Breweries – until it was demolished in 1978.

Hadley Highstone

At the end of Dury Road, turn right on the Great North Road and then, opposite the Old Windmill pub, cross the road into Old Ford Lane. As you do so, look right and you can just see a junction of roads and a patch of green. This is the site of the stone monument to the Battle of Barnet which was put up in the 18th century, supposedly on the spot where the Kingmaker fell, and which later gave its name to this part of Hadley, Hadley Highstone.

When Old Ford Lane bends right by the golf club (the clubhouse is a Regency house extended, in the Barnet direction, in the 1920s), turn left past Old Ford Manor House. Old Ford Manor was part of South Mimms, a village a couple of miles (about 3 kilometres) northwest of here. The moat of the original medieval manor house survives on the 18th tee of the golf course. This later house was built sometime around the middle of the 18th century.

Follow the path beside the green all the way back to Chipping Barnet. When you reach the junction of Gladsmuir Road and Christ Church Lane, turn right into the latter, passing on the left one of the old pumping stations of the East Barnet Gas and Water Company. When the road bends right, turn left into Christ Church Passage. At the end cross St Albans Road diagonally left and enter Stapylton Road. Walk all the way down this road, passing the library and the shopping centre. At the bottom Stapylton Road joins Union Street, one of the new roads built in Chipping Barnet in the 1830s. At the end of Union Street, turn right, past the Victorian almshouses of the Leathersellers' Company, one of the City livery companies, and then go left into Ravenscroft Park. The developer of this road, Thomas Smith, offered in 1880 to pay for the conversion of the last remaining patch of Barnet Common into the park here. Ravenscroft Park is sunken because it used to contain two large ponds that were only drained in 1992. The boundary stone at the end of the railings by the park marks the western limit of both Barnet parish (beyond it is South Mimms) and the long-defunct Whetstone and Highgate Turnpike Trust, which was once responsible for maintaining the main roads in the area.

Mrs Palmer and the Barnet poor

At the end of Ravenscroft Park turn left into Blenheim Road. At the junction with Wood Street you see the old tollgate-keeper's cottage across the road, and on the right the almshouses founded by Mrs Eleanor Palmer, the daughter of Henry VII's treasurer. Mrs Palmer left property in Kentish Town in 1558 to provide an income for the relief of Barnet's poor, but it was not until 1823 that the first almshouses were built with her money. They were subsequently rebuilt in 1930 and then modernized in 1987. About 100 yd (90 metres) beyond the almshouses you can see the junction with Wellhouse Lane. This leads – eventually – to the old chalybeate spring (the waters of a chalybeate spring contain dissolved iron salts) developed in the 1650s as a medicinal spa and visited by Samuel Pepys twice in the 1660s. Today the spring, in Well Approach and covered by a mock-Tudor well house, is surrounded by a 1930s housing estate.

Turn left along Wood Street. Bells Hill on the right shows you how steeply the ground falls away to the south into the valley of the Dollis Brook. The historic part of Wood Street really starts beyond the Black Horse pub and the roundabout. On the right the Elizabeth Allen free school functioned from 1824 until 1973. Local woman Mrs Allen actually left money for the school in 1727, but until the National School was set up in 1824 her bequest was used for the old grammar school seen later in the walk. The former Allen school building now provides sheltered accommodation for the elderly.

Barnet Museum

On the left is another almshouse, this one founded by John Garrett in 1728 for six elderly widows. A little further on from the Garrett almshouse and on the same side of the road is the fourth and last of Chipping Barnet's almshouses, the Jesus Hospital, founded by James Ravenscroft in 1679. Ravenscroft, of a prominent Barnet family, graduated from Jesus College, Cambridge, and went on to become a lawyer and a merchant. Just before the Registry Office, No. 31 Wood Street on the right is the **Barnet Museum**, run by the local history society. Ahead, Barnet church became a parish church in its own right in 1866. Since the Middle Ages until that time, it had officially been no more than subsidiary to the main parish church down in East Barnet. A wealthy brewer called John Beauchamp paid for the rebuilding of the original church in 1420. Then that 15th-century building was rebuilt and enlarged in the 1870s. Many of the old monuments were preserved, the best being that to James Ravenscroft's father, Thomas, who died in 1630.

Opposite the church and set back from the road is the last of Chipping Barnet's historic buildings to be seen on the walk. This is the Elizabethan grammar school, built in 1573 and the main school in the village until the 19th century. It was to this school that Elizabeth Allen's money was devoted for the century following her original bequest. The school moved to new premises in 1932. The old building, now part of Barnet College, is occasionally used for public concerts and other events.

Outside the old schoolhouse, cross back over the High Street to the north side and turn right. Make your way back down the hill past the Mitre and eventually to the station, where the walk ends.

Chiswick

Location	5½ miles (8.8 kilometres) west of Charing Cross.
Transport	Turnham Green Underground Station (District and Piccadilly Lines), Stamford Brook Underground Station (District Line).
Features	**St Nicholas's Church**; **Chiswick House and grounds**; **Hogarth's House**; old houses on Chiswick Mall; Church Street; riverside walk and views.
Refreshments	*Turnham Green Terrace/Chiswick High Road* (start of walk) variety of bars, restaurants and cafés; *in village* (on Great West Road) George and Devonshire and Mawsons Arms pubs; *grounds of Chiswick House* (halfway round walk) café/restaurant; *Chiswick High Road* (end of walk) Café Flo, Pitcher and Piano bar, Nachos Mexican restaurant.

Chiswick established itself on the north bank of the Thames a few miles west of London. Its one and only street – Church Street – led north away from the river towards the main road heading west out of London. At the river end of Church Street stood the church and vicarage (as they still do) and a cluster of cottages. A little to the east lay the manor house, called the prebendal manor house because the estate belonged to the Dean and Chapter of St Paul's Cathedral in the City of London, and its revenues were used to support one of the prebends, or members, of the Cathedral Chapter.

The river

'Chiswick' means something like 'cheese farm', but the village tended to regard the river rather than the land as its main livelihood and the occupations of its inhabitants were therefore generally river-related: fishing, boat-building, ferrying and so forth. The parish church was dedicated to the patron saint of fishermen – Nicholas – and a ferry ran from the foot of Church Street until 1934, the year after Chiswick Bridge opened.

From as early as the mid–15th century Chiswick was known to city-dwellers as an attractive and healthy place to live. The Russell family, later Earls and now Dukes of Bedford, lived at Corney House west of the village from 1542. In 1570 the still-existing Westminster School leased the old manor house as a retreat during times of plague. And about 1610 Sir Edward Wardour built the first Chiswick House to the north of Corney House. In the late 17th and early 18th centuries, people also began to build fine houses in Church Street and along the riverside lane leading from the church to the manor house. In time the whole of this lane to the manor house was built up to form a one-sided street called Chiswick Mall. Today Church Street, though mutilated at its top end, is one of London's most picturesque streets, while tranquil Chiswick Mall is one of its finest riverside promenades. Both feature on the walk.

Boot polish

Chiswick's riverside location attracted industry as well as wealthy and titled residents. In the 18th century there were two big breweries behind the Mall. Then, during the 19th century, when pollution killed off the fishing industry, came the Thornycroft shipbuilding yard and the Chiswick Soap Company, inventors of the famous Cherry Blossom boot polish. Polish and ships have both long since departed, but Fuller, Smith and Turner's Griffin Brewery, home of London Pride and Chiswick bitters, is still very much in existence (and often gives off a powerful smell of brewing to prove it).

As well as the village of Chiswick, the parish of Chiswick contained three other settlements: Strand on the Green, Little Sutton and Turnham Green. Like Chiswick, Strand on the Green was a riverside fishing village that later developed as a gentlemen's retreat. It is now another fine riverside promenade (see page 128). Little Sutton was a manor in its own right and in the 15th century boasted the king as tenant. It is now buried beneath suburbia. Turnham Green serviced traffic on the busy Great West Road. By 1700 it was as big as Chiswick itself and in the 19th century, boosted by the arrival of the railway, far outstripped the original village. Today most people think of Turnham Green as Chiswick. The old village is generally referred to as Old Chiswick.

Largely unscathed by its industrial past and cut off from modern Chiswick/Turnham Green by the new Great West Road built in the 1950s, Old Chiswick today is a peaceful and elegant backwater. Getting to and from it from the Underground line is not a particularly pleasant experience, but the village, with its old houses, luxuriant riverside gardens and fine river views, more than compensates.

THE CHISWICK WALK

Start Turnham Green Station.
Finish Stamford Brook Station.
Distance 2½ miles (4 kilometres).

Come out of Turnham Green Station and turn left under the railway bridge. Walk down to the lights and then go right on Chiswick High Road and immediately left into Devonshire Road. Towards the far end turn right into Bennett Street. Looking across the busy main road at the end you can see **Hogarth's House**, the little country house the painter and engraver, William Hogarth, used every summer from 1749 until his death in 1765. In those days it stood by a country lane surrounded by fields and market gardens. A local benefactor saved it from destruction early this century and it later opened as a museum with a large collection of the artist's well-known prints.

Turn left along the main road (here called, with unconscious irony, Hogarth Lane). The modern office block on the right stands on the site of the old Cherry Blossom polish works, originally founded as a soap works by brothers Dan and Charles Mason in 1878. Production ceased on the site in 1972 when Reckitt and Colman, who bought the company in 1954, transferrred operations to their main factory at Hull. Cherry Blossom is now owned by a private company called Grainger International.

At the roundabout go down into the subway. Take the first exit on the right if you want to visit Hogarth's House. Otherwise continue to the end and walk up the steps on the right. You come out opposite Chiswick Square, often billed as the smallest in London. At the far end stands Boston House, dating from the 1680s and named after Viscount Boston, later the Earl of Grantham, by whom it was extended

CHISWICK

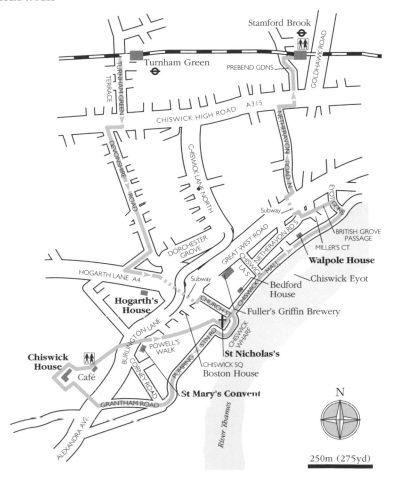

and refaced in the 1740s. Either side are two smaller houses. The one on the left has a plaque on its side relating to an incident in William Thackeray's novel *Vanity Fair,* of which more later when we reach Walpole House on Chiswick Mall.

The Lamb Brewery

Now turning to your left, you pass the George and Devonshire pub and enter Church Street, the high street of Old Chiswick. The street always curved round to meet you like this, but until the building of the new Great West Road in the 1950s it had shops, houses and a pub on the left-hand side where the entrance to the roundabout is. As you follow Church Street round to the right, you can see the bell tower of the old Lamb Brewery, in business here from 1790 till the 1950s. The Sich family founded it and owned it until 1920, and one member of the family still lives on Chiswick Mall. Beyond Ferry House the two old houses either side of the former brewery entrance were once Lamb Brewery pubs. Lamb Cottage was the Lamb Tap. The Old Burlington, built in the 16th century and the oldest building in Chiswick (apart from the church tower), was the Burlington Arms. Both became private houses in the 1920s. Opposite the Old Burlington, the Guardship acquired its name when it became a sea scouts headquarters in the 1920s. The nautical adornments were added by a later artist resident.

Walk on down Church Street between the Old Vicarage on the left (built in 1658 and refronted in the 18th century) and **St Nicholas's Church**. At the narrowest point notice the tablet in the churchyard wall saying that the wall was built in 1623 by Francis Russell to keep pigs out. Russell was one of the Corney House Russells and in 1627 succeeded as fourth Earl of Bedford. At the bottom of the street is the old ferry slipway. A gate just to the right leads to a riverside walk from which there are good views up- and downstream.

Chiswick Wharf

Turn right now into Chiswick Wharf. On the right at this point until 1950 stood the old village charity school, which was founded in 1707. On the left were the old fishermen's cottages, generally known as Sluts Hole and later as Fisherman's Corner. Now the modern development built over the site, which was cleared in the 1930s, is called Fisherman's Place. Further on along this road, which soon turns into Pumping Station Road, more modern housing is being built on the site of Thornycroft's Shipyard. Founded by sculptor's son, John Thornycroft, in 1864, the firm specialized in high-speed vessels, first launches and later torpedo boats and then torpedo-boat destroyers. It moved to Southampton in 1909 because it was building ever-bigger ships and finding difficulty in sailing them out into open waters.

Chiswick House

When you reach the roundabout (the approximate site of Corney House, demolished in 1832), take the second right by the off-licence – Grantham Road. This brings you out onto Burlington Lane, directly opposite the main entrance to **Chiswick House**. Go through the gates and walk towards the house. Modelled on Palladio's Villa Capra near Vicenza and one of the first Palladian houses in England,

Chiswick House was designed by its owner, the third Earl of Burlington, in the 1720s. The gardens, a pioneering naturalistic landscape, were laid out by Lord Burlington's friend, William Kent. Whereas in the 17th century the Russells had dominated Chiswick, in the 18th and 19th centuries it was the occupants of Chiswick House – first the Burlingtons and then the Dukes of Devonshire – who were the de facto squires of the village. The Devonshires, who also had a town house in Piccadilly, finally sold up in 1929.

Pass round the left of the house (with the lake to your left) and then turn right along the north front. Just before the gateway turn right and follow the path round to the left past the restaurant. This eventually brings you to a little lodge house. Exit the park by the little gate to the right of the lodge and turn left along Burlington Lane. At the lights cross over to **St Mary's Convent** and nursing home (here since 1897) and continue along the road. At the telephone box turn right into Powell's Walk, formerly a footpath connecting Chiswick House with the parish church. As you approach the church you pass the large railed tomb of 18th-century painter Philippe de Loutherbourg, a resident of Hammersmith Terrace just beyond Chiswick Mall. Several other artists are also buried here, including William Kent of Chiswick House (1748), William Hogarth of Hogarth's House (1765) and J. M. Whistler (1903).

Hogarth's tomb and grand houses

Turn right in front of the church tower (built in the 15th century – the rest of the church is Victorian) and then left through the south porch. Hogarth's tomb is the one with the urn on top on the right. Go down the steps out of the churchyard and carry straight on into Chiswick Mall. Beyond the Old Vicarage is the current vicarage. Soon after comes one of the two grandest houses on the Mall, Bedford House, now split into two. The original Bedford House, combining the current one and adjoining Eynham House, belonged to Edward Russell, a younger son of the earl who built the churchyard wall. Edward inherited Corney House but sold it and moved into the centre of the village in 1663. Years later, John Sich, founder of the Lamb Brewery, lived in the house until his death in 1836. Recent residents include the actor Sir Michael Redgrave, who lived there from 1945 to 1954.

More brewers

Further on, by the old draw dock, Belle Vue Cottage, Prospect Cottage and the warehouse on the corner of Chiswick Lane all belong to Fuller's Griffin Brewery. Belle Vue is the traditional home of the chief brewer. Next door to Belle Vue, Red Lion House was until 1916 a Fullers' pub, much frequented by reed cutters from the nearby island. Looking up Chiswick Lane you can see the entrance to the brewery and at the top on the left the Mawsons Arms pub. Thomas Mawson founded the brewery when he bought Bedford House's private brewhouse in 1701. The Fullers, Smiths and Turners all became involved in the 19th century. The Mawsons Arms pub, an early 18th-century building, was originally a private house and from 1716 to 1719 was the home of the poet Alexander Pope and his parents.

On the far side of the junction with Chiswick Lane, the Victorian villas stand where the manor house and College House stood until they were knocked down in 1875. College House, added to the manor house by Westminster School when it needed more room, was used by the school until well into the 18th century. From 1818 to 1852 it housed the Whittingham family's Chiswick Press, a printing firm famous for its hand-printed and finely designed books.

Inspiration for William Thackeray

A little further on near the end of the island you come to the second of the Mall's two finest houses. This one is called **Walpole House** and is named after a nephew of Prime Minister Sir Robert Walpole. Charles II's mistress, the Duchess of Cleveland, spent the last few years of her life in Chiswick, probably here. Much later the house became a school attended by the young William Thackeray in 1817. When he wrote *Vanity Fair* he is thought to have modelled Miss Pinkerton's Academy on it, though Boston House also claims that honour. The book starts at the academy, which is described as a 'stately old brick house' behind a great iron gate. Nowadays the house is home to members of the Benson banking family and the gardens are open each year as part of the National Gardens Scheme.

Passing more fine houses, you eventually come to modern Miller's Court, built on the site of a bakery, and, on the riverside, a row of small houses called Durham Wharf. Here, turn left into Eyot Gardens and then first left into British Grove Passage. Go past British Grove South and the entrance to Miller's Court. When you reach Netheravon Road South turn right and use the subway to cross the main road. Continue to the end of Netheravon Road North. At Chiswick High Road turn right and then left into Prebend Gardens. When you reach the railway viaduct go right through the station gates into Wilson Walk. This leads directly to Stamford Brook Station, where the walk ends.

Enfield

Location	11 miles (17.7 kilometres) north of Charing Cross.
Transport	Enfield Chase Station (overground trains from King's Cross and Moorgate via Finsbury Park); Enfield Town Station (overground trains from Liverpool Street).
Features	**St Andrew's Church**; Gentlemans Row; the New River; homes of the writer Charles Lamb; **Forty Hall** (not on walk – see map page 35).
Refreshments	*Church Street* pubs, fast-food outlets, Oliver's coffee house in shopping centre; *on the New River* (at halfway point of walk) Crown and Horseshoes pub; *Town Park* café.

Eight miles (13 kilometres) long by 3 miles (5 kilometres) across, Enfield was the largest parish in Middlesex after Harrow with Pinner. The village of Enfield, or Enfield Town as it became called, lay roughly in the middle. To the west was the 8,000-acre (3,250-hectare) royal hunting park known as Enfield Chase. To the east, open fields and later market gardens stretched down to the other parish settlement of Ponders End and the parish's eastern boundary, the River Lee. It was on the Lee that in 1804 the government established the arms factory that later produced the famous Lee-Enfield rifle.

In Enfield Town, settlement was restricted to just a few streets. Church Street was the high street, with the church and marketplace on one side and the manor house on the other. To the east London Road led south towards London and Silver Street led north to Forty Hill. The vicarage was in Silver Street and the rectory was a little to the north on the corner of Parsonage Lane and Silver Street's continuation, Baker Street. The ancient vicarage still survives in its original position, as you will see on the walk, but the rectory – which belonged to the Monastery of Walden in Essex up to the dissolution of the monasteries and to Trinity College, Cambridge, thereafter – was pulled down and its grounds were developed as Monastery Gardens in the 1920s.

The New River
At the west end of the village, the New River, an artificial canal constructed in the early 17th century to bring fresh water to the City of London from springs in Hertfordshire, divided the village from Enfield Chase. Along the village side of the river facing the Chase on the far side, a row of houses, many of them substantial,

grew up from the 17th century. In the 18th century it acquired the name Gentlemans Row. After 1779 when the old Enfield Chase was split up and enclosed, more houses, not so grand as the original ones, were built on the other side of Gentlemans Row, making it, at least for half its length, more like a regular street.

Royal connections

Many of the gentry who lived in Gentlemans Row's best houses and in other large houses in the village, notably Little Park and Burleigh House on the north side of Church Street and Chaseside on the south, were drawn to the village as much by its royal connections as by its proximity to London. For most of the Middle Ages the manor belonged to the de Mandevilles, Earls of Essex, and then to the de Bohuns, Earls of Hereford. But in 1421 it became part of the royal Duchy of Lancaster estate. Henry VIII's daughter Elizabeth inherited the manor after her father's death, along with Worcesters, the neighbouring manor to the north where she and her half-brother Edward – later Edward VI – spent a good deal of time as children. Elizabeth rebuilt Enfield's decaying manor house, but she is not believed ever to have visited it when Queen. She did, however, stay at the Worcesters manor house, Elsyng Hall, on a few occasions.

In the 17th century Sir Nicholas Rainton, a City merchant and twice Lord Mayor of London, acquired the Elsyng estate, pulled down the old house and built **Forty Hall** instead. This is now open to the public as the London borough of Enfield's local history museum, but it is unfortunately a little too far from the old village centre to be included in this walk.

Enfield's existence as a quiet country village came to an end in the mid-19th century when the railways arrived from two directions: first at Enfield Town Station in 1849 and then at Enfield Chase in 1871. In subsequent decades, and especially at the beginning of this century, the village lost its rectory, manor house and other fine houses, but it kept Gentlemans Row, the vicarage and the New River (which for a time was under threat). It also salvaged large tracts of gardens and orchards for use as a public park on the south side of the village and sports grounds on the north side, as you will see on the walk.

THE ENFIELD WALK
Start and finish Enfield Chase Station.
Distance 3 miles (4.8 kilometres).

Come out of the station and turn right under the railway bridge. Walk down the hill past the Wheatsheaf pub and Chase Green on the left. When Enfield Chase was enclosed in 1779, a portion was allotted to the villagers of Enfield as compensation for the loss of common rights in the Chase. When the common fields of Enfield were in turn enclosed in 1803, the allotment from the Chase, covering 12 acres (5 hectares), was preserved as Enfield's first public park. Cross Old Park Avenue and the bridge over the New River (more about the Old Park and the New River later). The gate into the Chase from Enfield stood just about here, on the village side of the bridge and at the entrance to Church Street.

ENFIELD

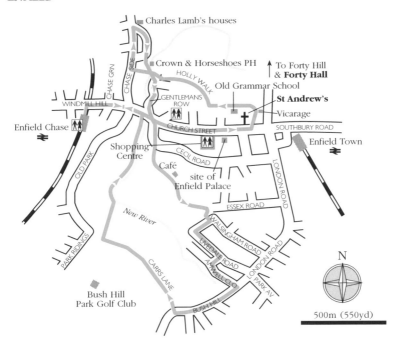

Cross Cecil Road and continue on into Church Street, the high street of the old village. Beyond Sarnesfield Road, Little Park Gardens on the left commemorates the old house called Little Park which, demolished in 1888, was one of the first of Enfield's mansions to fall victim to Victorian development. Burleigh House further on, commemorated in Burleigh Way, was knocked down in 1913. Opposite the marketplace, Pearson's department store on the right was built in the 1920s after Enfield's manor house, called the Palace because of its royal owner, was pulled down. As rebuilt during Elizabeth I's time, the manor was a two-storey gabled house with a central block and wings. Almost from the beginning it was let out, usually to royal servants. About 1670 Dr Robert Uvedale, who had been master of Enfield grammar school, opened a successful private boarding school in the manor, which survived right down to 1896. Destruction of the old house was finally completed in 1928. Nothing remains of it now except one panelled room with a fine plaster ceiling and a carved stone fireplace, re-erected in 5 Gentlemans Row.

Enfield market

When you reach Sydney Road, look across Church Street to the right-hand side of the bank and you will see the former parish beadle's house and lock-up, built in 1830. It later became the vestry house and is now a solicitor's office. Now cross Church Street to the marketplace. Although Enfield was first granted the right to hold a market in 1303, the modern one (on Thursdays, Fridays and Saturdays) was not started until 1612. From the beginning the proceeds were dedicated to parish poor relief. The original site of the market was a small green. Then it was enlarged by the acquisition in 1632 of a house called The Vine, which for a time served as the market house. The present octagonal market building dates only from 1904.

Fine memorials

From the marketplace go straight on into the churchyard. **St Andrew's** was the only church in the parish until 1831. Although it was extensively reconstructed in the 1820s, it retains its medieval appearance on the outside, and inside it has many of the monuments and memorials from the original structure. The best are in the northeast corner. One is a brass, said to be the finest in Middlesex, commemorating a soldier's wife, Lady Joyce Tiptoft, who died in 1446; the other is a fine 17th-century sculpture of Sir Nicholas and Lady Rainton, the builders of Forty Hall.

Make your way round the east end of the church. Now you can see to your left across the churchyard the original Elizabethan schoolhouse of Enfield grammar school. To the right is the handsome vicarage with its central Dutch-style gable. You can get a better view of it by standing on the plinth of the Mitton tomb next to the wall. Although the vicarage has all the appearance of a Georgian house, the oldest section of it, on the Silver Street side, is timber-framed inside and has been dated to the 13th century. Not many church houses of this antiquity survive in London, and certainly not still in church occupation.

Gentlemans Row

Walk on towards the churchyard gate. Just before you reach it, turn left along the footpath leading to the white house with black shutters. Continue past this house into Holly Walk. Follow this round by the car park on the left and the girls' school, founded in 1909, on the right. Keep right when the path forks. You now pass some cottages on your left, and on your right sports grounds bordered by the New River. Eventually you come out on Gentlemans Row. Turn right here, and at the end of the road by Brecon House turn left, cross the New River and carry straight on through the alley. You will emerge eventually on Chase Side next to Chase Green. Cross the road and turn right.

Development in this area started after the creation of Chase Green in 1803. After a while you come to an elegant terrace called Gloucester Place. The pretty little cottages here were built in 1823. At the end of the terrace look across the road to the white house (No. 87) and the brick house to the left of the white house (No. 89). Both these houses were successively home to the writer Charles Lamb and his mentally unstable sister Mary, and bear plaques to that effect. After retiring from the East India Company in 1825, Lamb occasionally took lodgings in Enfield. In 1827 he and his sister became tenants of The Poplars, the white house. After two years Mary's condition was so bad and she was away from home so much that Charles could not cope with the housekeeping and moved next door into Westwood Cottage to lodge with retired tradesman Mr Westwood and his wife. He stayed here for four years. In 1833 Charles and Mary left Enfield and moved to nearby Edmonton to live with Mary's keeper. Charles died there two years later.

Beer garden

Cross the road to the Lamb houses, turn right and walk along Cricketers Arms Road. Keep left into Chase Side Place and pass the modern Cricketers Arms pub. At the end of the Place turn left. Here you meet the New River again. Here also is the Crown and Horseshoes pub, which has a large beer garden behind. Turn right along the riverside. Having passed the wooden bridge, turn left across the next iron bridge (the one you crossed earlier in the other direction). Now you are at the top of Gentlemans Row. The next section of the walk follows the Row all the way down to its beginning in the centre of the village. The Row is lined with 18th- and 19th-century houses of varying sizes and styles, some cottages and some larger residences – Brecon House, for example, and a little further on, Archway, which arches over the entrance to Chapel Street, and which gave the Row its name.

Beyond Archway go left of the garden in the middle of the road and continue along the Row. Most of the houses have a special plaque indicating that they have been 'listed' (i.e. protected) by the local council. White-painted Clarendon Cottage, No. 17, was another of Lamb's Enfield homes (this was the one he occasionally rented before moving to The Poplars) and, like the other two, it bears a plaque recording the fact. At the end of the Row the biggest house provides offices for council services. To the right the New River flows through a pretty public garden. In the earlier section near the pub the river was roughly at the same level as the houses beside it. But here, as you can clearly see, it is several feet higher. This is because it was originally constructed to follow the 100-foot (30-metre) contour, a design constraint that produced some rather bizarre loops and diversions, including one all the way around Enfield village. In 1859 the Enfield section was straightened and then in 1890 piped underneath the village. Bypassed, the Gentlemans Row stretch then became superfluous and would have been filled in had there not been a public campaign to preserve it for its ornamental value. Today, therefore, the New River just here is not a river at all but a linear lake. The main channel still carries water to Stoke Newington, whence it is distributed via the mains.

Town Park

Gentlemans Row brings you out at the bus station. Turn right and then, in front of Trinity Church, go left across the road, using the zebra crossing. Walk on down Cecil Road and go straight on through the gates into the 27-acre (11-hectare) Town Park, created in 1903 out of the grounds of some large houses that formerly stood on the south side of Church Street. When the path forks, bear left beside the tennis courts. To your right you can see the embankment of the old New River course as it skirts the foot of Bush Hill.

Follow the path round to the right past the pavilion/café and then to the left towards the main gate. Just before you reach the main gate, cut right and go through the little gate leading into Walsingham Road. Immediately turn right. Follow the road round to the left (Uvedale Road) and then right into Whitethorn Gardens and left into Amwell Close (Amwell was one of the Hertfordshire sources of the New River). Keep to the high path on the right and then, when you reach the main road (Bush Hill), turn right and walk up the hill.

Bush Hill Park

At the top turn right at the Bush Hill Park Golf Club sign and join the footpath just to the right of the club gateway. The clubhouse, which you can see to your left at the end of the long straight drive, is in origin 18th century, but the history of the park in which it stands goes right back to before the Domesday survey of 1086. It is therefore much older than Enfield Chase, which was not emparked until a century or more later. After the restoration of the monarchy in 1660, Old Park, which was royal property, was granted to one of the major architects of the restoration, George Monck, Duke of Albemarle. Later the 550-acre (225-hectare) estate passed through many different hands before eventually coming into the possession of the Bush Hill Park Golf Club early this century.

The footpath goes straight through the middle of the golf course. When you reach the bollards at the end, turn right along the tarmac path leading down the hill back towards the New River. At the river go left (either side will do) and walk for some way beside the water. Eventually you come out back on Church Street. Turn left up Windmill Hill and make your way back to the station, where the walk ends.

Hampstead

Location	4½ miles (7.2 kilometres) north of Charing Cross.
Transport	Hampstead Underground Station (Northern Line), Hampstead Heath Station (overground North London Line trains).
Features	**St John's Church** and Constable's grave; **Fenton House**; **Burgh House and Hampstead Museum**; **Hampstead Scientific Society's Observatory** and meteorological station; High Street and **Antiques and Crafts Market**; Church Row and 18th-century houses; views of London; **Keats House** (not on walk – see map page 41).
Refreshments	*High Street and Heath Street* wide selection of cafés, bars, restaurants and pubs; *Holly Mount* (first half of walk) Holly Bush pub; *Well Walk* (second half of walk) Burgh House Buttery, Wells Tavern.

Hampstead was established a thousand or more years ago on the slope of the Northern Heights overlooking London to the south. At that time it belonged to the great Benedictine Abbey of Westminster. The abbot was the lord of the manor and he ruled the village through a bailiff based at the manor farm on the west side of the village. On the east the village was bounded by its great common, now Hampstead Heath. After the dissolution of the monasteries in the mid-1500s Hampstead passed into lay hands. Over the next 300 years it had a succession of lay lords, starting with a Tudor courtier, Sir Thomas Wroth. Descendants of the last lord, Sir Thomas Maryon Wilson, still own much property in the area.

From early times Hampstead was a pleasant resort for wealthy Londoners seeking a cool summer retreat or a refuge from the plague. Its slightly greater distance from the City and its hilly, uneven site meant that it did not attract quite the same quality of newcomers as Highgate, its neighbour across the heath. But what it lacked in quality it more than made up for in quantity. As early as the 1640s locals were complaining about outsiders taking over the village and forcing them out of their homes. Many of these outsiders must have built themselves fine houses, but thanks to wholesale rebuilding in the 18th century, none has survived – with the notable exception of the beautiful Fenton House, which is featured on the walk.

'Snowbound' village

Besides its healthily elevated position – the top of the village is 440 feet (135 metres) above sea level – Hampstead's other claim to fame in olden times was its water, which was both abundant and unusually pure. No fewer than four rivers, the Brent, the Fleet, the Tyburn and the Westbourne, rose in the area, and the quality of their water was such that in the 1500s a significant number of Hampstead's women inhabitants earned their living by taking in washing from the city. So much linen was regularly hung out to dry that viewed from London the village appeared permanently snowbound.

Around 1700 a chalybeate (iron-containing) spring with medicinal properties was discovered on the heath next to the village and developed as a spa. In fact there were two spas, one following on from the other after a space of 20 years or so. Neither was hugely successful, but the spas nevertheless attracted a lot of people and money to the village and led during the course of the 18th century to its virtually complete rebuilding, and also to significant expansion and population growth. Many of the houses put up at this time – though sadly not the spa buildings – have survived. Thus modern Hampstead is largely a Georgian village, though the houses are mostly of mellow weathered red brick, not stone or stucco.

Writers and artists

At the time of the Romantic movement in the 18th century still-rural Hampstead, with its wild heath, was discovered by writers and artists – John Keats and John Constable to name but two. Two of Constable's Hampstead homes are seen on the walk. Keats' house in the hamlet of South End has been made into a museum and is only a few minutes off the walk (see map opposite). Thanks to Keats, Constable and the numerous fellow-workers that followed them, Hampstead acquired something of a bohemian reputation in the 19th century. In the 20th century – and particularly during the 1930s when Communism was fashionable – that reputation has gained a distinctly avant-garde, left-wing, edge. Today, although it has become hugely exclusive and expensive, Hampstead is still the archetypal trendy liberal's village and the spiritual home of the so-called chattering classes.

THE HAMPSTEAD WALK

Start and finish Hampstead Station.
Distance 1¼ miles (2.8 kilometres).

Come out of Hampstead Station and turn left down the hill. This, the very centre of Hampstead, is largely Victorian in appearance, having been rebuilt towards the end of the 19th century. Heath Street, above High Street, is much more as it used to be in the 18th century, as you will see later in the walk. Cross on the zebra, go a little further down the street and then turn right into Perrin's Court, a narrow lane named after a family that used to own land in the area. Since 1938 it has been the home of the local paper, the *Hampstead and Highgate Express,* familiarly known as the *Ham and High.* Halfway along the Court is an entrance (on the right) to the **Antiques and Crafts Market**.

At the end of the Court turn right into Heath Street, then immediately left into Church Row. Built at the beginning of the 18th century as Hampstead spa was developing into a fashionable resort, and designed to form a grand approach to the parish church, this is now the village's oldest and finest street. Many people of national significance have lived here, but the only plaque (No. 18 on the left) is to a local worthy, John Park, Hampstead's first historian. No. 14 is the rectory.

Bailiff's house

Just before you reach the church, a path called Frognal Way leads off down the hill to the left. This connects with a road called Frognal behind the church, and then continues on the other side of Frognal as Frognal Lane. At the junction of these two roads stood the manor farm and the bailiff's house in the last century and before. The farm has long since disappeared but the bailiff's house, rebuilt in the early 19th century and recently much restored, still survives as No. 40 Frognal Lane. There are many other fine old houses in large gardens in Hampstead's Frognal quarter.

Hampstead's medieval parish church of **St John** was cramped and dilapidated and hardly worthy of the village's new status as a pleasure resort, so in the 1740s the

HAMPSTEAD

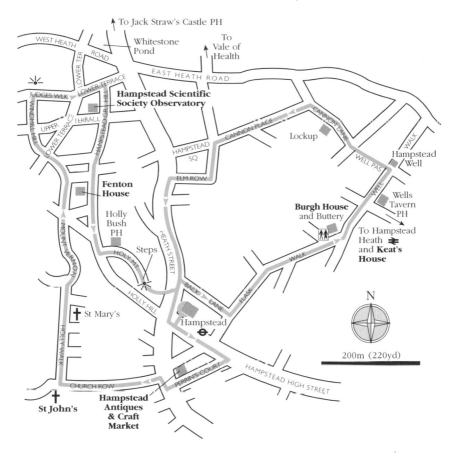

decision was taken to rebuild, leading to the construction of the present church. The churchyard is well worth exploring: tomb guides are available for a modest fee inside the church. The painter John Constable's tomb, surrounded by railings, is in the southeast corner and easily identifiable.

Holly Walk

From the church and Church Row turn right into Holly Walk. This part of Hampstead was developed in the early 19th century. First the churchyard extension was opened in 1812. Then, in succeeding years, came the little rows of houses at the top – Prospect Place, Benham's Place, Holly Place and Hollyberry Lane. St Mary's Catholic Church in the centre of Holly Place was built in 1816, mainly for French refugees, many of whom had settled in the village from the 1790s onward. The house on the corner of Hollyberry Lane served as the parish watch-house and lockup from 1830 until a proper police station was built nearer the High Street.

At the top of the hill Holly Walk meets Mount Vernon. The path left leads to Frognal. Looking back down Holly Walk there is a fine view towards London. Turning right into Mount Vernon, Abernethy House on the corner was built around 1820 as a parish girls' school. By the 1870s it had been converted into a lodging house and Robert Louis Stevenson, author of *Treasure Island*, stayed here several times for the sake of his health. Abernethy House faces the 18th-century Mount Vernon House, named after General Charles Vernon, and the former TB (tuberculosis) hospital, currently being converted into flats.

Constable's holiday home

Follow the road to the left behind Mount Vernon and descend to the green on Holly Bush Hill. On the left Frognal Rise goes down the hill to connect with Frognal. The walk goes straight on into Windmill Hill, named after the two windmills that used to stand in this part of the village. Follow Windmill Hill as it winds along the side of the hill past the gravelled back entrance to Fenton House, of which more later. When you reach Lower Terrace, a row of houses faces you across the green. The little one on the left with the blue door (No. 2) was Constable's summer home in 1821 and 1822. Constable first came to Hampstead for the sake of his family's health, but he found it such a wonderful place to paint that he returned every year for the rest of his life. He loved to study the great open skies and billowing clouds.

Cross Lower Terrace and continue on up Windmill Hill past Upper Terrace. Right at the top you come to Judges Walk, the place where the village ends and Hampstead Heath begins. Judges Walk is so called, it is believed, because of the number of lawyer tenants of nearby Branch Hill Lodge in the 18th century. In those days the view from the hilltop avenue was much better than it is today and the spot was one of Constable's favourites. Any of his pictures entitled *Branch Hill* would almost certainly have been painted from here.

Turn right along the gravel path and then cross the road and go straight on beside the reservoir on your right. Built in 1856 by the New River Company, this was Hampstead's first reservoir. Since 1909 it has provided an ideal base for the **Hampstead Scientific Society's Observatory** and weather station.

Fenton House

At the end of this small road look left and you will see the famous Whitestone Pond and beyond it a large pub called Jack Straw's Castle. The pond takes its name from the milestone standing in the bushes to your left ('IV miles to St Giles's pound' it says, i.e. roughly to the eastern end of Oxford Street). Turn away from the milestone and head off down Hampstead Grove back towards the village. Just beyond the junction of Admiral's Walk and The Mount Square you come to New Grove House, home of *Trilby* author George du Maurier until the year before his death in 1896. Opposite is the National Trust's **Fenton House**, a beautiful example of 1690s' architecture and the finest house in Hampstead. It is not known who built it but its name comes from Philip Fenton, the merchant who bought it exactly a century after its construction. Fenton is buried in the churchyard. His family subsequently played an early part in the long-drawn-out campaign to save the heath from developers. Fenton House is now owned by the National Trust.

Carry on down Hampstead Grove to the green on Holly Bush Hill. The weatherboarded house on the left was used as a studio by the artist George Romney at the end of the 18th century. Later it was turned into the village assembly rooms and used for meetings and lectures. In the 1930s it belonged to Clough Williams Ellis, builder of the resort of Portmeirion in north Wales. Go past the house and turn left into Holly Mount. Follow this hilltop cul-de-sac right to the end where there is a superb viewpoint to the south and west. To the left you can make out the British Telecom Tower in the West End. To the right the main feature is North Kensington's Trellick Tower, with its distinctive detached lift shaft.

Threepence a bottle

Go down the steps and cross straight over Heath Street into Back Lane. At the bottom is the Victorian version of The Flask pub. In the original one water from the spa was bottled and sold in London for 3d a bottle. Turn left on Flask Walk, the main route from the village centre to the spa. In the 19th century, after the spa had closed, this was a working-class area, as is indicated by the public baths and washhouse built near the end of the road in 1888 (they have now been converted into flats). Beyond the baths you come to the junction with New End Square. Here stands **Burgh House**, built in 1703 and the residence of Dr William Gibbon, the official physician at the spa. A local trust now runs it as an exhibition centre and local history museum. New End was an extension of the village begun in the decade before the spa opened.

Keats museum

Go straight on from Flask Walk into Well Walk. The original village stopped here. All the streets down the hill to the right are suburban developments added in the 19th century. Right at the bottom is the early 19th-century Keats Grove, site of **Keats House**, where the poet lived from 1819 to 1821 and now a Keats museum.

On the left, post-World War II council flats stand on the site of the buildings of the second spa, which were bomb-damaged during the war and demolished in 1948. Crossing Christchurch Hill, you pass the imposing Wells Tavern and then a row of Georgian houses. No. 40 was rented by Constable in 1827. His wife died here the following year, but he stayed on with his seven children until his own death in 1837. Just beyond is the gated entrance to Gainsborough Gardens, the Victorian development laid out over the side of the first spa. Opposite the entrance on the left side of Well Walk is a Victorian drinking fountain that marks the site of the original chalybeate spring.

Squire's Mount

Turn left here up Well Passage. At the top cross Well Road (Hampstead Heath is to the right) and continue up Cannon Lane. On the way you pass the old parish lockup built into the garden wall of Cannon Hall and in use until superseded about 1830 by the one seen earlier in Holly Walk. The lockup is now part of a house built in the grounds of Cannon Hall. At the top of the hill you come to Squire's Mount and Cannon Place. Squire's Mount, named after Joshua Squire who built the house on the right in 1714, leads to Hampstead Heath and the Vale of Health. The Vale of Health is a little hidden suburb of Hampstead, first developed in the late 18th/early 19th centuries, when it was given its current name. Originally it was called Hatch's Bottom, but clearly that would not have been very effective in attracting prospective tenants to the somewhat out-of-the-way location.

Cannon Hall

Turning left into Cannon Place you pass Cannon Hall, named after old cannon brought here for use as bollards by a 19th-century resident. During this century the house's most famous residents have been the actor Gerald du Maurier and his writer daughter Daphne. Gerald was the son of George, whose house in Hampstead Grove you passed earlier.

Carry on right to the end of Cannon Place. Beyond Christ Church (1852), turn left into Hampstead Square and then right into Elm Row. Here there are many more early 18th-century houses, reflecting the development of the village east of Heath Street and High Street once the spa had started to attract visitors in large numbers. From Victorian times until well into the 20th century these older properties were relatively cheap, which is why so many impoverished writers and artists could afford to live in them. But now they are expensive again. In 1996 No. 1 Hampstead Square, dating from 1721, was on the market at £1.5m.

From Elm Row turn left on Heath Street, along with Hampstead High Street the main thoroughfare of the old village and still an extension of the High Street today. The station, where the walk ends, is down the hill on the left.

Harrow-on-the-Hill

Location	10½ miles (17 kilometres) northwest of Charing Cross.
Transport	Harrow-on-the-Hill Station (Underground Metropolitan Line; overground trains from Marylebone Station).
Features	**St Mary's Church**; **Harrow School and Old Speech Room Gallery**; Byron's Peachey stone; High Street; **Cat Museum**; views east and west; **Harrow Museum and Heritage Centre** (not on walk – see map page 47).
Refreshments	*High Street* French restaurant, Drift In tearooms (heavily used by boys from Harrow School), hotel and bar, tapas bar, Chinese restaurant, bar-brasserie; *West Street* Tea at Three tearooms, Castle pub; *Station Road Shopping Centre* (down by station) range of fast-food outlets.

Harrow-on-the-Hill must be the most conspicuous village in London. Perched on top of a high hill, largely bare for three-quarters of its circumference, it is visible for miles around. The 200-foot (60-metre) spire of **St Mary's Church** rising up above the trees further advertises its presence. In fact, the church is probably the reason why Harrow is here at all, for the name 'Harrow' is thought to be an ancient word meaning temple or sacred grove. In pagan times the summit of a hill would have been a natural site for a shrine or some other place of religious significance.

If this theory of the origins of Harrow is correct, it is all the more fitting that the Lord of the Manor of Harrow should have been the Archbishop of Canterbury. In 1094 Anselm, then archbishop, consecrated the first St Mary's Church. Nothing remains of that building, but sections of the existing church date from only half a century later. The chancel was constructed out of local oak in 1242. The nave and roof and the great spire – a landmark in every direction – were added in the 1400s.

The manor house of Harrow was reserved for the use of the archbishops when they came on a visit to their estate. Originally the manor house was at Sudbury Court down the hill to the east, but in the middle of the 14th century it was moved to Headstone northwest of Harrow and rather closer to Pinner. The moated manor house constructed at the time still survives and is now, with its huge tithe barn, the **Harrow Museum and Heritage Centre**.

Yeoman farmer

Big changes came to Harrow in the 16th century. First, having already shut down all the monasteries and seized their property, Henry VIII virtually forced the then

Archbishop of Canterbury, Thomas Cranmer, to hand over the Manor of Harrow to the Crown. Secondly, in 1572 a public-spirited yeoman farmer petitioned Queen Elizabeth I to allow him to found a free school at Harrow, funded by the rents from his various local properties, including his farm in the nearby village of Kenton. From this petition has grown the modern boys' public school of Harrow, second only to Eton in terms of social exclusivity and alma mater of such illustrious figures as Palmerston, Byron, Sheridan, Trollope and Churchill.

Since the 19th century, when numbers rose from under 70 to 500 and more, the school has dominated the village, and protected it from the pressures towards development that began to build up in Victorian times, especially when the railway arrived in 1880. The result is that the old village, centred on the High Street, Crown Street and West Street, still retains much charm. Also it remains islanded in a largely rural setting of parkland and playing fields, and even farmland. When the founder's farm at Kenton was sold for development in the 1920s, another small farm was created in the angle of Watford Road and Pebworth Road to replace it. The farm now adjoins the golf course and the school playing fields where games – including the unique Harrow football – take place most afternoons in term.

THE HARROW WALK
Start and finish Harrow-on-the-Hill Station.
Distance 1¾ miles (2.8 kilometres).

Take the south exit from Harrow Station, walk straight down to the end of the road and turn left with the rising ground of the park to your right. After a while turn right into Grove Hill and begin the climb up to the top of the hill. Just before the junction with Davidson Lane you pass between two large houses: Elmfield and The Copse. These are the first of the **Harrow School** boarding houses in the village. There are 11 in all. Another three are below you to your left on Peterborough Road. The remaining six are strung out along the High Street on top of the hill. Around the corner ahead you come to the main complex of school buildings, with more boarding houses on the left and the first classrooms on the right.

King Charles's Well
Just beyond the path on the right ascending to Church Hill there is a metal plaque high on the Art School wall recounting how Charles I stopped here in 1646 to water his horse and take a last look at London before going on to surrender himself to the Scottish Army. King Charles's Well, as the place came to be called, was just one of three places on Harrow Hill where villagers could obtain water until the Harrow Waterworks Company started piping in supplies in 1855. The difficulty of obtaining water on this hilltop site was an important factor in limiting the expansion of the village before the mid-19th century.

Speech Room
Opposite the massive Speech Room (assembly hall) built to commemorate the school's tercentenary in the 1870s, there is a plaque in the wall at the junction of

HARROW–ON–THE–HILL

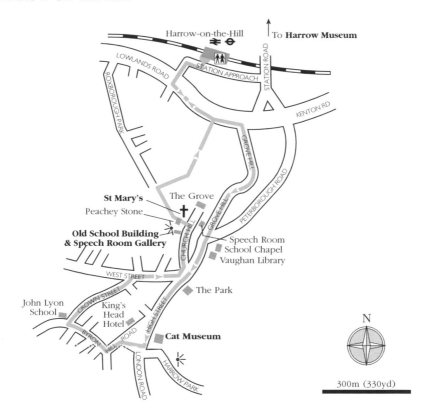

Grove Hill and the less steep road to the east, Peterborough Road. Headed 'Take Heed', it was placed here in 1969 on the 70th anniversary of what is thought to have been Britain's first fatal car accident, or, at least, Britain's first car accident in which the driver of the car died. Edwin Sewell was the man in question and the accident happened on 25 February 1899 when the brakes of his Daimler Wagonette failed as he was going down Grove Hill. He was killed instantly; his passenger died later. Peterborough Road had been constructed 20 years earlier to provide a less precipitous route up and down the hill – a pity he did not use it instead.

Passing the New Schools, the Vaughan Library and the Chapel on the left, you are now in the heart of the school. It is concentrated here at the north end of the High Street because this is where the school originally started, but all the buildings are much later in date, reflecting the great era of expansion and reconstruction in the mid- to late-19th century when Harrow transformed itself into a progressive, modern public school. As Church Hill joins from the right, you pass between two of the oldest boarding houses, Druries on the right, where Bryon and Palmerston lived, and Headmaster's on the left. The headmaster used to live here as well, but now has his own house elsewhere.

Flambards

Now you are in the High Street proper, dipping and winding along the crest of the hill in a north–south direction. At certain times of day it will be packed with boys in their straw boaters and blue blazers going off to eat or hurrying between classes. Beyond Headmaster's are the school bursary and bookshop. Opposite, at the beginning of West Street, are the outfitters and school tuck shop. On the far side of the bookshop are three more boarding houses: Moretons, Flambards and The Park. Flambards and The Park are connected historically because they are both relics in their way of another estate in Harrow that existed side by side with the Archbishop of Canterbury's. Flambards is the successor to the original manor house of this estate, named after the family that owned it in the Middle Ages. There are 14th- and 15th-century brasses to some of the Flambards in St Mary's Church. In 1797 James Rushout acquired the estate through marriage, but finding Flambards too small for him, proceeded to build The Park. The school acquired The Park as a boarding house in 1831.

The Cat Museum

In the little square ahead cat lovers should look out for an antiques shop called The Other Shop on the left-hand side of the road for they will surely not want to miss the **Cat Museum** here. Actually, it is not really a museum as such, more a private collection of feline memorabilia put together by the owner of the shop, Kathleen Mann, over the past 20 years and now, in response to public demand, put on show by her in the converted Victorian scullery beneath the shop. Admission is free, but the premises are rather cramped, so only two people can visit at a time.

The other Harrow school

After slipping into the private road called Harrow Park to see the easterly views from the first corner, exit from the square via the road going downhill next to the King's Head Hotel. The next section of the walk is a circuit that takes in Byron Hill Road, Crown Street and West Street to see the other old streets that have always been part of Harrow village. There are some pretty houses of varying ages and descriptions and some good views off to the west.

At the bottom of Byron Hill Road turn right into Crown Street. To the left now is the John Lyon School, another school set up with funds left by the founder of Harrow School, but long after the original Harrow School. John Lyon established the original Harrow School for local children, but also made some provision for fee-paying children from elsewhere. Over the centuries the fee-paying children gradually ousted the local children, even though the school tried to encourage local children to attend. In the end, following the passage of the Public Schools Act in 1868, Harrow School ceased to provide free places for local children and established the John Lyon School for them instead.

Workhouse and Old Schools

At the end of Crown Street turn right into West Street. The large white building on the left now is the former parish workhouse, dating from the 18th century, where poor people who could not maintain themselves were given spartan accommodation in return for their labour. When you get back to the High Street at the top of the hill, turn left and walk along the left-hand side of the road past Druries and into Church Hill. Now you are really at the heart of the school, for the building on the left with the clock on top is the original Harrow School building, called the Old Schools. John Lyon petitioned for permission to endow the school in 1572, but funds were not actually available for it until after both he and his wife were dead and that was not until 1608. Work on the new school then began and the building opened in 1615 with a single large classroom, masters' accommodation above and storerooms below. This Jacobean building is the left-hand section of the Old Schools and survives unchanged. Inside, every available surface in the classroom, known since the 19th century as the Fourth Form Room, is covered with the carved names of generations of pupils, including, close together, those of Byron and Sheridan. In 1820 the original school building was extended in identical style to the right. This now houses the **Old Speech Room Gallery** with its collection of school treasures. From the yard outside, where the game of squash was invented, there are wonderful views west as far as the North Downs and the Chilterns.

Byron's daughter

From the Old Schools make your way up Church Hill and into the churchyard (the big house up ahead is The Grove, another school boarding house, and there are good views east here, sometimes as far as Westminster Abbey and the British Telecom Tower). Byron's daughter Allegra, who died when she was only five, is buried somewhere in the churchyard and there is a little plaque to her fixed to the south porch. Inside the church there are various memorials to John Lyon and a large collection of brasses. The path takes you past the church to a famous viewpoint with a viewfinder to help you identify the various sights. This spot is also a place of pilgrimage for Byron lovers, for it is the site of the Peachey stone, the flat-topped tomb, now railed in, where as a boy the poet used to spend hours musing and gazing over the countryside.

If you go straight on here you will pass through the lower cemetery on to the western slope of Harrow Hill. But the route of the walk goes to the right to descend the northern slope. When you meet the road coming up the hill, take the signposted path to the right and follow it down to the main road. The station and the end of the walk is 100 yards (90 metres) or so to your left.

Highgate

Location	4½ miles (7.2 kilometres) north of Charing Cross.
Transport	Highgate Underground Station (Northern Line).
Features	**St Michael's Church**; **Highgate Cemetery**; Highgate School; High Street; fine collection of 17th- and 18th-century houses; Waterlow Park; Hampstead Heath and Highgate ponds (facilities for bathers); views of London.
Refreshments	*High Street* wide selection of pubs, cafés, bars and restaurants; *Waterlow Park* café/restaurant in Lauderdale House; *Highgate West Hill* (in the centre of the village and on the walk) The Flask pub.

Back in the Middle Ages the Bishop of London had a large hunting park, fenced to keep the deer in, on top of the hills to the north of London. In the early 1300s the then bishop decided to start charging travellers using the roads across the park. He put up three gates at various points and installed gatekeepers to collect the tolls and see to the maintenance of the roads. The most easterly gate was the most important because it controlled the main road from London to the northern counties. Here the gatekeeper and road-mender was a hermit. With pilgrims visiting the hermitage chapel, and thirsty travellers requiring refreshment and accommodation, a settlement soon grew up, centred on the road to the south of the gatehouse. In time, being on a hilltop site, the settlement acquired the name of Highgate.

At Highgate the Great North Road formed the boundary between the parishes of Hornsey and St Pancras. So to begin with Highgate was no more than an outlying hamlet of these two places. But as early as the 1500s it began to overtake its parent villages, and by the 1660s it had become the largest centre of population in both parishes. Even so, Highgate had to wait until 1834 before it became a parish in its own right.

Cholmeley's school

An important factor in Highgate's rapid development in the 1500s was its discovery by merchants and lawyers from London, attracted by its healthy position and fantastic views over the city a few miles to the south. One newcomer was Sir Roger Cholmeley, Lord Chief Justice in 1552. He first came to the village in 1536, living in a large house called Fairseat on the west, St Pancras, side of the High Street. After nearly 30 years in the village he began to evolve plans for the foundation of a boys' grammar school. It opened six years after his death in 1565, and like Harrow has since grown into a well-known public school.

In Elizabethan times aristocrats and courtiers began to settle in the village, particularly to the west of the High Street where there was a plateau offering good sites for houses. Here, beside the village green (now Pond Square), several great mansions were built on the edge of the escarpment looking west and south. All have since disappeared, but some largish houses remain, including Cromwell House, the finest early-17th-century house in London, plus whole rows of smaller 17th- and 18th-century houses in the High Street, Southwood Lane, North Road, Pond Square and The Grove. All these places are included on the walk.

Public open spaces

In the 19th century Highgate's hilltop position, and the fact that it was always able to attract the wealthiest and most influential residents, saved it from being engulfed by the tide of suburbia. Such development as there was occurred mainly on the east and less fashionable side. Here in 1813 was built a new and less steep stretch of the Great North Road, so giving the village a bypass. Here, also, the railway was built in 1867. Meanwhile, on the west and smarter side, the village benefited from the preservation of both Hampstead Heath and the private estate of Kenwood as public open spaces. To the north, the Bishops of London continued to own land until well into the 19th century. The site of the Bishops' hunting lodge in the medieval Hornsey Park is now covered by the 14th tee of Highgate golf course. Thanks to all these restraining influences Highgate is now one of the most elegant and best-preserved villages in London, as you will see on the walk.

THE HIGHGATE WALK

Start and finish Highgate Station.
Distance 3½ miles (5.6 kilometres).

Take the 'car park' exit from the Underground station and walk up to the junction with Shepherds Hill and Archway Road. The latter is the new road driven through a cutting in 1813 to avoid the steep slope up to Highgate village. Cross Archway Road into Jackson's Lane and walk on up the hill. Shepherd's Lane and Jackson's Lane are part of an old road connecting Hornsey and Highgate. Jackson's Lane gets its name from an early-19th-century fox-hunting colonel who lived in the house with the overhanging window which you pass at the top just before the junction with Southwood Lane.

Continue straight on along Southwood Lane towards the High Street, which comes into view as you approach the junction with Castle Yard on the right. On the left, detached houses once lined the road looking down the steep hill towards London. One, **Southwood Lodge**, survives in Kingsley Place: here you first see the panoramic views that have long been one of Highgate's main attractions.

Further along, on the right, are the village almshouses, founded by City goldsmith (i.e. banker), Lord of the Manor of Hornsey and Highgate resident Sir John Wollaston, who died in 1658. The almshouses, much decayed, were pulled down and rebuilt by Sir Edward Pauncefoot of Lauderdale House in 1722. In the rebuilding of them Pauncefoot doubled the accommodation to 12 and added a school for girls

HIGHGATE

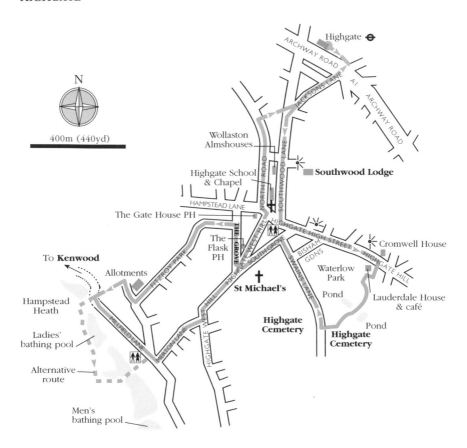

in the middle. The boys of Highgate had already been provided for by Sir Roger Cholmeley 150 years earlier. Cholmeley's school, much expanded, is behind the almshouses. Opposite the almshouses is Avalon, the childhood home of Mary Kingsley, writer and traveller, and niece of Charles Kingsley. She died in South Africa in 1900 while working as a nurse in a prisoner of war camp.

As you approach the village centre you pass on the right the main buildings of Highgate School and then, on the corner, the school chapel. The original chapel, which replaced the medieval hermitage chapel, doubled up as the village church until the early 1800s. By this time the village had grown so much that a new church was needed, but the school claimed ownership of the chapel and would not allow the village to rebuild it. So the village built a brand new church for its own use on a different site, which we will pass later.

Turn left into High Street, until you reach the opening of Archway Road, the Great North Road out of London. As you walk down it in the direction of the City, you can see what a gruelling climb it must have been for horses pulling heavily laden wagons and carts. With its restricted site, Highgate was a cramped village, hence the numerous yards – side streets really – leading off the High Street, particularly on the left-hand side. Townsend Yard, leading to a garden centre on the eastern slope of the hill, is a good example. It is named after a family of local builders called Townshend [sic] who lived in the 18th-century house on the south side of the entrance. Opposite the yard is the Prickett and Ellis estate agency, founded by John Prickett in 1767 and probably the oldest business in the village. Frederick Prickett, born in 1821, was the first historian of Highgate.

The Bank

Below Cholmeley Park you come to a raised road called The Bank, parallel with the main road. The first buildings belong to the Channing School, a private girls' school founded in 1885 (the large house on the other side of the road is the Channing Junior School). Then there is a row of fine 17th-century houses culminating in No. 104, Cromwell House, one of the very finest in the whole of London. Built about 1638 by the Sprignell family, it is certainly contemporary with Cromwell, but no one is sure why exactly it is now named after him. Possibly the Sprignells were admirers of the great Roundhead leader.

Lauderdale House and Highgate Cemetery

At the end of The Bank, cross the High Street and go through the gates into Waterlow Park, originally the grounds of Lauderdale House, which is now right in front of you. Go round to the left of the house and onto the terrace in front. Lauderdale House was built as the country home of London goldsmith Richard Martin in the 16th century. In the 17th century it was modernized by the Earl of Lauderdale, the 'l' of the ministerial grouping of Charles II's day called the 'cabal' (see pages 117–118). By the 19th century the house was part of the estate of Fairseat, the home of Sir Sydney Waterlow, head of the Waterlow printing firm and Lord Mayor of London in 1873. Waterlow generously donated the house and grounds to the London County Council in 1889.

From the front of the terrace go through the gap in the wall and then left and right down to the lakes. Cross the bridge over the cascade and continue along the main path. This brings you out of the park into Swains Lane, just by the entrance to **Highgate Cemetery**. The cemetery was opened on the other side of the road in 1839, just a few years after the new parish church. By 1856 it was already full, so an extension was consecrated on the eastern side of the road. It is in this new cemetery (entrance to your left) that Karl Marx is buried.

Turn right up Swains Lane. This ancient thoroughfare, more properly called Swines Lane, climbs steeply up to the village centre and brings you out on South Grove, west of the High Street. Immediately on your right is the Highgate Literary and Scientific Institution, founded in 1839 and the only surviving such organization in London. Ahead is Pond Square, the original village green. The ponds from which it takes its name were the principal source of water for the village's poorer inhabitants until piped water arrived in the mid-19th century. The old ponds – possibly former gravel pits – were then filled in.

Refrigeration experiments

Turn left along South Grove. Along here, right on the edge of the hill, used to stand the largest mansions in Highgate. The Old Hall, built in the 1690s, stands on the site of the most famous of them, Arundel House, built in the 16th century by one of Elizabeth I's courtiers, but from 1610 the home of the great art collector and connoisseur, Thomas Howard, Earl of Arundel. Many illustrious contemporaries stayed with Arundel here, including the lawyer, philosopher and scientist Francis Bacon. In fact, Bacon died in the house in 1626 after catching a chill while he was carrying out refrigeration experiments with a dead chicken and some snow!

Next door to The Old Hall Sir William Ashurst, Lord Mayor of London, built Ashurst House, also in the 1690s. Little more than a century later it was demolished and **St Michael's**, the new parish church, built on the site. The grounds were incorporated into the new cemetery.

The Grove

At the church, which stands exactly where Ashurst House stood, hence the fore-court in front, turn right across Highgate West Hill into **The Grove**. The first six houses were built on the site of Dorchester House in the late 17th century. At No. 3 the poet and writer Samuel Coleridge, by this time a laudanum addict, was looked after by Dr James Gillman and family from 1823 until his death in 1834. He was buried in the old churchyard and then re-interred in the new church in 1961. The author J. B. Priestley was a later resident of the same house.

No. 7 The Grove and following houses, obviously later in date, stand on the site of The Grove, demolished in the 18th century. At the end of this row of houses, turn left into Fitzroy Park. In the 18th century Charles Fitzroy, the first Lord Southampton, built himself a large house here with grounds laid out by Capability Brown. This road is the old drive to the house, demolished after barely half a century. Now it leads to houses of various dates, including some spectacular modern ones on the left-hand side.

Millfield Lane

At the second big left bend, turn right into a road leading along the foot of the allot-ments. At the end of the road carry on along the gravel path and then, just beyond some railings, go left down the bank and into Hampstead Heath. Follow this path down to the bottom of the hill where you join up with an old farm track called Millfield Lane, which leads up to **Kenwood** and Hampstead Lane. If you want to see more of the heath, go straight on across the bridge and then turn left beside the ponds (see alternative route shown on the map on page 52). Otherwise turn left on the lane, keeping the ponds to your right.

By damming the River Fleet, which rises near here, the Hampstead Waterworks Company created these ponds in the 1690s in an attempt to provide London with a reliable new water supply. There are six ponds altogether: the second, which you are passing now, is the ladies' bathing pool (the men's is number five). Millfield Lane passes the entrances to Fitzroy Farm (once the Fitzroy estate farm) and the Water House (the Waterworks estate farm) before – eventually – turning into a tarmac road by pool number four, the model boat pond. Here turn left up Merton Lane and then left again at the top into Highgate West Hill.

Royal thanks

On the right is the gated entrance to Holly Terrace, a long row of houses built about 1809 with its back sensibly to the main road and its front facing south to catch both the sun and the views. Opposite, No. 40 stands back at the end of the fore-court of the old Fox and Crown pub (see the plaque on the front). The landlord of the pub, James Turner, won heartfelt royal thanks in 1837 when he managed to prevent the young Queen Victoria's carriage careering down the hill out of control as she returned from a drive with her mother. Above the house on what must be Highgate's prime site stands, appropriately, the vast Witanhurst, reputed to be the largest house in London after Buckingham Palace. Millionaire soapmaker Sir Arthur Crosfield built it in 1920 as a platform for his young socialite wife, who had great ambitions to be a society hostess.

The Gate House

At the top of the hill, keep going along Highgate West Hill, passing the old Flask pub on the right and then the covered reservoir, dating from the 1840s, on the left. Beyond the heavily restored No. 47 at the end (the doctor's house in the 18th century) you come to the Gate House pub facing down the High Street. This stands on the site of the original gatehouse. Opposite is the old village churchyard and the Highgate School chapel of 1867, which stands on the site of the original hermitage chapel. Behind the chapel is the new school building, completed the year before.

Go round the corner by the pub. The sign shows what the gatehouse looked like before its demolition in 1769. Cross the zebra at the entrance to Hampstead Lane and carry on along North Road. As its name suggests this is the continuation of the old main road to the north. There are more 17th- and 18th-century houses here, including No. 17, Byron Cottage, where A. E. Housman lived from 1886 to 1905 and where he wrote his most famous work, *A Shropshire Lad*. Castle Yard on the right alludes not to a real castle but to the Castle Inn, which until 1928 stood at the right of the entrance to the road.

Highgate Wood

When North Road begins to lose height, cross over via the traffic island to the right-hand side. Here, No. 92 has a plaque commemorating the brief residence of the 20-year-old Charles Dickens in 1832. Continue on a few doors to the Wrestlers pub and turn right between it and the Indian restaurant into Park Walk. This brings you back to Southwood Lane and its junction with Jackson's Lane. The 'south wood' of the manor of Hornsey, now represented by Highgate Wood and Queens Wood, lies down the hill to the left. There are paths in Highgate Wood (and also a café) for anyone who has the energy for more walking. Otherwise, cross Southwood Lane and retrace your steps down Jackson's Lane to the station entrance, where the walk ends.

Isleworth

Location	10 miles (16 kilometres) west of Charing Cross.
Transport	Isleworth Station (overground trains from Waterloo).
Features	**All Saints Church**; Duke of Northumberland's River; boat-yards on the Thames; Ingram's Almshouses; historic London Apprentice pub; riverside walk and views; **Syon House** (walk passes entrance to park but not the house).
Refreshments	*outside station* burger bar/café, bistro and Chinese restaurants; *village centre* various pubs and cafés; *riverside* (and passed by the walk) Town Wharf pub (new), London Apprentice pub (old).

Isleworth is a riverside village on a great bend in the Thames opposite the Old Royal Deer Park at Kew. Originally it was no more than an enclosure belonging to one Gislhere; hence, apparently, the name. After the Norman Conquest of 1066 the manor was granted to the St Valery family of Picardy. In 1227 Henry III seized it and gave it to his brother Richard, Earl of Cornwall. Richard built himself a new moated manor house on the south bank of a little stream called the Bourne, just where it entered the Thames. Here the village grew up, with houses clustered around the manor house and the church, rectory, vicarage and manor farm on the north side of the stream. Further north and west lay the open fields of the manor. South at Railshead, where the River Crane entered the River Thames, there was a manorial corn mill for grinding flour and a salmon fishery (the stakes in the river forming part of the fishery gave Railshead its name). Further south lay the manorial hunting park.

Abbey and estate

In 1415 Henry V granted this park and the rest of the manor to a group of Swedish Bridgettine nuns who wished to found an English branch of their order. But the nuns preferred an alternative site to the north of Isleworth and it was here that they laid the foundation stone of their new abbey in 1426. Five years later they moved in and in 1488 the abbey church was finally consecrated. Half a century later, Henry VIII seized the abbey during the dissolution of the monasteries. It then passed into secular hands and was converted into a nobleman's mansion. The Earl of Northumberland acquired a lease of it from Elizabeth I in 1594 and the freehold from James I ten years afterwards. The now-ducal Northumberland family still owns the estate today and it is the last one in the vicinity of London to remain in the possession of its ancestral occupants.

Duke's river

After the dissolution of the Bridgettine convent the manorial corn mill moved to the mouth of the Bourne and a new channel was dug from the Crane to provide the Bourne with the extra water it needed to drive the mill. The new river was acquired along with the old abbey by the Northumberland family and inevitably became known as the Duke of Northumberland's River.

The extra power in Isleworth's river led to the building of several new mills upstream of the flour mill. At various times these turned out brass and copper, paper, dyes from mahogany imported from Brazil, and calico. Increased industrial output in turn stimulated the village's Thames-side wharves and in time Isleworth became quite a little port, complete with its own customs facilities. It handled not only local products but also swords and gunpowder from the nationally important mills on Hounslow Heath. More than once the village was badly shaken by gunpowder exploding in the wharf area.

Royal retreat

The impact of industrial development on Isleworth was not so great as to damage its attractions as a pleasant, healthy place to live. In the 17th and 18th centuries – and particularly when the royal family adopted Kew as a country retreat from the 1720s – it was a popular resort of courtiers and rich merchants. The whole area abounded in delightful country seats of all shapes and sizes. Most of the big houses have been demolished, but Gumley House, Isleworth House and Gordon House survive and are pointed out on the walk. Along with the big houses, much of the historic centre of Isleworth has also disappeared, a victim mainly of World War II bombing and of redevelopment, especially during the property boom of the 1980s when the old wharf area and Lower Square behind it were almost rebuilt. But there is still much to see – particularly the riverside grouping of church, pub and houses which is undoubtedly one of the prettiest sights on the Thames in the London area.

THE ISLEWORTH WALK

Start and finish Isleworth Station.
Distance 3 miles (4.8 kilometres).

Turn left out of the station and walk down through the car park to St John's Road. Turn left under the bridge and then second right by the Woodlands Tavern into Woodlands Road. After 100 yards (90 metres) or so you meet the Duke of Northumberland's River coming towards you from the Twickenham direction and then turning sharply east towards the centre of Isleworth and the Thames. Carry straight on, with the river on your left, and walk all the way along Riverside Walk (developed in the 1930s when the Middlesex County Council bought the river from the Duke of Northumberland) until you reach the bridge. Here, in the 18th century, there used to be two calico mills. A little further upstream near the disused railway embankment there is a road called Weavers Close.

Apart from the river there is not a great deal to see either on this or on the next section of the walk, but these suburban streets have to be negotiated in order to

ISLEWORTH

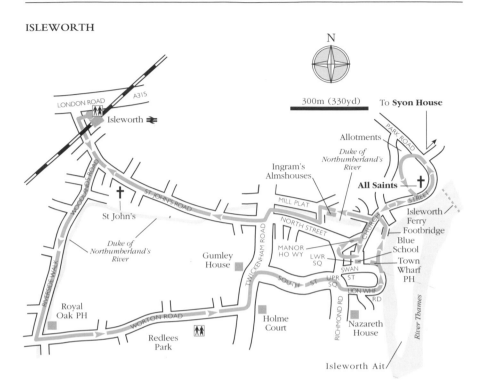

reach Isleworth village centre. Turn left over the bridge past the Royal Oak pub and carry on down Worton Road quite some way until, having passed the entrance to Redlees Park, you reach the junction with busy Twickenham Road. Holme Court, the old house on the far side of the road, is now an office but in the 1870s it was a Methodist boys' boarding school run by the Reverend J. S. Jones. In 1876–77 the young Vincent Van Gogh spent six months teaching here before returning to Europe and devoting himself to art.

Commissary-general

Cross Twickenham Road and turn left, passing Gumley House Convent School on the left. Gumley House, where the school started in 1841, is the large brick mansion straight ahead. It was built about 1700 by John Gumley, glass manufacturer, cabinet-maker and commissary-general to the army, after his marriage to Maria, daughter of Sir John and Lady Whittewronge of Isleworth. John and Maria's daughter later married the Earl of Bath, one of the aristocratic residents of 18th-century Isleworth.

Catholic centre

When you reach the road junction you will see, opposite Gumley House, the Roman Catholic church of Our Lady of Sorrows and St Bridget, built in 1909 to replace a small Catholic chapel on the riverside. After the Reformation Isleworth remained something of a Catholic centre. More Catholics came here from the 1680s onwards after James II built a Catholic chapel for his army encamped on Hounslow Heath. From 1744, by which time things were a little easier for Papists, a Catholic priest held regular services in the village.

Turn right at this junction into South Street, the beginning of Isleworth village proper. At the far end, the junction of roads – with a few original village houses on the left-hand side – is known as Upper Square. Shrewsbury Walk, to the right, commemorates Shrewsbury Place, where the Duke of Shrewsbury, an ex-Catholic, died in 1718. On the far side of Richmond Road, and away to the right, Nazareth House is another Catholic institution: a Poor Sisters of Nazareth convent and home for the elderly, founded in 1892 in Isleworth House. The house, once the home of Sir William Cooper, George III's chaplain, is still standing close to the riverside, but you cannot see it from this vantage point. Cooper enlarged his grounds both by buying up and demolishing houses north and south of Isleworth House and by diverting the Richmond road away from the riverside to its present course.

Lion Wharf

Cross Richmond Road and head off down Lion Wharf, the site of the Duke of Shrewsbury's house. From the riverside you can see the boatyard on Isleworth Ait (ait, or eyot, means island), reachable on foot at low tide. To the left there is a fine view of the old wharf area and, beyond the solitary surviving crane, the church and London Apprentice pub on the bend of the river. Turn left in this direction, walking through the Town Wharf pub. Beyond, look back for another fine view, this time of Gordon House, the residence of Lord and Lady Frederick Gordon in the 19th century and now part of the West London Institute of Higher Education.

Having passed the crane, cross the entrance to the Duke of Northumberland's River and then pass along beside the new houses covering the site of the old flour mill. As Kidd's Mill, it was bought by Rank in 1934 and immediately closed and then knocked down in the 1940s. Follow the path out – via the gate into this new development – into Church Street and turn right. Church Street has most of Isleworth's remaining original houses. Richard Reynolds House on the left (No. 43) commemorates a senior monk of Syon Abbey, executed in 1535 together with the vicar of Isleworth for resisting Henry VIII's attempt to make himself head of the English Church. Further on, No. 59 is called the Manor House, but is not really and is not even on the same site as the real manor house (which we come to later).

City apprentices

Here, by **All Saints Church**, you are in the most attractive part of Isleworth village. The old church is but a carcase of its former self, having been burnt down in 1943, not by German incendiaries but by two local, and youthful, arsonists. There is more about its history on the reverse of the signboard. To your right, the London Apprentice pub claims to date from the 15th century, but does not appear in the licensing records until the 1730s. The name alludes to the time when City apprentices used to row up river on their days off in search of recreation, exercise and, of course, beer. Church Wharf is a free draw dock, which means that boats can moor here free of charge. The wharf is also a ferry landing and the Isleworth Ferry uses it at the weekends during the summer months.

Carry on past the church and round the corner past the Headmaster's House and then the old Green School, a charity school for local girls. Ferry House, opposite, was the artist J.M.W. Turner's home from 1804 to 1806. Beyond Ferry House is the entrance to **Syon House**. On this side of the road you pass, first a pair of Syon estate cottages and then a house called The Limes. Immediately beyond The Limes, turn left into the lane by the allotments. Follow this round into the churchyard. At the top of the avenue leading up to the church there is a large yew tree on the left covering the mass burial pit of 149 victims of the Great Plague in 1665.

Blue School

Go right of the church tower and then exit from the churchyard, turning right on Church Street. Now retrace your steps along the street. When you reach the entrance to the riverside walk, carry straight on over the bridge and then keep going straight when the road bends right. You now enter Lower Square. Although it was comprehensively redeveloped in the 1980s, a few original buildings remain, notably the old village school in the centre. Founded as a charity school for boys in 1630, the Blue School (so called because of its blue uniforms) moved to another site at the end of the last century, but the school building, erected in 1841, continued to be used by the local elementary school until 1939.

Turn right by Waverley House – built as the Northumberland Arms in 1834 and an inn until 1983 – and exit from the square through the first arch on the right (by the sandwich bar). Head diagonally right across the green and then turn right along North Street (until around 1960 lined with houses at this point), with the relocated Blue School on your left. When the road turns left, turn right into Manor House Way, the site of Richard of Cornwall's medieval manor house.

Almshouses

At Church Street turn left, cross back over the bridge with the old mill sluice on your left and then turn left again into Mill Plat ('plat' just means a small piece of flat ground). This path eventually brings you to the oldest of the several sets of almshouses in Isleworth, Ingram's Almshouses, which were founded in 1664 by Sir Thomas Ingram, Chancellor of the Duchy of Lancaster, Lord Mayor of London and an earlier owner of the house later inhabited by the Duke of Shrewsbury. Each tiny single-storey almshouse has a bed-sitting room, a kitchen and a bathroom and, at the back, a little garden beside the river.

Silver Hall

When the path widens out, turn left, cross the river and then go right, through the gate, into Silverhall Neighbourhood Park, formerly the grounds of a handsome old North Street house called Silver Hall, demolished about 1950. Follow the winding riverside path to the main road, and then turn left and right into St John's Road. This is the final section of the walk and it takes you back to Isleworth station. The river is now behind the houses to your right. At Kendall Road it crosses underneath you and also joins with the Bourne, Isleworth's original stream, coming from the right. In the 'V' of land ahead between the river and St John's Road – where new houses are currently being built – the Isleworth Brewery stood until 1991. This was both the largest and the oldest commercial enterprise in the village. Founded in 1726, it gradually expanded to incorporate other mills on the river and was eventually sold to Watneys in 1924. Brewing ceased at Isleworth in 1952, although bottling continued till later.

St John's Church

Carry on up St John's Road. Copper Mill Drive on the right recalls John Broad's 16th-century brass and copper mill. Further on, St John's Church, paid for by the brewery owners and completed in 1857 along with almshouses, a parsonage and an infants' school, was needed by the growing population of the area brought in by the railway from 1849 onwards. On a site behind the houses on the opposite side of St John's Road, Pears soap was made between 1862 and 1962. The station, and the end of the walk, is up ahead on the right.

Kensington

Location	3 miles (4.8 kilometres) west of Charing Cross.
Transport	High Street Kensington Underground Station (District and Circle Lines).
Features	**St Mary Abbots Church**; **Kensington Palace**; **Commonwealth Institute**; **Kensington Roof Gardens**; **Leighton House Museum and Art Gallery**; Holland Park and remains of Holland House; Kensington Square and Edwardes Square; **Linley Sambourne House** (not on walk – see map page 64).
Refreshments	*Kensington High Street* pubs, cafés, sandwich bars and all manner of restaurants and fast-food outlets; *Holland Park* café and restaurant; *Kensington Church Street* Pierre Pechon's patisserie (and café).

The village of Kensington grew up at the junction of Church Street and High Street, the latter being a section of the Great West Road to the western counties. Traffic along this road accounted for most of the village's prosperity up to the 17th century. After that time it was the royal court and the capital itself that provided most local inhabitants with a living.

Throughout the Middle Ages the village was dominated by two owners. The larger of the two was the de Vere family, Earls of Oxford. Hailing originally from Vers in France, they came over to England during the Norman Conquest and added the manor of Kensington to their other estates before the end of the 11th century. The other landowner was the Abingdon Abbey near Oxford. One of the first de Veres granted a portion of Kensington to the abbey in the early 1100s out of gratitude for medical services performed by the abbot for a family member. From that time the abbey's property was a separate manor, distinguished by the name of Abbot's Kensington. The manor covered most, if not all, of the village of Kensington and gave its name to the local parish church, St Mary Abbots.

Sir Walter Cope's house
Following the destruction of Abingdon Abbey and sales by the de Veres, most of Kensington came into the possession of Sir Walter Cope around 1600. Choosing an elevated site a little to the west of the village, Cope built himself a fine country house with views south across the fields to the Thames glinting in the distance. This was one of the first modern country houses to be built on the fringes of London and it started something of a local trend. Lord Campden built Campden House up

on the hill behind the village, and on the London side Sir George Coppin erected a third mansion, later acquired by the Earls of Nottingham. Campden House disappeared long ago, but Cope's and Coppin's mansions survive respectively in Holland House (remains only) and in royal Kensington Palace.

Royal Kensington

In the 1680s Thomas Young, a carpenter, built a square in Kensington. Although people had already started to build them in London, it was probably a bit early to put one up so far from the West End. But Young was saved in 1689 when the asthmatic William III, unable to cope with the smogs and fogs of riverside Whitehall Palace, moved out to salubrious Kensington and transformed Lord Nottingham's house into a royal palace. Naturally he was followed by a huge retinue of servants, officials, courtiers and hangers-on. They soon acquired the empty houses in the new square and before long the High Street was buzzing with all kinds of new shops that catered to the wealthy new clientele. These were halcyon days for Kensington, but they did not last long: the palace was neglected after Queen Caroline's death in 1737 and deserted completely after her husband's demise in 1760. Thereafter, the village was thrown back economically on its traditional mainstay: its fertile nurseries and market gardens to the south.

Victorian suburb

Despite the departure of the court, Kensington never quite lost its reputation as a smart place to live. When London began to break out of its old historic confines in the 19th century, it became *the* Victorian middle-class suburb, home especially to the new rich of Victorian society, artists. Along with the middle classes came shops, and from these shops developed, from the 1870s onwards, department stores, notably Barkers. These stores, made accessible by the underground railway, which arrived in 1866, transformed Kensington into London's most fashionable shopping centre outside the West End.

Since those days, the 'old court suburb' as writer Leigh Hunt famously called it in the 1850s, has hung on to its reputation as a fashionable place to live and shop. But underneath the character of the old village survives, as the following walk shows.

THE KENSINGTON WALK

Start and finish High Street Kensington Station.
Distance 2¼ miles (3.6 kilometres).

Turn left out of the station down Kensington High Street and then cross Wrights Lane. Opposite Safeway, turn left through the arch into Adam and Eve Mews, which developed out of the yard and stables of a former inn. This was about as far as the high street of the original village extended before the era of expansion in the 19th century. Follow the mews round to the right at the bottom, then turn left by the Kensington Chapel (1854) – evidence of Kensington's expanding population – onto Allen Street. Go first right into Abingdon Villas, walk to the end and turn left into Earls Court Road.

Edwardes Square

Take the first right into Pembroke Square, walk to the end past Rassell's Nursery and the tennis court, and then turn right. Having passed the Scarsdale Tavern (named after a former mansion – Scarsdale House), turn left into Edwardes Square. This is the later of Kensington's two old squares. By the time it was begun in 1811, demand was building up locally for this type of house, but even so the developer took things steadily, building one side at a time. The north side, called Earls Terrace, was built first, then the east, west and finally the south sides, the latter completed in 1819. When you get to the little gardener's house halfway along, notice the artists' studios with their large north-facing windows on the left-hand side. First is a freestanding one used from 1940 to 1980 by the portrait painter Cowan Dobson. Then there is a purpose-built block of four, converted to offices. The East End is now the artists' quarter of London, no doubt because of lower property prices.

Artists' colony

Turn right at the end of the square and walk up to the main road, turning right by the lodge of Earls Terrace. The orientation of the terrace – facing the main road

KENSINGTON

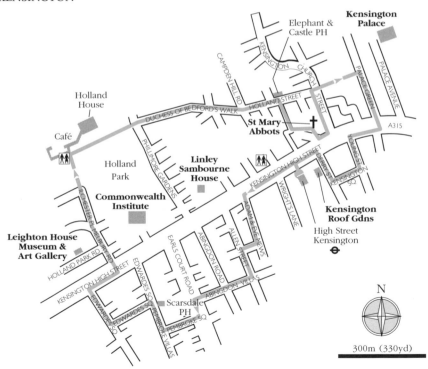

with gardens behind – proves that the developer was hedging his bets. It was only when the houses sold well that he proceeded with the square behind (perhaps it was even an afterthought). Cross the main road at the traffic lights, carry on a little way and then turn left into Melbury Road.

Attracted by the relatively clear air and the cheapish property, artists settled all over Kensington in the 19th century. The more successful congregated in the Melbury Road area, where they built themselves houses with studios attached. The sculptor G. F. Watts started the influx when he moved into Little Holland House on the edge of Holland Park. Before long there were no fewer than six Royal Academicians living in the colony. Chief among them was Frederick Leighton, president of the Royal Academy and the first painter to be made a peer. He lived in Holland Park Road where his house-cum-studio survives as **Leighton House Museum and Art Gallery**. Look left as you cross the entrance to Holland Park Road and you will see it with its glass-roofed studio sticking out at the back. Further on up Melbury Road, No. 18 carries a plaque to the Pre-Raphaelite painter William Holman Hunt.

When the road begins to bend round to the left, keep right into Ilchester Place. The house in the 'V' here was built for the artist Sir Luke Fildes, almost totally forgotten now, but a very successful painter in Victorian times. To the left, the house with the tower was the home of Cardiff Castle architect William Burges. He designed the house in the 1870s and made the inside – a riot of detail, colour and ornament that still survives – as medieval in style as the outside. Walking up Ilchester Place beside Fildes' house, look back to see the painter's huge studio, topped by a cupola, attached to the back.

Holland Park

Go straight on through the gate into Holland Park and walk up the hill towards the old stable block and garden arcade (the café is behind the arcade). Turn right here and walk eastwards across the park in front of the remains of Holland House (the green-roofed building away to your right is the **Commonwealth Institute**). The old Jacobean mansion was a private house until World War II, but it was badly damaged by bombs in 1940 and subsequently sold, with its surrounding parkland, to the local authority. Later the west wing was salvaged and converted into a youth hostel, which you can see today.

In the 18th century the house came into the possession of the Edwardes family, descendants of Sir Walter Cope. They sold it to Lord Holland, father of the famous Whig politician, Charles James Fox. During the time of Fox's nephew, the third Lord Holland, the house enjoyed several decades of fame when it served as the nerve centre of the Whig party, out of office almost continuously between 1784 and 1830. Later the Hollands, who were great entertainers, fell on comparatively hard times and had to start developing parts of their estate to make ends meet. The majority of the park survived, however, and, just as Holland House had been one of the first country houses on the fringes of London, so it was also the last private estate in central London to pass into public ownership. This belated transition helped protect Kensington's western flank from total obliteration by the developers. On the eastern side Kensington Palace performed a similar service.

The Phillimore estate

Having walked past the house, carry straight on out of the park into Duchess of Bedford's Walk. Phillimore Gardens on the right indicates that you are now entering the Phillimore estate, still privately owned after some 250 years. The Phillimores were one of the first Kensington landowning families to start developing their property. They began with a terrace of shops and houses on Kensington High Street in the 1780s. Then between 1812 and 1817 they built a group of seven country villas on the hill to your left. They intended these for markedly superior tenants, and got them, three dukes included. Immediately on your left stood the grandest of the villas, Bedford Lodge, which was the London home of the Duke and Duchess of Bedford.

Lesbian novel

Walk down to the end of Duchess of Bedford's Walk and cross over Campden Hill Road into Holland Street. Ahead the 250-foot (80-metre)-high steeple of St Mary Abbots Church rising above a row of gabled houses makes a picturesque view. Crossing Hornton Street and carrying on down Holland Street, you pass two of the many blue plaques in Kensington, a reminder of the large number of successful – often creative – people who have lived in the village over the past two couple of hundred years. Charles Stanford (terracotta house on the corner) was a leading English musician and teacher; Radclyffe Hall (No. 39 on the right) is best remembered for her lesbian novel *The Well of Loneliness,* published when she was living here and banned after an obscenity trial.

When you reach Gordon Place by the Elephant and Castle pub you are crossing the main drive that led left up the hill to Campden House, demolished about 1900. Beyond the pub you are in the oldest section of Holland Street and the heart of the former village. Further on, narrow lanes and passageways lead off the road on both sides and the houses almost all date from the 18th century. Take the first turning on the right – Kensington Church Walk – and walk on down to the churchyard. Most of it has been converted into a small park and playgrounds for the local school, but the section in front of the church's west door has survived. Turn in here and walk round to the right of the church, noticing the brightly coloured figures of the boy and girl high up on the wall of the school. The original parish school was designed by the architect Nicholas Hawksmoor, who was then clerk of works at Kensington Palace. It used to stand nearby on the High Street, with these charming little figures adorning its façade.

St Mary Abbots

The present **St Mary Abbots** is certainly the third and possibly the fourth parish church that has stood on this site. The arrival of the court led to the building of one new church in the 1690s; the coming of the Victorians, with their taste for Gothic, led to another nearly 200 years later. Fortunately, memorials from both replaced churches were preserved so that St Mary Abbots today, with its fine collection of over 250 inscriptions, is not unlike a miniature Westminster Abbey. The oldest memorial, dating from 1653 and commemorating Henry Dawson, MP and mayor of Newcastle, is on the west wall.

Barker's of Kensington

Leave the church by the covered passageway. This brings you out at the very centre of Kensington (the junction of Church Street and High Street) and presents you with a fine view of Barker's department store. Founded in 1870, Barker's gradually took over all its main rivals in Kensington and in the 1920s began work on this flagship store. But by the time the building was completed 30 years later, the firm had lost its independence and been taken over by the House of Fraser. Now it is merely a brand of another company, but its building remains a fine architectural adornment to Kensington's much rebuilt High Street.

Turn left and walk up Church Street as far as Holland Street and the traffic lights (Pierre Pechon's patisserie is on the left). Cross Church Street here and walk down York House Place, the name recalling another of Kensington's lost mansions. The path brings you out on Palace Green. Ahead is William and Mary's palace (or **Kensington Palace** where, later, Queen Victoria was born) and Kensington Gardens. To the right is the original palace coach house and stable. Either side of you are rows of vast mansions built in the mid-19th century as a Crown Estate speculation. Apart from a smattering of aristocrats, early tenants were mostly rich industrialists and businessmen. Today virtually every house is an embassy. Should you want to take a closer look at the palace, you can do so from the park, accessed by the gate in the park wall directly ahead across the green. Otherwise, turn right and walk down the hill to Kensington High Street.

Thackeray's novels

Turn right. Cross safely where you can and then take the first left into Young Street (the Victorian novelist William Thackeray lived in the house with bow windows on the right while writing *Vanity Fair, Pendennis* and *Henry Esmond*). Emerging in Kensington Square you are in Thomas Young's creation of the 1680s, the radical development only saved from disaster by the arrival of the court a few years later. Quite what Young thought he was doing building an urban square in a country village three miles (5 kilometres) from London is not clear, but that it was a premature development is surely proved by the fact that it backed directly onto open fields until as late as 1840. Then development started and the square's long-term future was at last assured. Turn right into the square. Except for those on the east side, most of the houses are original, but they have all been much altered and now each looks different from the rest. But this variety only adds to the square's charm.

Derry and Toms

At the west end of the north side, turn right out of the square into Derry Street. The Barker's building is on the right; the former Derry and Toms store, taken over by Barker's in 1920, is on the left. Should you want to see the famous **Kensington Roof Gardens** on top of what was Derry and Toms, the entrance is through the glass doorway marked No. 99. Otherwise, carry straight on to the end of the road and turn left into the High Street. The station entrance, and the end of the walk, is ahead on the left.

Pinner

Location	13 miles (21 kilometres) northwest of Charing Cross.
Transport	Pinner Underground Station (Metropolitan Line).
Features	**St John's Church**; High Street with 16th-century pubs and Georgian houses; timber-framed cottages and farmhouses scattered among suburban roads; views over park and farmland to Harrow Weald; **Harrow Museum and Heritage Centre** (not on walk – see map page 70).
Events	**Pinner Fair**.
Refreshments	*High Street* Italian restaurant, café/wine bar, Queen's Head and Victory pubs, Pizza Express; *Bridge Street* Oddfellows Arms pub, McDonald's, Wenzel's bakery and coffee house, Chinese restaurant, fish and chip shop.

Pinner. No name is more redolent of comfortable Home Counties suburbia. Yet few of London's villages are more ancient and picturesque. Pinner's chief glory is its wonderful High Street, a broad sloping thoroughfare stretching uphill from the River Pinn at one end to the parish church at the other. Lined with houses, shops and pubs built over the last four centuries or so, it is a wonderful lesson in architectural styles and building materials. Here, and in neighbouring Bridge Street, is held Pinner's famous fair, first authorized in 1336 and a regular annual event since at least the 18th century. Surrounding the old village centre, many of the timber-framed cottages and farms that once lay scattered about among the fields also survive. They are now embedded in more modern housing developments and the best of them feature on the walk.

South of the High Street in the early days lay the village's common fields reached by Rayners Lane. Traces of medieval ridge and furrow ploughing can still be seen in Pinner Village Gardens. East and west of the village were two outlying settlements called East End and West End. The sadly mutilated West House and Sweetman's Farm, a 16th-century timber-framed house, survive from the hamlet of West End in West End Lane.

Two lanes, Paines Lane and Moss Lane, stretched north to farms such as Waxwell Farm and Woodhall Farm. The former is included on the walk. At the latter, which still exists in Woodhall Drive, but which is a little too far to be included in the walk, John Claudius Loudon, the famous gardening writer, spent some time in the early 19th century convalescing from rheumatic fever and helping his tenant farmer father. A designer of elegant cottages and farm buildings, he also did some work on his father's farmhouse at the same time and it still bears his neo-Gothic Regency touches to this day.

High ground

On the high ground to the north of Waxwell and Woodhall farms – again, too far away to be included in the walk – lay more farms and, later, one or two large houses where Pinner's grander residents lived. From the 17th century, the village began to attract an increasing number of these types, usually City merchants and lawyers in search of country homes close to their London offices. The finest of these houses, Pinner Hill, a late-18th-century mansion, survives as a golf club.

Away to the east of Pinner – beyond East End – lie two large open spaces, Pinner Park and Headstone Manor Recreation Ground. Pinner Park, a former deer park and now a dairy farm, features on the walk. The Headstone Manor Recreation Ground, which surrounds Headstone Manor Farm, a moated medieval farmhouse with a massive tithe barn and an 18th-century granary, is unfortunately too far away. In the Middle Ages Headstone Manor was the manor house of Harrow. Pinner at that time was merely an outlying hamlet within both the manor and parish of Harrow. Harrow and its parish church were some distance away, however, so from early times Pinner had its own church. Today, Headstone Manor is home to the **Harrow Museum and Heritage Centre** and the Harrow Show takes place here over the August Bank Holiday.

THE PINNER WALK

Start and finish Pinner Station.
Distance 2¼ miles (4.4 kilometres).

Come out of the station and turn left down the hill. At the bottom turn right onto the main road and then right again into the High Street. Bridge Street is really Pinner's main shopping street and has most of the big stores you would expect to find in any modern town centre. Fittingly, High Street is reserved for more individual shops, including Corbett's bookshop and one or two antique shops. It also has a couple of ancient pubs, the Queen's Head on the left and the Victory on the right. The latter is dated 1580, but while the building itself might be that old, the pub has only been here since the late 1950s. They have been pulling pints at the Queen's Head, on the other hand, since at least the days of Charles I (1625–49).

At the top of the street on the left – beyond the green donated to the village in 1924 – is the long, low Church Farm, one of the oldest buildings in Pinner. The fact that this was a farmhouse as late as 1906 shows just what a modern phenomenon the modern suburb of Pinner is. Opposite, the Hilltop Wine Bar was a butcher's shop from the 1600s until the 1930s. Animals were slaughtered in the building to the right with the louvred roof (now a chiropodist's surgery). Between Church Farm and the wine bar is a house with an unusually large window facing down the High Street. As the Harrow Heritage Trust plaque says, this was a Victorian temperance tavern and tea garden called Ye Cocoa Tree. Opened in 1878 by 45-year-old local resident and property lawyer William Barber, who must have been something of a temperance enthusiast, it was popular with day trippers from London (the Metropolitan Line railway arrived at Pinner in 1886) and lasted well into the 1920s, by which time much of the central area of the village had been developed.

PINNER

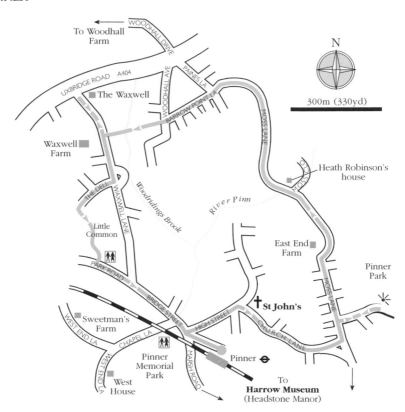

To Woodhall Farm

WOODHALL DRIVE

PAINES LA

WOODHALL AVE

UXBRIDGE ROAD A404

The Waxwell

BARROW POINT LA

N

300m (330yd)

Waxwell Farm

MOSS LANE

THE DELL

WAXWELL LANE

Woodridings Brook

River Pimm

Heath Robinson's house

Little Common

PARK ROAD

East End Farm

Pinner Park

BRIDGE STREET

HIGH STREET

St John's

MOSS LANE

CHURCH LANE

WEST END LA

Sweetman's Farm

CHAPEL LA

Pinner Memorial Park

MARSH ROAD

Pinner ⊖

WEST END LA

West House

To **Harrow Museum** (Headstone Manor)

St John's Church

Continue to the right into Church Lane. Built in flint, the only building material available in any quantity locally, **St John's Church** was dedicated in 1321, though it did not become a parish church in its own right until 1766 when Pinner broke away from Harrow. St Johns' great tower, which dominates Pinner High Street, is a 15th-century addition. The entrance to the church is via the lychgate and the sunken path leading to the south door. To the right, the curious monument with the stone coffin sticking out either side commemorates John Claudius Loudon's parents and is no doubt another product of their son's fertile, if slightly eccentric, imagination. Inside the church there is a memorial to the poet laureate Henry Pye, of whom more later when we come to East End.

Pinner House

Carry on past the church. Round the corner you come across Pinner House, the grandest house in Pinner village proper. Dating from around 1700, it has a very gracious aspect and must at one time have enjoyed wonderful views southwards across the fields towards Harrow. Apart from Pinner Hill away to the north, it is the only one of Pinner's mansions to survive into the late 20th century. Since the late 1940s it has been an old people's home. Further on around another corner you come to a cluster of comfortable-looking old houses: on the right The Grange; on the left the grey-painted Bay House (timber-framed behind a deceptive Victorian façade); and then, on the right again, the substantial Elmdene facing Nower Hill Green. Here, in the 19th century, lived the natural daughter of Horatio Nelson and Lady Hamilton, Horatia Nelson Ward. Horatia died when she was 81 and is buried in the village cemetery in Paines Lane. More recent occupants of the house include the comedian Ronnie Barker and the actor David Suchet, star of the TV series *Poirot*.

Nower Hill Green is sometimes known as Tooke's Green because of the Victorian drinking fountain in the centre that commemorates village benefactor William Tooke. Tooke, who lived at Pinner Hill, was as near to a squire as Pinner could have in the 19th century. He paid for the rebuilding of the church in 1880. His clergyman grandfather – whose inheritance of a fortune in 1792 enabled him to devote himself to historical studies – was one of the first historians of Russia.

From deer park to farm

Walk past the memorial to the top of the green and turn left and then right into Wakehams Hill. At the top where the road bends right, bear left down the track. From the gate, where there is a thoughtfully provided seat, there is a splendid view north over Pinner Park towards the high ground beyond. Up in that high ground near the River Pinn's source are two of Pinner's three surviving farms: Pinnerwood Farm and Oxhey Lane Farm. The third is the one you can see in the middle of Pinner Park, just beyond the main road. Sometimes called Hall's Farm, it is named after the family that have tenanted it (from St Thomas's Hospital in central London) since the end of the last century. Before that the Halls were at Headstone Manor. In medieval times Pinner Park was a 250-acre (100-hectare) deer park used for hunting. Farming gradually took over in the 16th century.

East End

Re-trace your steps down Wakehams Hill. Facing you across Moss Lane at the bottom is The Fives Court, a notable Arts and Crafts house designed at the beginning of this century by Cecil Brewer for Ambrose Heal of Heal's furnishing store in Tottenham Court Road. Turn right into Moss Lane. A fairly long section now ensues until you come to the nucleus of the old outlying settlement of East End. You will know it when you see it, for the ancient houses are conspicuous among the newer buildings. Three houses remain out of the original half dozen or so. First, on the left behind a crazy wall, is Tudor Cottage, an old house tarted up with an assortment of architectural antiques. Beyond is East End Farm, the brick indicating a later date and greater prosperity. Here lived George III's poet laureate Henry Pye (1745–1813), whose memorial is in the church. Ridiculed even in his own day, he is only remembered now, if at all, because of fellow writer George Steevens' punning put-down of his first birthday ode to the king using the line 'When the PYE was opened' from the 'Sing a song of sixpence' nursery rhyme. At the end of the farmyard is the 15th-century East End Farm Cottage, the oldest house in Pinner, if not in the whole of Middlesex. Amazing enough from the outside, inside it has a superb, roughly contemporary, wall painting. Clearly the house must have been grander when it was built than the farm labourer's cottage it later became. The old farmyard on the right survives virtually intact and is still in semi-agricultural use (by a firm of fruit and potato merchants).

River Pinn

Carry on along Moss Lane, around the corner and down the hill. At the bottom you cross over the River Pinn: the name Pinner is thought to mean 'settlement on the banks of the Pinn'. The path on the left by the postbox leads through to Paines Lane. No. 75 on the right has a blue plaque to the illustrator William Heath Robinson, a resident of Pinner for some 13 years. He actually lived in this house for five years from 1913.

Another long section now ensues until you reach the junction of Moss Lane with Paines Lane (Moss Cottage is on the left). If you would like to catch a glimpse of Loudon's Woodhall Farm, turn right here, walk to the end of the road, cross the main road into Woodhall Drive and walk up the left-hand side for about 100 yards (90 metres). Otherwise, cross Paines Lane diagonally to the left into Barrow Point Lane and carry on to the bottom.

Waxwell Lane

Where the lane turns sharp left, bear right through the hedge and then immediately left into the footpath, signposted Waxwell Lane, though the name has been painted over. At the low point in the middle of the path you cross over Woodridings Brook, a tributary of the Pinn. Emerging in Waxwell Lane, Waxwell Farm is immediately opposite. No longer a farm, it still has a huge garden and is another reminder of Pinner's not too distant agricultural past. The house is now used by the Holy Grail, a Roman Catholic organization.

Waxwell Lane takes its name from a medieval spring or well, which until the arrival of piped water was a major source of fresh drinking water in the area. If you turn right in Waxwell Lane you will find the well, reached by a short flight of steps but now bricked up, just by the junction with the main road, on the right-hand side. The main route of the walk turns left along Waxwell Lane and then, opposite Waxwell Close, an elegant crescent of 'artisan' housing dating from the 1920s, right into the Dell. The great hollow of the Dell, now filled with modern houses, was man-made over the centuries by locals digging for lime and flint. Both were used for building, but lime, of course, was also applied as a dressing to farmland. Elsewhere in Pinner, people mined underground for these valuable materials. Some of the mines, which still exist but are not open to the public, are over 100 feet (30 metres) below ground level.

Pinner Common

As you approach the Dell, keep on the left-hand side and walk along the pavement as the ground drops away to the right. Just beyond White Cottage, turn left through the gate into Little Common, relic of a once much larger piece of common land

Plate 11: *The Flask in West Hill, Highgate, has been a popular drinking place for over 300 years (see page 55).*

Plate 12: *One of the five lakes that make up Highgate Ponds on Hampstead Heath: this one is used by model boat enthusiasts (see page 54).*

Plate 13: *The narrow stretch of the Thames between Isleworth and Isleworth Ait provides a sheltered location for a boatyard (see page 59).*

Plate 14: *Kensington Church Walk: a quiet corner close to the parish church in the heart of the village (see page 66).*

Plate 15: *A profusion of flowers decorates the exterior of the Elephant and Castle in Holland Street, one of Kensington's most popular pubs (see page 66).*

Plate 16: *The Wax Well in Pinner is now disused but it was once an important source of drinking water (see page 72).*

Plate 17: *The timber-framed East End Farm Cottage dates from the 15th century and is probably the oldest house in Pinner (see page 71).*

Plate 18: *Once the boyhood home of Arts and Crafts designer William Morris, this Georgian mansion in Walthamstow is now the William Morris Gallery (see page 78).*

(another area, called Pinner Green, survives to the north). Follow the path out of the park and turn left on Park Road. Ahead you can see the spire of Harrow church breaking out of the trees on top of Harrow Hill. Carry on down the hill to the Oddfellows Arms pub at the junction with Waxwell Lane. Here there is an old milestone giving the distance to London. Around the corner in Waxwell Lane there are two charming old timber-framed cottages, Orchard Cottage and Bee Cottage, which are well worth a look.

Carry on down Bridge Street. At the bottom you pass the entrance to Chapel Lane, leading to West End and West House whose grounds are now a public park. You then cross (although you are not really aware of it) the bridge over the Pinn, from which, of course, Bridge Street takes its name. The Pinn flows to the right here in a southwesterly direction and eventually joins the Colne (and thence the Thames) a few miles south of Uxbridge. Pinner Station, and the end of the walk, is 100 yards (90 metres) or so ahead, *this* side of the railway line.

Walthamstow

Location	7½ miles (12 kilometres) northwest of Charing Cross.
Transport	Walthamstow Central Station (Underground Victoria Line; overground trains from Liverpool Street), Walthamstow Queens Road Station (overground North London Line trains between Gospel Oak and Barking).
Features	**St Mary's Church**; Monoux and Squires Almshouses; **Vestry House Museum**; 15th-century Ancient House; **William Morris Gallery**.
Events	**Village Festival**.
Refreshments	*Orford Road in Walthamstow village* bakery, café/takeaway, Chinese takeaway/fish and chip shops, two pubs, two Italian restaurants, Indian takeaway; *High Street in town centre near station* cafés, restaurants, sandwich bars and fast-food outlets.

The village of Walthamstow – meaning 'a place where travellers are welcome' – grew up on high ground east of the River Lea, opposite Tottenham on the London bank. The village was well established by the time of the Domesday survey in 1086 and subsequently expanded to include several outlying settlements; for example, Kings End in the south and Chapel End (where there was a chapel-of-ease to the main parish church) in the north. Subsequently, the centre of the village, where the main parish church was situated, became known as Church End.

After the Norman Conquest, the manor of Walthamstow was granted to the de Toni family. They are credited with building the present church, which is certainly medieval in origin and appears to date from the 13th century. There is some doubt about the location of the de Toni manor house. Some sources say that it was at a place called High Hall between the village and the river; others that it stood opposite the church on the site of the present Ancient House, a half-timbered 15th-century house featured on the walk. Either way, the last de Toni died childless and his sister took the property into the Beauchamp family, earls of Warwick. From the 15th to the 17th centuries it passed through many, including royal, hands. The last squires were the Maynards, first baronets and then viscounts. Charles Maynard, auditor of the exchequer, acquired it in 1639 and a Maynard was still lord of the manor 300 years later.

Walthamstow benefactor
From the late Middle Ages rich City merchants built country houses in the beautiful wooded countryside around the village. One of these in the early 16th century was

Sir George Monoux, Lord Mayor of London in 1514. Although not lord of the manor, Monoux was one of Walthamstow's most generous benefactors, founding the Monoux Almshouses and Grammar School, and paying for the rebuilding of the church. He died in 1544 and was buried at St Mary's, where there is a commemorative brass to him. His house in the north of the parish near Chapel End survived until 1927 and is now covered by Monoux Grove.

Gentlemen's residences
By the middle of the 19th century, the still-rural parish was well sprinkled with fine gentlemen's seats. Several of these are still standing today, including Walthamstow House in Shernhall Street to the east of the village and The Chestnuts to the south in Hoe Street. These do not feature on the walk, but the 18th-century Water House and Brookscroft and the 19th-century Orford House do. Although some distance from the village centre, Water House, a fine Georgian mansion on a low-lying site to the north of the village, has been included on the walk because it was the boyhood home of the great designer and socialist William Morris and is now a gallery devoted to his life and work. The walk between the village and the house is not particularly attractive, but it cannot be avoided.

Following the arrival of the railways in the 1840s and the enclosure of all the old common land in the 1850s, the way was clear for the speculative builders to transform the old village into a modern suburb. Elsewhere in London this process usually involved the destruction of the old village. But at Walthamstow new village/town centres were built (first in Orford Road and then in Marsh – now High – Street). As a result the original Walthamstow village survives today, complete with medieval church, 15th-century Ancient House, 16th-century almshouses, 18th-century workhouse and vestry room, and 19th-century cottages and schools. It is a rare little oasis of history in the otherwise rather ugly sprawl of contemporary east London.

THE WALTHAMSTOW WALK
Start and finish Walthamstow Central Station.
Distance 2¾ miles (4.4 kilometres).

Turn right out of the station and walk up Selborne Road to the traffic lights. Cross the main road and go straight on into St Mary Road. At the end of the road continue on into Church Path This takes you past some pretty Victorian cottages, and then a row of rather older ones built in 1825, before bringing you out in the centre of Church End, the original village centre of Walthamstow. On the right are the old school and workhouse, of which more later. On the left are the Squires almshouses, founded in 1795 by Mrs Squires for six tradesmen's widows. Mrs Squires lived at Newington and died the year after the almshouses were founded.

Ancient House
Carry on past the almshouses into Church Lane. On the left now is **St Mary's Church**, standing in its three-acre (1.2-hectare) churchyard. The many fine tombs reflect Walthamstow's former status as an up-market residential area. Opposite the

75

church is the so-called Ancient House, a timber-framed structure dating from the 15th century. In the 19th century it was converted into four shops, hence the large windows on the ground floor. Now it is a private home again. The bare plot on the other side of the entrance to Orford Road was the site of the village inn, the Nag's Head, until it was rebuilt behind the Ancient House in Orford Road in 1859.

Walk on past the Ancient House. The small but elegant house on the far side (No. 10 Church Lane) was built in 1830 for a family of local builders called Reed. A little further on in Bishop's Close is the Chestnuts, built by the Rev. J. Roberts, headmaster of the Monoux School from 1820 to 1836. It was partly a residence for himself and partly a boarding house for the private pupils he taught at the school. Bishop's Close was later built in the grounds of the house.

Vinegar Alley

Continue on down Church Lane for some way. Just beyond the pillar box near the end, turn left into Vinegar Alley. This takes you back through the churchyard towards the east end of the church. To the right, opposite the church, are the Monoux Almshouses and Grammar School for boys, founded by Sir George Monoux in 1527 and completed before his death in 1544. The school was in the

WALTHAMSTOW

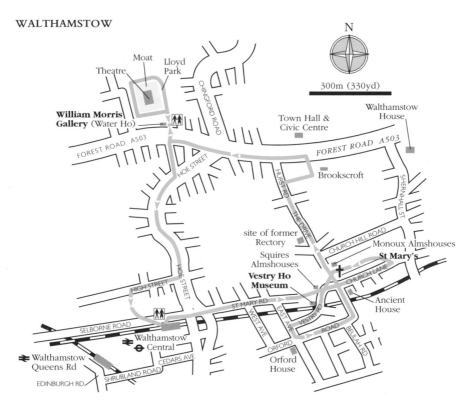

brick part at the far end (rebuilt in 1955 following bomb damage during World War II) and the master lived in the protruding section in the middle. The much-expanded school moved to a new site in Chingford Road in the last century and is still there today.

At the west (tower) end of the church, turn left and bear right at the fork. On the right now, on the far side of the churchyard, is the old St Mary's infants school, founded in a barn on the vicar's glebe in 1824 and then provided with this handsome building four years later. The vicar at the time, the Rev. William Wilson, was a pioneer of infant education and St Mary's was the first school of its kind established by the Church of England. The building was last used as a school in 1978 and is now the church's Welcome Centre.

Parish workhouse

Back in Church End, cross the road, turn right and follow it round to the left as it becomes Vestry Road. The road takes its name from the building on the right, built by the parish in 1730 as a combined workhouse and vestry office (the vestry was the local authority in those days). The parish poor were moved to a new workhouse in Stratford in 1840 and the building subsequently became, among other things, a police station and a private house before being turned into a local history museum in 1931, now the **Vestry House Museum**. A plaque on the wall by the barrel marks the site of the old parish watch-house and lockup. Nearby stands the top of a column from the old General Post Office in St Martin-le-Grand in the City. The building was demolished in 1912 and this relic brought here by a local resident. On the other side of the road is the National School. This was built in 1819 to take the overflow from the old Monoux School and was in use till 1906. Since 1924 the building has been used by the National Spiritualist Church.

Carry on along Vestry Road, crossing the deep railway cutting made in 1870, and following the road round to the right past the playground and the old (1903) postal sorting office on the left. As the plaque on the sorting office says, this area was once the Bury Field, or Church Common, one of three large areas of common land in the old rural Walthamstow. All the commons were enclosed in 1850 and subsequently built over with streets and houses.

New centre of Walthamstow

At the end of Vestry Road, turn left into East Avenue. The large house ahead is Orford House, built on the edge of Church Common in the early 19th century for Whitechapel merchant John Case. Now it is a social centre with a bowling green in the garden behind. Before you reach the house, turn left by the Queen's Arms pub into Orford Road and walk along past the shops. Orford Road was built from the 1860s onwards as the new centre of Walthamstow: further on you pass the new school (now the Asian centre) and the new town hall (now a nursery school), which were put up at that time. As Walthamstow continued to expand, the centre of the growing town moved to yet another new site, still further from the old village. Today Orford Road serves the Walthamstow Village conservation area and surrounding streets.

Follow the road when it bends round to the left and crosses back over the railway line, passing the rebuilt Victorian Nag's Head pub on the far side. Cross straight over Church Lane and walk past the west end of the church once more, but this time in the opposite direction. Carry on past the almshouses into Church Hill. Beyond the almshouses on the right is the new rectory; on the left is the old vicarage, absorbed into Walthamstow High School in 1974. The old rectory, owned all through the Middle Ages by the Priory of Holy Trinity, Aldgate, in London, stood across the road ahead to the left until its demolition at the end of the last century.

The Ching valley
Cross straight over the road ahead (Church Hill/Prospect Hill) and walk along The Drive. Although you cannot see it, the ground now drops away on all sides as you approach the top of the hill that once protected Walthamstow village from the worst of the north winds. At the end of The Drive the steepness of the descent into the Ching valley becomes apparent. Go straight over into Hurst Road, and halfway down turn right by the Hurst Road Health Centre sign into the path to the right of the railings. This brings you out in front of a block of flats. At the far end there is a car turning area and next to it more railings. Turn left here and follow the path downhill again to the junction with Forest Road. On the right now is Brookscroft, another of old Walthamstow's surviving 18th-century mansions. Once it looked out over woods and fields. Now, converted into a YMCA hostel, it surveys the borough of Waltham Forest's impressive civic centre, opened in 1941.

William Morris's home
Turn left along Forest Road. At the lights cross straight over and at the zebra cross the road and go through the gates into Lloyd Park surrounding the **William Morris Gallery**. Go through the gate to the right of the house and walk around the moat in the park behind in either a clockwise or an anti-clockwise direction. The original house stood on the island in the centre of the moat. The present house was built in the mid-18th century. William Morris was born at Elm House further along Forest Road in 1834 and moved here with his parents in 1848. Eight years later Morris senior lost a lot of money in the City and the family had to leave. The house was bought by newspaper publisher Edward Lloyd. In 1950 it was turned into a museum celebrating William Morris's achievements as a designer, craftsman, poet and socialist.

Walthamstow Market
Exit Lloyd Park by the same gate and cross straight over the main road into Gaywood Road. At the top, turn right on Hoe Street. Follow this winding road for some distance until you pass the cinema and reach the lights. Here turn into the modern High Street, the post-Orford Road town centre and the site of Walthamstow's mile-long (1.5-kilometre) street market. Originally called Marsh Lane, High Street connected the village with the marshes down by the Lea. As Walthamstow expanded, costermongers started setting up the stalls here from the 1880s and so the market, now one of the longest in Europe, grew up. When you reach the town square, turn left along the tree-lined avenue and make your way back to the station, where the walk ends.

Villages South of the River Thames

Barnes

Location	5½ miles (8.8 kilometres) west of Charing Cross.
Transport	Barnes and Barnes Bridge stations (overground trains from Waterloo).
Features	**St Mary's Church**; Barnes Terrace; site of Barn Elms manor house; Barnes green and common; Thames and Beverley Brook riverside walks; **Barn Elms Nature Reserve**.
Events	**Barnes Village Fair**.
Refreshments	*overlooking river* Café Uno, Bulls Head pub (start of walk) White Hart pub (end of walk); *High Street* fish and chip shop, pub, café/patisserie, bakery, vegetarian takeaway, brasserie; *Barnes Green* Sun Inn; *Church Road* Délice de France café (village end), cafés, Indian restaurant, Red Lion pub (Barn Elms end); *White Hart Lane* (junction with The Terrace near end of walk) Thai, Indian and Chinese restaurants.

Long before the Norman Conquest King Athelstan gave to the Dean and Chapter of St Paul's Cathedral in the City of London an estate to the west of the city on the south bank of the Thames. The estate consisted of a neck of land opposite Chiswick and Hammersmith bordered on three sides by the Thames. The whole of the peninsula was low-lying, between about 14 and 20 feet (4 and 6 metres) above sea level. The top end was marshy and subject to flooding. But the bottom, landward, end was firmer. Here a road ran between Putney and Mortlake. Barnes grew up at the west, Mortlake, end of the road, just at the point where it intersected with the river.

At the intersection point, where the Bulls Head pub now stands, the village had its own wharf. Shops and houses lined the road approaching the wharf, in time forming today's High Street. At the other end of the High Street was the common. The part of the common nearest the village, where there were several ponds, became the village green. Several large houses in spacious grounds were built overlooking it. Beside the green, a lane led off from the High Street past the church to the grounds of the manor house, called Barn Elms after the great elm trees that populated its large park.

Bridge and waterworks
North of the village and manor house, the bulk of the peninsula was a quiet, remote farming district traversed by no roads except a lane leading to Chiswick ferry (now

represented by Ferry Road). Progress arrived in the early 19th century in the form of the Hammersmith Bridge Company which, in 1825, bought the Barn Elms estate in order to build an approach road to Hammersmith Bridge, opened in 1827. The bridge company was followed almost immediately by the West Middlesex Water Works Company. In 1828 it built the first of several massive reservoirs and filter beds, which in time came to occupy a substantial chunk of the peninsula. As the 19th century advanced, the rest of the peninsula was covered by roads and houses, especially after the opening of Barnes Station in 1846. The Barnes Bridge Station line was built three years later, but Barnes Bridge Station, where the walk starts and finishes, was not constructed until 1916.

Barnes today

Although it has lost its manor house and several of the fine houses that once surrounded the green, Barnes is still an exceedingly attractive London village. It has its terrace of elegant 18th- and 19th-century houses overlooking the river – a popular vantage point for the closing stages of the annual Oxford and Cambridge University Boat Race; its High Street with its individual shops; its green and church with some lovely old houses along Church Road; and finally its common and its open parkland, once the grounds of Barn Elms House. Barnes also has something that many other London villages lack – a strong community spirit, carefully nurtured by the local community association. This should be evident on the walk, along with all the physical features just listed.

THE BARNES WALK

Start and finish Barnes Bridge Station.
Distance 3¼ miles (5.2 kilometres).

Come out of Barnes Bridge Station and turn right along The Terrace, keeping to the raised riverside walkway on the left and walking in the direction of Chiswick, which you can just make out in the distance on the opposite side of the river. The Terrace dates from the 18th century when people began to move to Barnes from the city in increasing numbers. Several houses survive from that time, including No. 10, the red brick house on the corner of Cleveland Gardens, which has a plaque recording the residence of Gustav Holst. Best known for his suite *The Planets*, the composer lived here from 1908 to 1913 while teaching music at St Paul's girls' school in Hammersmith.

The Bulls Head pub stands opposite the site of the old village wharf. At the roundabout here turn right into the High Street. This has been largely redeveloped since Barnes became a railway suburb, but it still contains many small shops offering specialist products and personal service. At the far end you pass the 18th-century Rose House – once a pub and now the headquarters of the local community association – before arriving at the village green, part of the old village common. The pond is the only one of four to survive. It used to be fed by the Beverley Brook (which you will see later), but now it depends on a mixture of rainwater and mains top-up, rather like the ponds at Carshalton.

BARNES

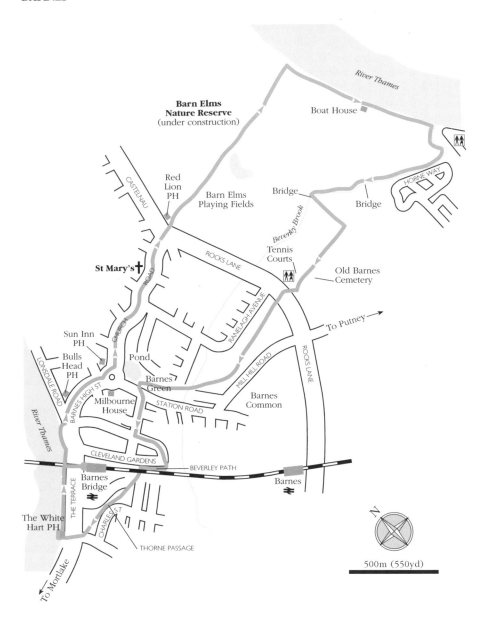

River Thames

Barn Elms
Nature Reserve
(under construction)

Boat House

CASTELNAU

Red
Lion
PH

Barn Elms
Playing Fields

Bridge

Bridge

HORNE WAY

St Mary's

Beverley Brook

Tennis
Courts

Old Barnes
Cemetery

ROCKS LANE

CHURCH ROAD

RANELAGH AVENUE

To Putney

Sun Inn
PH

Bulls
Head
PH

Pond

Barnes
Green

MILL HILL ROAD

ROCKS LANE

LONSDALE ROAD

BARNES HIGH ST

Milbourne
House

STATION ROAD

Barnes
Common

River Thames

Cleveland Gardens

Beverley Path

Barnes

THE TERRACE

Barnes
Bridge

The White
Hart PH

CHARLES ST

THORNE PASSAGE

To Mortlake

N

500m (550yd)

Gothic novel

Turn left at the green into Church Road and walk past the Sun on your left and the green on your right. The building in the middle of the green is a Victorian girls' school, closed in the 1920s and now used as a senior citizens' day centre. At the end of the Victorian developments and just before the terrace of shops you come to a handful of 18th-century houses (one, pink Gothic) making a very pretty little group next to the little green with tree and bench underneath. The last house in the row is The Grange (now an old people's home run by the Julian Memorial Trust). Behind The Grange, in the appropriately named Hermitage Cottage, the author 'Monk' Lewis lived on and off from about 1801 to his death in 1818. Lewis earned his nickname and his reputation (though not his living which came from slave-ownership in Jamaica) from his 1795 publication, *The Monk,* an early and very successful Gothic novel. The site of his cottage is now covered by a modern development called The Hermitage.

Now follow the road round by the parade of shops. On the right the green, ringed by a low white post and rail fence, extends right up to Glebe Road. Glebe Road was built on the glebe land belonging to the rector; the rector himself lived in the large Georgian house on the far side of the junction of Kitson Road on the left (Kitson Road, laid out in 1907, is named after Canon Kitson, rector of the parish at that time).

St Mary's churchyard

Beyond the former rectory (now called Strawberry House) is the parish church of **St Mary's**. The original church was destroyed by a fire in 1978 but the 15th-century tower survived. In the attractive old churchyard most of the gravestones date from the 18th and 19th centuries, though on the south wall there is a 17th-century plaque to Edward Rose, citizen of London, who died in 1653. He obviously had a sense of humour because he left £5 a year to the parish for roses to be planted on his grave.

From the churchyard carry on along Church Road, passing on the left the handsome Homestead House, dating from about 1700 and one of the finest of Barnes's surviving historic houses. At the end of Church Road you come to the junction with Castelnau, left (the new road built in 1827 as an approach to Hammersmith Bridge), and Rocks Lane, right. Cross straight over by the Red Lion into Queen Elizabeth Walk and walk on down beside the Barn Elms Playing Fields. The Walk was the drive to the manor house: one of the entrance lodges survives on the right-hand side. On the left redundant reservoirs built by the West Middlesex Water Works company a century ago are currently being dismantled and converted into a housing development and the 100-acre (40-hectare) **Barn Elms Nature Reserve** to be created by the Wildfowl and Wetlands Trust. You may have noticed as you passed the old entrance lodge that the Trust has taken it over for its Barnes office.

Pepys picnicking

When you reach the entrance to the Wandsworth borough sports centre, keep to the left along the footpath. A small wood in the centre of the sports centre covers the site of Barn Elms House. The original manor house was home to several historical characters, including Elizabeth I's spymaster, Sir Francis Walsingham. In the 17th century the grounds appear to have been at least partly public, for they were often used for picnics (by Samuel Pepys among others) and for duels. In 1698 the Cartwright family built a new house, which was extended in the 1770s by the Hoare banking family. The last tenant (apart from the army during World War II) was the Ranelagh Club, an upper-class social and sporting club, founded in Fulham in 1878 and based at Barn Elms from 1884 until its demise in 1939. The much-abused house was finally demolished in 1954. Its ancient elms fell victim to Dutch elm disease 20 years later.

Along the towpath

When you reach the end of Queen Elizabeth Walk turn right along the towpath beside the Thames. On the towpath you pass a couple of boathouses. Across the river is Fulham Football Club. Ahead is Putney Bridge. After some distance you come to a little bridge crossing the mouth of the Beverley Brook. This little river is thought to be named after the beavers that once inhabited its banks. Turn right just before the bridge and follow the path as it winds along between the stream and the sports centre. The brook rises in the vicinity of Nonsuch Park in south London and flows for 8 miles (13 kilometres) before arriving here to join the Thames.

After a while you pass a modern bridge with green railings, wide enough to take a vehicle. Carry on past it along the path. Later, opposite a corner in the sports centre fence, you come to a similar but much narrower bridge. Cross this bridge into Barnes Common and follow the path along the wire fence to the right. Keep to the path as it first goes to the right round the corner of the fence and then bears slightly left through a belt of trees. You emerge by some tennis courts. Keep going along the path between the courts and the Victorian cemetery – opened in 1854 when the old churchyard you passed in the village was full – until you come to a car park.

Sir William de Milbourne and Milbourne House

Cross the car park and turn right on the road. At Rocks Lane cross slightly to the left into the tarmac path across the common (there is a 'Toilets' sign at the entrance to the path). Follow this path for some distance until you meet another, obviously more important one, crossing diagonally. Turn right on this and follow it back to the Beverley Brook. Here cross the bridge into the village green and take the left-hand avenue. When you reach the pond at the far end look diagonally left to the long house with the pebble-dash front. This and Essex House on its far side are the only two survivors of the colony of large houses that used to surround the green. Of the two, Milbourne House is by far the older and more important. Whereas Essex House only dates from the middle of the last century, Milbourne House has a history going right back to the 1400s when it belonged to Sir William de Milbourne, MP for Surrey in the 1370s. Later tenants included the 18th-century novelist Henry Fielding, to whom there is a commemorative plaque on the front. He lived here in the early 1750s and probably wrote his last book (*Amelia*) here.

From the pond turn left onto Station Road and then immediately right into Cleveland Road. Take the second left into Cambridge Road and follow it round to the right. As it bends right again into Cleveland Gardens, turn off it to the left to join Beverley Path and then immediately right along the path past some 19th-century cottages. Go under the railway line into Archway Street and then almost immediately right into Thorne Passage. You are now in the Westfields district of Barnes, the site of the great west field of the medieval manor. In those days Thorne Passage and Beverley Path formed a short cut across the fields by-passing Barnes for people walking between Mortlake and Putney. In the 19th century Westfield House, lived in by local brewer Benjamin Thorne, stood here. At the far end of the passage you pass, first, the old brick wall of Mr Thorne's residence and then the old coach house – now, appropriately, part of a garage.

Emerging from Thorne Passage, turn right on White Hart Lane and go straight over at the road junction into the short alley to the left of the riverside White Hart pub. This alley represents the boundary between the parishes of Barnes to your right and Mortlake to your left. Turn right now along the towpath and follow it past the upper section of The Terrace to Barnes Bridge Station where the walk ends.

Bexley

Location	12½ miles (20 kilometres) southeast of Charing Cross.
Transport	Bexley Station (overground trains from Charing Cross).
Features	**St Mary's Church**; **Hall Place and Bexley Local History Museum**; River Cray and water meadows; winding High Street with many 18th-century houses; Styleman's almshouses; **Bexley Cricket Club**.
Refreshments	*High Street* 16th-century King's Head pub, Chinese, Italian, Greek and Indian restaurants, fish and chip shop, Bon Appetit tearooms and sandwich bar, wine bar and brasserie, Bexley bakery, Old Mill pub-restaurant; *Bourne Road* Dennis the Butcher for award-winning pies; *Hall Place* (see map page 88) café and pub-restaurant.

The Kentish village of Bexley – meaning 'clearing among the box trees' – grew up at the point where two roads converged to cross the River Cray. One road led from Eltham to Dartford and the other from Crayford to Orpington. Today, these are represented respectively by Parkhill Road, Bexley High Street and Vicarage Road, and by Bourne Road, the High Street and North Cray Road.

The village was well established by the time of the Domesday survey. During the Middle Ages the Church of St Mary and the little rectory estate belonged to the Priory of Holy Trinity in Aldgate in London. From the Priory came the village's vicars. They lived in the medieval vicarage south of the church, which survived until the 1770s.

The main manor of Bexley, which included not just the village but the outlying hamlets of Blendon, Danson, Hurst, Upton and Welling, belonged to the great estate of the Archbishops of Canterbury. The archbishops did not live in the village, but they had a manor house there from which the village was governed. The manor house, rebuilt in the 18th century, still survives and can be seen – or rather glimpsed – on the walk.

In the 1530s the Crown acquired the manor and almost immediately leased it to a rich London merchant and ex-Lord Mayor of London, Sir John Champneis. Using old stone salvaged from demolished monasteries, Champneis built himself a fine house about 1 mile (1.6 kilometres) northeast of the village, on the north bank of the Cray. In the early 1600s James I granted the manor and Champneis' house to the antiquary and herald William Camden, author of Camden's *Britannia*. When Camden died in 1623 he left the estate to Oxford University to fund a history professorship. The university remained Lord of Bexley Manor into modern times.

Local history museum

In the meantime, the house – known as Hall Place – was acquired by Sir Robert Austen in 1649, the year of Charles I's execution. Adding a brick section on the south side that faces the river, he more than doubled the house in size. Today, half silvery Tudor stone and half weathered 17th-century brick, the building is more or less as Austen left it at his death in 1666. Now owned by the council, it houses offices and the **Bexley Local History Museum**, and together with its immaculate gardens, forms one of the highlights of the walk.

Hall Place was the big house of Bexley village, but there were several more mansions in the parish, mostly to the north and west, for the village is in the southeast. The two most important were probably Blendon and Danson. In the early 15th century Blendon was home to the archbishop's park keeper, Henry Castilayn, to whom there is a brass memorial in the village church. Danson was acquired by East India Company director Sir John Boyd in the mid-18th century. The architect Sir Robert Taylor built him a Palladian house in the 1760s and Capability Brown landscaped the park. Both house and park survive, but are unfortunately too far from the village to be included in the walk. Blendon was demolished and built over in the 1930s.

Water meadows and woods

In the 1770s Bexley was described as having many handsome, modern-built houses, inhabited by genteel families of fortune. Many of these houses survive today and are seen on the walk. Also still in existence and seen on the walk are the old water meadows bordering the river and the woods crowning the high ground to the south. What Bexley has lost as a result of suburbanization – following the arrival of the railway in 1866 – are its farmland and the great heath on the high ground to the north, crossed by the main road from London to Dover.

Once the villagers' common grazing land, the heath was enclosed in 1819 and subsequently developed. Within a few decades the village of New Bexley – now Bexleyheath – was bigger than the old one. Its growth took the pressure off Old Bexley and helped ensure the latter's survival as a pretty little village literally right on the edge of London, with one side built up and the other meadow and woodland. Today, with the new Dover road cutting it off from Hall Place and a constant stream of cars thronging the narrow High Street, traffic is Bexley's main problem, but as a London village it is hardly unusual in that.

THE BEXLEY WALK

Start and finish Bexley Station.
Distance 3¾ miles (5.2 kilometres).

Turn right out of the station and follow Station Approach down the hill to the junction with the High Street. Turn right and then immediately right again into Tanyard Lane. This takes you through the former tanning yard and under the railway line into the riverside meadowland. Across the meadows you can see the backs of some of the houses in North Cray Road. Follow the path until you reach **Bexley Cricket Club**. Founded by 1746, the club is one of the oldest in Kent and has been based at this pitch since about 1840. Match scores survive from 1802. The most celebrated match in club history took place in 1805, the year of the Battle of Trafalgar, when Bexley dismissed Kent for only six runs.

Turn right at the car park and go back under the railway line into Manor Way. When you reach Hurst Road cross slightly to the left and go into a footpath (the entrance is marked by a 'No Cycling' sign). This brings you out on Parkhill Road, the old main road from Eltham to Dartford. The houses on the other side of Parkhill Road, built from 1869 onwards for middle-class commuters attracted to Bexley by the new railway, were the first signs that the old country village was changing into a London suburb. St John's Church was completed for the new inhabitants in 1881 and became a parish church in its own right in 1936.

Almshouses and workhouse
Turn right past the church, and playground, and walk down the hill into the winding village High Street, which begins at the junction with Hurst Road. On the left,

BEXLEY

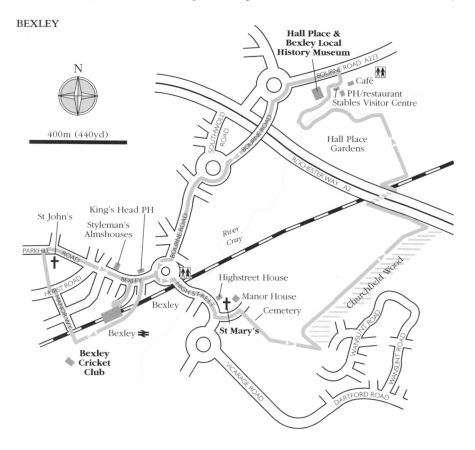

the long low building is Styleman's Almshouses. John Styleman made a fortune in India and owned Danson before Sir John Boyd. He died in 1734 and left money for the almshouses, but they were not built until several years after his widow's death in 1750. Ahead, the Georgian house with steeply pitched roof on the corner by the station entrance represents another 18th-century method of dealing with the poor: from the 1780s until 1834 this house served as the parish workhouse.

Beyond the old workhouse is the Railway Tavern, and then on the left is No. 57 High Street, otherwise known as Jackson House. Built in 1676 with a double-height porch, this is one of Bexley's finest houses and in the 18th century was lived in by the local builder. Still on the left, the building with the clock tower is the Freemantle Hall, built in 1894 as a public hall for the village. Just beyond is the 16th-century King's Head pub, probably the oldest building in the village centre apart from the church.

The mill

When you reach the little roundabout at the junction with Bourne Road, follow the High Street round to the right past the George pub (dating from at least 1717) and cross under the railway line once more. On the far side of the railway line you come to the river crossing. The Old Mill restaurant on the right is a modern replica of the 18th-century corn mill, built in 1775 and burned down in 1966. Beyond is Cray House, built at the same time as the mill, possibly for the mill owner. The cottages on the opposite side of the road are mainly early 19th century with the exception of No. 101 in the middle, which has a bit of style and which probably dates from the mid-18th century.

Following the High Street round to the right you come to the wisteria-clad Highstreet House, the finest house in the village with the exception of the Manor House. Built in 1761 over the foundations of an earlier house, it was, as the plaque on the front states, the home of the Kent historian and antiquary John Thorpe. Born in 1715, the son of a Rochester surgeon, he lived here until 1789, when his wife Catharina died. Thorpe died three years later. There is a plaque to his wife on the churchyard side of the garden wall.

Brasses and monuments

Walk beside the churchyard wall and turn left into Manor Road. **St Mary's**, with its unique cone and pyramid spire, dates from the early Middle Ages. Inside, besides the Castilayn brass, there are Champneis, Austen and Styleman monuments. Outside, the oldest tomb – belonging to the Payne family – dates from 1603. On the right you pass the entrance to Manor Farm House and then the footpath leading up the hill to an area that used to be called, for obvious reasons, Coldblow. Then go past the modern church hall, built on the site of the medieval tithe barn demolished about 1910, and the Victorian Manor Cottage.

Manor Road finishes at the entrance to the old manor farmyard, now the Bexley Sand and Ballast Company. The Manor House is to the left, but is hardly visible unless you go into the churchyard and peer over the fence. The walk turns right here into the lane leading to the churchyard extension, opened in 1857 and in 1990 turned into a protected ecological area. If you look back when you reach the corner of the wall, there is a good view of the upper part of the manor house across the old farm orchard.

Carry straight on along the now narrow path heading uphill through the cemetery. At the end, go through the gate and continue up the hill on the tarmac path leading through meadow land towards Churchfield Wood on top of the hill. Just before the path forks, turn left into Churchfield Wood (there is a Cray Riverway waymark here) and follow the lower of the two paths (the one on the edge of the wood next to the fence). From the path you can clearly see the sand and gravel workings beside the Cray.

When you reach the far side of the wood by the main road, exit via the stile and turn left down the tarmac path towards the railway line. Follow the path underneath the road and then round to the right, keeping tight to the embankment. When you reach the path leading up to the road level, take it and cross the bridge over the railway line, walking into the face of the oncoming traffic. On the far side, turn right down the steps back onto ground level and go through the gate into the grassy area beside the railway line, following the Cray Riverway waymark. Walk straight along here with the railway on your right and the hedge boundary of Hall Place gardens on your left. At the corner of the hedge turn left and follow the hedge all the way up to the river. Here turn left again and go straight on through the gate into the Hall Place grounds and walk along beside the river.

Hall Place and gardens

Beyond the first bridge – leading into the maintenance yard and marking the approximate site of the old watermill demolished in 1926 – **Hall Place** comes into view, presenting its 17th-century brick face. At the second bridge, cross the river and turn back towards the house, aiming for the gap in the hedge. You can then see the older stone part of the house and how the later section was simply added onto the south side. The Tudor part has two wings projecting to the north, but the 17th-century part is a quadrangle with a courtyard in the middle.

Once through the hedge look left and you will see the topiary garden started by the last private occupant of the house, the Countess of Limerick. She died in 1943. The figures at the front – looking like large teddy bears, but in fact intended to be heraldic beasts – were added by Bexley Council a decade after the countess's demise to mark the Queen's coronation. Follow the path round to the east side of the house where the public entrance is and then turn right past the granary (brought from Manor Farm in Bexley village in 1988) and the stables (now the Visitor Centre). Go out of the gate into the car park (café and toilets ahead) and turn left.

Victorian and Edwardian building

Turn left again out of the car park and walk along Bourne Road in front of the north front of the house, screened from the road by a fine pair of 18th-century gates. Continue on up to the roundabout and turn left. Follow the pavement over the motorway and River Shuttle back towards Bexley, which you re-enter at the second roundabout. As you approach the village centre once more, you pass on the right various institutions that reflect the growth of the village in the Victorian era and later: the National Schools, opened in 1834 and converted to industrial use 140 years afterwards; the Victoria Homes almshouses, built to mark Queen Victoria's Diamond Jubilee in 1897; the local library built at the junction of Albert Road in 1912; and the 1905 Baptist chapel across Albert Road from the library.

Across Bourne Road from the library is the old Refell's Brewery, in business from 1874 until 1956 and now converted into a business park. Further on, also on the left, you pass the entrance to a row of old workshops leading down to the railway viaduct, and then the original 1846 Baptist chapel with a louvre in the roof, converted into shops many years ago. At the roundabout you meet up with the High Street once more. Turn right here and make your way back to the station (the entrance is by the Costcutter Supermarket), where the walk ends.

Blackheath

Location	6½ miles (10.5 kilometres) southeast of Charing Cross.
Transport	Blackheath Station (overground trains from Charing Cross).
Features	Black Heath; some of the finest Georgian architecture in London (notably The Paragon); **All Saints Church**; Morden College; the Cator Estate.
Refreshments	*Tranquil Vale* pubs, tapas bar, bakery, patisserie, delicatessen and Indian restaurant;
	Montpelier Vale Café Rouge, Italian restaurants and wine bars, Indian/Nepalese restaurant;
	on the walk Hare and Billet pub (first half of walk – see map page 94), Princess of Wales pub (second half of walk – see map page 94).

Blackheath takes its name from the heath that divides it from Greenwich, its riverside neighbour to the north. Some say the name comes from the black, barren soil of the heath, but it is more probably a corruption of 'bleak'. Certainly the heath, a treeless plateau 125 feet (38 metres) above sea level, is empty and windswept enough today. In the days when it was covered with gorse and scrub and infested with highwaymen and footpads it must have been truly forbidding.

The heath was originally waste or common land for the inhabitants of the four neighbouring manors of Lewisham, Greenwich, Charlton and Kidbrooke. In those days Blackheath village did not exist in the way it does today. There were just a few large houses on high ground overlooking the valley of the Kid Brook and the heath beyond, and some cottages and a pub down in the dip where the roads from Lee and Lewisham met to cross the Kid Brook.

Having come together to cross the Kid, these two roads then divided again, one heading east to join the main road across the heath (now the A2 from London to Dover) and the other heading west to join the same road but going in the London direction. It was at this latter junction – on the west side of the heath – that the first developments in Blackheath took place when the new Lords of Lewisham manor, the Earls of Dartmouth, built Dartmouth Row and neighbouring streets in the 1690s.

Speculators move in

Later, in the 18th century, fine houses were built by speculators along the south side of the heath, first on the western side and then, right at the end of the century, on the eastern side. Tradesmen moved into the area to service these houses and so the village gradually came into existence – but at the low point where the Lee and

Lewisham roads crossed the river and not on the main road close to Lord Dartmouth's mansion and surrounding streets.

In the 19th century the river was covered over and the railway laid out along its length. Development proceeded apace after the opening of Blackheath Station in 1849. Much of this development took place on the largest single property in the area, the 293-acre (118.5-hectare) Cator Estate. The old name for the Cator Estate was Wricklemarsh and it was as such that the Blount family bought it in the late 16th century. In 1669 the estate was sold to Turkey merchant Sir John Morden and his wife. Having no children to leave their property to, the Mordens founded a large almshouse on the eastern edge of their estate for Turkey Company merchants who had been rather less successful than Sir John. Attributed to Wren, Morden College was built in spacious landscaped grounds on a knoll overlooking the Kid Brook in 1695. It survives, much expanded, to this day and features on the walk.

After Lady Morden's death in 1721, Wricklemarsh was bought by Sir Gregory Page. One of the few people to escape from the South Sea financial scandal in 1720 with his fortune intact, he demolished the old Tudor house and built a vast new one on the heights overlooking the Kid valley and the heath beyond. It was all in vain, however, for his nephew and heir found it far too large and promptly sold it to a self-made businessman from Beckenham, timber merchant John Cator. Cator auctioned off the fabric of the house and developed the northern fringe of the estate beside the heath into what is now Montpelier Row, South Row and The Paragon. Building on the interior of the estate started a little later – in about 1806 – and continued over a considerable period of time.

Starting and finishing at Blackheath Station, the walk takes in the Cator Estate and other Georgian and Victorian developments on the surrounding heights. It also, of course, includes the village centre and parts of the heath, but unfortunately not the Dartmouth streets of the 1690s, which are a little too far away.

THE BLACKHEATH WALK
Start and finish Blackheath Station.
Distance 3 miles (4.8 kilometres).

Turn left out of the station and walk through the centre of Blackheath village. This is the low point where originally the two roads from Lee and Lewisham joined to cross the Kid Brook. In early days it was known as Blount's Hole, after the residents of the nearby Wricklemarsh estate. During Lady Susannah Morden's long widowhood in the early 18th century it acquired the new, and somewhat less flattering, name of Dowager's Bottom!

When the road divides in front of the triangle, bear left into Tranquil Vale and walk up the hill. Before the village developed in the second half of the 18th century there were just a few cottages here, a public well called Queen Elizabeth's Well (its site is in Tranquil Passage which runs through the middle of the triangle) and the Crown pub, which you soon come to on the corner of Camden Row. Tranquil Vale was the beginning of the road that led off across the heath towards London; its sister, Montpelier Vale, headed off west in the Dover direction. Go past the

entrance to Camden Row and the well-known Mary Evans Picture Library and
you come out on the southern edge of the 275-acre (111-hectare) Black Heath. To
the right is **All Saints**, the parish church, not built until the mid-19th century. Ahead
is a cluster of buildings in the middle of the heath, hiding what is known as
Blackheath Vale. The Vale is actually a huge pit dug in the days when Blackheath
was an important source of sand and gravel. After World War II most of the pits
were filled in with bomb rubble, but the Vale had long since been colonized, not
just by cottages, but by a livery stable, a school and even a brewery. Today only the
houses and the school survive.

City merchant

Walk on up the hill. At the top you come to a handsome semicircle of houses composed of Lloyd's Place, Grote's Buildings and Grote's Place. Lloyd's Place was built
in the 1770s by John Lamb and takes its name from John Lloyd, a resident of No. 3
in the 1780s. Grote's Buildings and Place were a largely speculative development
by City merchant Andrew Grote in the 1760s. The land belonged to Morden
College, which wanted to create a fund for paying its chaplain. Grote built Lindsey
House – the red-brick detached house behind the trees at the left end – for himself
and then sold the other, terraced, houses to recoup his investment. All these houses
enjoy fine views across the heath to All Saints Church and South Row and,
beyond, to the houses along Shooters Hill Road and the spire of St John's Church.

Walk straight on across the green towards the clump of trees surrounding the
Hare and Billet pond, probably an old gravel pit. As you pass between the pond and

BLACKHEATH

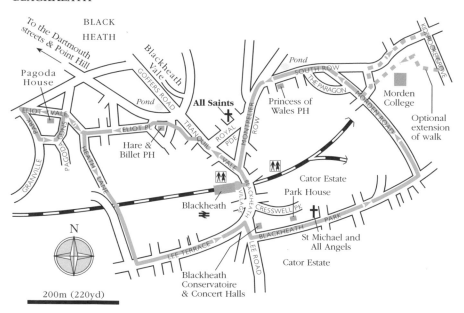

the pub you can see to the right the roofs of the houses in Blackheath Vale. Straight ahead in the distance are houses built on the west side of the heath close to Lord Dartmouth's original development of the 1690s. The most prominent house – white stucco with a pitched roof – is actually a pair and dates from 1776.

Turn left at the pub and cut across past Eliot Cottages to Eliot Place. The houses here were built between 1795 and 1802 on land belonging to the Eliot family, Earls of St Germans (hence St Germans House at No. 11). The central house, No. 6, is perhaps the most handsome. Built in 1797, it became the home and private observatory of merchant and amateur astronomer Stephen Groombridge five years later. Now Morden College almshouse uses it for out-pensioners. The last house in the terrace, No. 2, was the home of naval officer and polar explorer Sir James Clark Ross, after whom Ross Island and Ross Sea off Antarctica are named. Next door is the grand Heathfield House, built for Rotherhithe shipowner John Brent. The earliest and grandest house in Eliot Place, it has now been given a modern extension and divided up into flats.

Pagoda House

Go straight on down the hill into Eliot Vale and then up the far side, following the road round to the right. As you cross the entrance to Pagoda Gardens look left and you will see the house with the curly roof that gives the road its name. Standing by the pillar box, you can see away to the right on the other side of the heath a red-brick house called Ranger's House (see page 115). Next to it another mansion used to stand called Montagu House. Montagu House's grounds were mainly on this side of the heath, laid out on the south-facing slope of the hill, and the 18th-century Pagoda House was a kind of summer house. When George IV's wife Caroline was living at Montagu House in the early 19th century she was a regular user of Pagoda House and it was here that she was rumoured to have had her affairs and to have housed her illegitimate children. In reality she probably got up to nothing more suspicious than overseeing her little nursery school and tending her garden. The king had Montagu House knocked down in 1815 and divorced the unfortunate Caroline five years later.

Follow the road round to the left past Aberdeen Terrace, which consists of large 19th-century houses built on land once belonging to the Pagoda. When the Terrace turns left, keep going and on the far side of the green, behind the bushes, turn left down Granville Park. When you get to Pagoda Gardens turn left and then at the T-junction turn left again. Now you have a close-up view of Pagoda House.

Quaggy valley

Back on Eliot Vale, turn right and then a little further on right again into Heath Lane. Passing Eliot Vale House on the left and turning into a footpath, this goes down the hill into the former valley of the Kid Brook, crosses the railway line and the old course of the river and then climbs up the far side to meet Lee Terrace, the road connecting Blackheath (to your left) with Lewisham (to your right). Some distance ahead, down in the valley of the Quaggy river, lies Lee. The church here, St Margaret's, is Lee's new parish church, built in 1841. The ruins of the original one stand in the closed graveyard 100 yards (90 metres) or so to the right. The astronomer Edmond Halley, of Halley's Comet fame, is buried here.

Turn left on Lee Terrace and head back towards Blackheath, passing some fine 19th-century houses and some less impressive 20th-century infilling. As you pass Dacre Park there is a good view to the right over the Quaggy valley.

The Cator Estate

You arrive back in the village at the point where Lee Terrace meets Lee Road coming in from the right. Cross over to the partly ivy-covered Blackheath Conservatoire (founded 1881) and turn right. Immediately beyond the Concert Halls turn left through the gates into Blackheath Park and the Cator Estate. With the exception of Kidbrooke Grove near Morden College and the fine houses round the heath, the Cator Estate was, and indeed still is, the most select part of Blackheath village.

Laid out along the crest of the ridge dividing the valleys of the Kid and the Quaggy rivers, Blackheath Park is the main thoroughfare of the estate and the location of some of its earliest and finest houses. The row on the left starting at No. 7, for example, dates from about 1806. Just beyond it is a wooden fence atop a low brick wall. Behind here, set well back in a large garden, is the earliest and finest house on the estate, a silvery stone mansion constructed in 1788 with materials salvaged from Sir Gregory Page's house. Since the end of the last century it has belonged to the Catholic Church.

Now comes a row of three pretty detached villas and then St Michael and All Angels church, built in 1828. The junction of Blackheath Park with Pond Road next to the church marks the site of the great house built by Sir Gregory Page in the 1720s. From its hilltop site it had wonderful views north over the heath to Greenwich and south over the Quaggy valley.

Gounod's plaque

Carry on along Blackheath Park and then at the end turn left into Morden Road. No. 17 just beyond The Plantation on the right has a blue plaque on it recording the stay of French composer Charles Gounod in October 1857. At the end of Morden Road you leave the Cator Estate by another set of gates and return to the heath. To the right is Morden College, set in immaculate grounds. It is not very easy to see the actual College building from this point, but a better view can be obtained from the footpath (illustrated on the map) which starts to your right at the end of the green railings and runs all the way through the College grounds.

The Paragon

Walk straight on up the hill onto the heath. To your right is St German's Place. Ahead you can see Greenwich Park and the Canary Wharf Tower beyond. To your left is The Paragon, the first section of the line of houses built along the northern perimeter of the Cator estate from 1795 onwards. As its immodest name suggests, The Paragon is the finest Georgian set piece in Blackheath and one of the finest of its period anywhere in London. As you walk past you will see that it is composed of seven blocks linked by colonnades to form a crescent looking northeast across the heath towards St German's Place. They were designed, as were South Row and Montpelier Row which follow, by surveyor Michael Searles. Each block contained two houses so there was a total of 14 residences in all. Unfortunately they were very badly damaged during World War II, but afterwards they were acquired by a responsible developer to whom their restoration was something of a personal crusade. The original 14 houses are now split up into 100 flats.

Colonnade House

South Row continues the Cator Estate perimeter development. Cator Manor, the first house, is not an old manor house but a neo-Georgian house built on the site of outbuildings blitzed during World War II. Pond Road, named after the remnant of an ornamental lake that existed up until 1955, is the old drive up to Sir Gregory Page's Wricklemarsh. Beyond Pond Road more modern housing replaces another section of South Row destroyed during World War II. Then comes Colonnade House, built in 1804 for William Randall, shipbuilding partner of John Brent whom we encountered earlier at Heathfield House. Brent, Randall and a third partner made a fortune building warships at the time of the Revolutionary Wars with France.

At the end of South Row you come to the Princess of Wales pub (named after George IV's wife Caroline, who was never actually crowned). A plaque on the front records the fact that it was here in 1871 that the English team for the first-ever rugby international was selected. The team included four players from Blackheath Rugby Club, one of the oldest in the country.

Blackheath has always been used for sport. Golf was played here from early times, the old sand and gravel pits making excellent bunkers. James I (also James VI of Scotland, the 'home' of golf) is said to have introduced the sport to the area while staying at Greenwich Palace in the early 17th century. The local club, in existence by the 1780s, later developed into the Royal Blackheath Golf Club and is now generally regarded as the oldest in England. Since 1923 it has been based at Eltham.

Round the corner from the Princess of Wales pub, South Row turns into Montpelier Row. At the far end of the Row you return to the centre of the village. Follow Montpelier Vale down the hill to the junction with Tranquil Vale and make your way back to the station, where the walk ends.

Carshalton

Location	10 miles (16 kilometres) southwest of Charing Cross.
Transport	Carshalton Station (overground trains from Victoria).
Features	**All Saints Church**; the source of the River Wandle; **Carshalton House and Water Tower**; Carshalton Park and grotto; **Sutton Ecology Centre** and nature reserve; **Sutton Heritage Centre**; Grove Park, **Little Holland House** (not on walk – see map page 100).
Refreshments	*village centre (east of church)* pubs, Bon Appetit sandwich bar and deli, Village bakery and coffee house, fish and chip shop, burger bar, Indian restaurant/takeaway, Woodman's wine bar; *village centre (west of church)* Greyhound Hotel, tearoom in Heritage Centre.

Carshalton lies on the old road from Croydon to Sutton, about 1 mile (1.6 kilometres) east of Sutton. Behind are the chalk downs where the Epsom Derby is raced. North stretches a flat plain through which the Wandle river snakes its way towards the Thames. The larger of the two streams that join at Hackbridge to form the Wandle begins in the ponds at Carshalton. Originally these ponds were filled naturally by springs in the chalk. Now they have to be topped up from the mains because of a general lowering of the water table in the area. This general lowering has also caused all Carshalton's other streams and ponds – streams and ponds that once made the village famous for its trout and water cress – to dry up, as you will see on the walk.

The village High Street runs east–west along the foot of the downs. To the south, ascending the hill to the former common fields on the plateau, the old roads were Park Hill and Park Lane, embracing Carshalton Park between them. To the north, the main roads were West Street and North Street, converging after about three-quarters of a mile (1.2 kilometres) at Wrythe Green and then branching into three – one highway leading to Morden and Wimbledon, the middle one to Merton and Wandsworth, and the easterly one to Mitcham and thence to London, crossing the Wandle at Hackbridge. West Street Lane connected West Street and North Street and then continued east along the Wandle as Mill Lane, its name reflecting the presence of many water mills in this industrial part of the village.

Wandle mills

From at least the time of the Domesday Book there was a corn mill in the village. But from the late 17th century onwards, various entrepreneurs began to harness the

Wandle's power to drive other kinds of mills. Industrial milling reached its peak in the late 18th century and finally died out about a century after that. At various times the Carshalton mills produced – besides flour – paper, leather, snuff, drugs, linseed oil, sheet copper and gunpowder.

When it was just a small country village, Carshalton was dominated by three large houses whose estates intruded right into the centre of the village. To the west was Carshalton House, built in the time of Queen Anne (1702–14) by Edward Carleton and later added to by Sir John Fellowes. In the centre, between the High Street and the Wandle, was Stone Court, later The Grove. The original Stone Court – its name indicating the strangeness of the building material in an area where chalk and flint, and then brick, predominated – was built in the 15th century by Nicholas Gaynesford, at one time sheriff of Surrey. Then, south of the High Street, on the slope of the down, stood Mascalls, later Carshalton Place and later still Carshalton Park. Carshalton Park was bought in 1696 by merchant Sir William Scawen. The Scawens sold up in 1781 and were succeeded by the Taylors, a family of West Indian sugar planters and slave owners. Mascalls was the manor house of the village and the Scawens, followed by the Taylors, were the lords of the manor. Carshalton House and The Grove still stand and feature on the walk. All that remains of Mascalls is a large part of its park (also seen on the walk): the house itself was demolished in 1927.

Unlike its neighbour to the north, Mitcham, Carshalton never became a rural retreat for merchants and courtiers from London. The extra few miles needed to reach it seem to have made all the difference. Or maybe it was the paucity of good sites for houses. Whatever the reason, Carshalton's transition from rural village to London suburb had to wait until the arrival of the railway in 1868. Even then it was some decades before pressure for development really built up. As late as 1890 the three large estates strait-jacketing the expansion of the village were all still in private hands and undeveloped. The following year the first new roads were laid out in Carshalton Park and suburbanization then proceeded apace.

THE CARSHALTON WALK
Start and finish Carshalton Station.
Distance 2¾ miles (4.4 kilometres).

Come out of Carshalton Station and turn right down the hill. At the bottom turn left into West Street and walk in the direction of the village. Traditional weatherboarded houses, painted white, are a feature of this part of Carshalton. Beyond the Racehorse pub, the park wall and the Water Tower of Carshalton House come into view. Just beyond the Water Tower a gate in the wall allows you a view of the house.

Carshalton House
Having built **Carshalton House** around 1707, Edward Carleton went bankrupt in 1713. Two years later merchant Sir John Fellowes purchased it but, having become head of the South Sea Company, he encountered problems of his own in 1720 when the Company went bust. Carshalton House was confiscated to compensate

the victims of the crash and in 1724 Fellowes' brother had to buy it back for the family for twice the amount Sir John had paid for it less than ten years before. In possession once more, Sir John added the **Water Tower** to the amenities of the mansion. Its prime purpose, achieved through a rooftop reservoir, was to supply water to the house – even to the upper floors – but it also contained an orangery, a changing room and a Delft-tiled plunge bath, one of the earliest in the country.

In 1850 the last of Carshalton House's private occupants moved out and the Board of Ordnance moved in, using the house as a school for its military cadets. In 1892 the Daughters of the Cross arrived and opened St Philomena's girls' school. Over 100 years later the school is still here. Founded in Liège in 1833, the Daughters are a Roman Catholic organization and carry on the educational work of the convent of St Philomena.

CARSHALTON

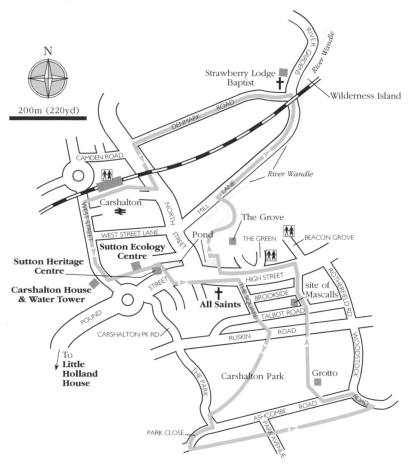

Ecology Centre

Cross West Street at the gate into Carshalton House and walk along Festival Walk by the side of the dried-up watercourse. Long ago a stream from the chalk downs used to flow into a lake in the grounds of Carshalton House and thence down this channel into the Wandle. The Old Rectory on the left, built about the time of Queen Anne, like Carshalton House, and raised well up to protect it from flooding was never the rectory as such, but the private home of a number of well-to-do rectors in the 18th century. The village's official rectory was in the High Street until it was pulled down for a shopping precinct in the 1960s. The present rectory is a modern house up the hill behind the church. Since the 1930s the Old Rectory has been public property and is now used, along with the grounds of a large 19th-century house called The Lodge, as the **Ecology Centre** of the Borough of Sutton. The Centre's nature reserve is well worth a visit. Just outside the main entrance stands the tallest London plane tree in Britain (see the plaque at its base).

Festival Walk takes you past the Ecology Centre and brings you out at Carshalton's famous ponds, one of two major sources of the Wandle (the other is at Whaddon ponds a few miles to the east, near Croydon). Originally there was only one pond here, but the building of a causeway across the middle into North Street during the Middle Ages divided it into two. Since that time the near pond has been public property and the far one part of the Stone Court/Grove estate.

Arts and Crafts

The Lodge to your left was built in 1866 on what had been the orchard and kitchen garden of Stone Court. Ahead right is a fine view of the church and the High Street. Immediately to the right is Honeywood, a house dating from the 17th century and once the home of the 19th-century author and civil servant Mark Rutherford, real name William Hale White. White lived in several houses in the neighbourhood and, being a friend of William Morris and John Ruskin, eventually built himself an Arts and Crafts-inspired house in Park Hill. Honeywood was later bought by the council and in 1990 converted into the **Sutton Heritage Centre** and local history museum. (Coincidentally, a few doors up from White's Park Hill house there is another Arts and Crafts house – **Little Holland House**, the home of the 20th-century designer and craftsman Frank Dickinson.)

Anne Boleyn's Well

Turn right past the entrance to Honeywood (note the dry watercourse running under the house) and walk up to the main road. This is the east end of Pound Street: the name comes from the village pound where stray animals were rounded up pending collection by their owners. Ahead is the elegant Greyhound Hotel, Carshalton's oldest and principal inn. Cross the road to the hotel and turn left. Opposite the entrance to North Street, the disused well surrounded by railings at the foot of Church Hill is known locally as Anne Boleyn's Well, Anne Boleyn being Henry VIII's second wife. A modern statue of the Queen is set into the corner of the new house in Church Hill. Legend has it that the Queen's horse kicked at a boulder here one day and in doing so brought a spring gushing forth. The truth is that in pre-Reformation days there was a little chapel here dedicated to Our Lady of Boulogne. Over time the name Boulogne simply became corrupted into Boleyn.

Monuments and stables

Pass to the right of the well and follow the raised path that leads past the entrance to the church. Medieval in origin, **All Saints** was enlarged to such an extent in the 1890s that the old nave was relegated to the status of a subsidiary chapel. Here is to be found the Purbeck marble tomb of Nicholas Gaynesford, the builder of the original Stone Court. Many other old monuments, including those of Sir William Scawen and Sir John Fellowes, are also in the church.

Just beyond the church is one of the oldest buildings in Carshalton, an ancient butcher's shop, now a wine bar. Carry on past the shop, turn right into The Square and walk up past the library. On the other side of the road is the remaining section of the Carshalton Park orangery, later used as stables. Before streets were built along the bottom side of Carshalton Park, The Square was a wide cul-de-sac, its top end closed off by the park wall and the stable entrance. Carry on up the road, cross Talbot Road into the path, cross Ruskin Road and enter Carshalton Park.

Squire of Carshalton

After he became squire of Carshalton in 1696, Sir William Scawen planned to replace the ancient Mascalls with a brand new house. Unfortunately, he died before he was ready to start building. His nephew and heir managed to complete the 2-mile (3-kilometre) park wall, the orangery and various other structures, but then the money ran out. So the great new house Thomas Scawen had commissioned from the Italian architect Giacomo Leonie was never built and Mascalls remained the mansion of the estate until the property was sold for development in 1895. Part of the park was developed and part – complete with some fine old trees – preserved as a public open space.

Ahead, the deep hole called the Hogpit started out before the Scawens' time as a chalk pit and was later excavated to form a deep pond, now dried up. Branch right up the hill, with the Hogpit on your left, and when the path stops continue straight on across the park. Exit opposite the hospital and turn left, occasionally glancing back for the views. At the top, before the road bends left, turn right into The Park cul-de-sac. Walk to the far end, continue on along the footpath and then turn left when you meet the track. This was formerly an old road that ran across the hill just outside the park wall: large sections of the latter survive on the left-hand side. Cross the first road you come to – Park Avenue – and continue on down into the low point. Then climb. At the end you will have to negotiate an overgrown section before finally emerging on Woodstock Road. Here turn left, and then left again, into Ashcombe Road and then right into the park once more.

The grotto

At this point you are right on top of the grotto, one of the park features built by Thomas Scawen in the 18th century. From the shell-covered grotto, which housed a source spring of the Wandle, water flowed down towards the High Street over a series of cascades, passing close by Mascalls near the bottom. Near where it joined the Wandle the stream powered a mill forming part of the Carshalton Park estate. Nowadays the grotto is derelict and the canal dry, but the whole structure is still a most impressive feature.

Mascalls

Walk down the left-hand side of the canal under the avenue of trees. Exit the park crossing Ruskin Road and continue. Talbot Road crosses the canal by means of a handsome little balustraded bridge, possibly a feature of the gardens around Mascalls, for the old house stood just here on the left until the 1920s.

When you reach the High Street, turn left, cross at the traffic lights and continue. Opposite the Coach and Horses turn right through the gates into the grounds of The Grove. In common with both Carshalton's other main estates, The Grove – named after a grove of trees with a temple in the middle cleared away during the 19th century – has passed through many hands since its early days as Stone Court, or Gainsford's Place, as it was later known. The present house, a Victorian-Edwardian hotchpotch, is largely the work of Sir Samuel Barrow, a wealthy tanner who owned the house between 1896 and 1923. The local authority bought it the following year and now uses it for offices.

Follow the path round to the left by the lake and then, before crossing the 18th-century bridge over the outflow, turn right, keeping the water on your left. Near the first bridge you come to stood what was called the Upper Mill, the original Carshalton corn mill, which finally went out of service in the 1880s after at least 800 years of operation. Barrow later used the mill's power source to drive electricity-generating turbines for his house. At the second bridge, cross the Wandle and turn right into Mill Lane. On the left the 19th-century mill workers' cottages still survive, but on the right the mills where so many of Carshalton's population once worked (nearly 60 per cent in the early 19th century) have recently been cleared away and replaced by housing.

Butter Hill

Continue along Mill Lane. Just before the railway bridge you pass one of the original bridges over the river leading into Butter Hill. The snuff mill driven by the grotto canal in Carshalton Park stood about halfway up the hill on the right. Carry on under the bridge to the entrance of Denmark Road. Ahead on the right you can see the signboard at the entrance to Wilderness Island, a 6-acre (2.5-hectare) nature reserve bordered by the Wandle and run by the Ecology Centre. Long before the railway arrived, the land covered by the reserve formed part of the rather larger Shepley estate, an industrial area first developed by gunpowder-maker Josias Dewye in 1692. Dewye lived across the road in a large house rebuilt in the 18th century as Strawberry Lodge. This still stands opposite the reserve entrance and is now owned by the Baptist Church, by whom it has recently been comprehensively restored.

Turn left now into Denmark Road. Follow this round to the end and then turn left into North Street. Go under the railway line and then right up the incline to the station entrance, where the walk ends.

Dulwich

Location	5 miles (8 kilometres) south of Charing Cross.
Transport	North Dulwich Station (overground trains from London Bridge), West Dulwich Station (overground trains from Victoria).
Features	Dulwich College (old and new versions); **Dulwich Picture Gallery**; Georgian houses in Dulwich Village; Dulwich Park and Dulwich Woods; last surviving tollgate in London; views of the City and West End from Sydenham Hill.
Refreshments	*Dulwich village* Greyhound pub, Le Piaf café-bar-brasserie, Bella Pasta restaurant; *Dulwich Park* café (see map page 106); *Sydenham Hill* Dulwich Wood House pub (see map page 106).

Although one is hardly aware of it today, Dulwich lies in the bottom of a shallow valley, bounded on the north by Denmark Hill and Dog Kennel Hill and on the south by Sydenham Hill and One Tree Hill, Honor Oak. The name is supposed to mean 'the meadow where dill grows'.

The village is one of the oldest in London. The earliest reference to it occurs in a Saxon charter dated 967. After the Norman Conquest the manor was granted by Henry I to the Priory of Bermondsey (see Rotherhithe and Bermondsey, page 136). The Priory continued to own it throughout the Middle Ages until the dissolution of the monasteries when it was seized by Henry VIII and granted to the Calton family (remembered today in Calton Avenue).

The most significant event in Dulwich's history occurred in the early 17th century, when the estate was bought by Edward Alleyn. Born in 1566, Alleyn (pronounced Allen) was one of the leading actors of the Elizabethan stage. He was also a successful businessman and impresario, with stakes in a theatre and in a bull- and bear-baiting arena. In 1604 he reached the summit of his career when he was appointed Joint Master of the Royal Bears, Bulls and Mastiff Dogs, a lucrative post which made him an extremely wealthy man.

College of God's Gift

Alleyn bought the Manor of Dulwich in 1605. At first he used the old moated manor house – known as Hall Place – as a summer residence, much as the prior of Bermondsey had done. But in 1613 he left his London home in Southwark and moved into Hall Place permanently. In the same year he began work on the College of God's Gift, a combined school and almshouse. The almspeople and

schoolchildren came from the three London parishes with which Alleyn had connections, and from St Giles, Camberwell, of which Dulwich was part (it did not
become a parish in its own right until late in the 19th century). Alleyn managed
and paid for the College until his death in 1626 and then left the bulk of his estate
to support it after he was gone.

Both almshouse and school still survive and feature on the walk. The almshouse
is still in the original building, but the school, which has grown into one of Britain's
leading public schools, moved into new premises on Dulwich Common to the
south of the village in 1870.

With the improvement of roads in the 18th century, it became possible for merchants and stockbrokers in the City, and for civil servants in Whitehall, to live in
Dulwich and commute daily to work. The College estate let off building plots to
these commuters and they built fine Georgian houses down the eastern side of the
long village street, set back from the road behind elm and chestnut trees and little
green verges protected by white posts and chains. Opposite were the village shops
and other business premises.

Dulwich Common

In 1805 the Common was enclosed and more fine houses were built along its
northern fringe, along what is now the busy Dulwich Common road. The arrival
of the railways in mid-century (West Dulwich, 1863, and North Dulwich, 1868)
further increased pressure for development, and gradually all the land in the vicinity
of Dulwich was built up, with the manor house and manor farm on the outskirts
of the village disappearing in the process.

But the village itself was preserved, as was a green belt around it, composed of
former farm, common and park land. Preservation of the historic village centre in
its green oasis was due mainly to control exercised by the College estate and its resident architect and surveyor, first Sir Charles Barry, architect of the Houses of
Parliament, and then his son, also called Charles. Today, even though leaseholders
have the right to buy their freeholds, the College Estate retains control over the
appearance of the village so it is likely to remain one of the most attractive and
unspoilt in the capital for some time to come.

THE DULWICH WALK

Start and finish North Dulwich Station.
Distance 4¼ miles (6.8 kilometres).

Come out of North Dulwich's elegant station, designed by Dulwich College architect Charles Barry in 1868, and turn left down Red Post Hill (named after a red
post that once stood at the summit of the hill pointing the way to Dulwich). At the
crossroads go straight over and keep walking. Already you can tell you are on
College property because of the old-fashioned finger posts and the post and chain
fences around the grass verges.

After a while you come to a parade of shops called Commerce Row, built by
the College in 1860 on the site of an old pond to cater for new Victorian housing

DULWICH

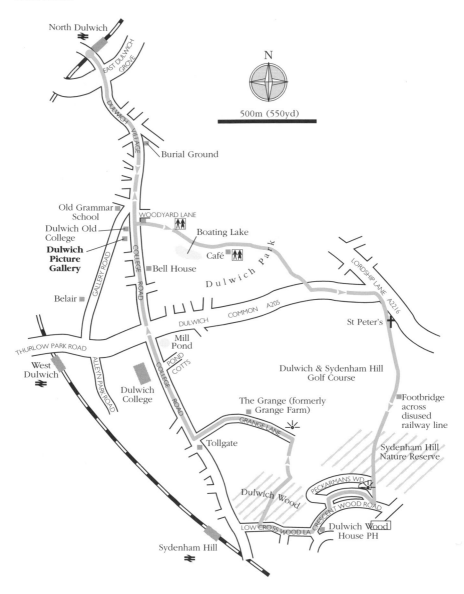

developments in the area. Opposite is another Victorian building housing the Dulwich Hamlet school and the Dulwich Society, one of the two local amenity societies. The building was originally constructed for the James Allen Girls School, an institution that grew out of a 'reading school' for poor girls and boys established over a century earlier by James Allen, Master of the College from 1721 to 1746.

The school became an all–girls' school in 1857 when it was taken under the wing of the College foundation, and moved to this new building in 1866. Twenty years later it moved out of Dulwich Village to East Dulwich Grove, where it still is.

Gypsy queen

At the end of Commerce Row, Calton Avenue leads left, past Ash Cottage and the entrance to Court Lane, to St Barnabas's Church, built in 1894 when Dulwich first became a parish in its own right. Until then it had been part of Camberwell parish. All through the Middle Ages villagers had to trek 2 miles (3 kilometres) north to Camberwell parish church to attend divine service on Sundays. Then, in 1616, they at last had their own place of worship when the chapel in Alleyn's almshouse was consecrated. At the same time Alleyn donated to the village the burial ground you can see straight ahead. Those laid to rest in the cemetery before it was closed in 1898 include Dulwich's 35 plague victims in 1665, Old Bridget, queen of the Norwood Gypsies, in 1768, Samuel Mathews, the Dulwich Hermit, murdered in 1802, and Richard Shawe, solicitor to Warren Hastings during his famous impeachment trial, in 1816. Shawe, whose tomb can be seen from Court Lane, lived at Casina, a country house built for him on the high ground north of Dulwich ten years earlier.

Cross Calton Avenue and walk along Dulwich Village beside the burial ground. Now you are entering the village proper. The fine Georgian town houses start immediately on the left, the eastern side of the village street. The first one still has its original coach house. Opposite is the original row of village shops, built at various times between 1765 and 1837. The one with the wrought-iron canopy over the front used to be a butcher's shop. Bella Pasta on the corner of Aysgarth Road is a 1930s' reproduction of the Georgian coaching inn that used to stand on the site.

Belair

Continue on down the left-hand side of the road, past the Crown and Greyhound and Le Piaf and then more shops and houses. At the junction ahead the road divides. Gallery Road on the right leads to Belair, one of several country houses built in the neighbourhood of Dulwich in the 18th century. Acquired by the local council after World War II, the grounds were turned into a public park, protecting Dulwich's western flank, and the house was expensively restored. Now it is in a sorry state, in stark contrast to properties belonging to the College.

The Tudor-style building on the right of the entrance to Gallery Road is the Sir Charles Barry-designed Old Grammar School, set up by the College in 1842 after complaints from local people that it was not doing enough to promote education for village boys. Like the girls' school, it was taken under the wing of the College foundation in 1857. Thirty years later, having grown from its original complement of 60 boys, Alleyn's School moved to Townley Road near St Barnabas's Church. It has been there ever since. In 1975 it became co-educational.

The old College

Across the road from the Old Grammar School is the original College of God's Gift. The building has inevitably been altered over the years, but it is essentially as

107

it was when first constructed. Looking at it from the front gates surmounted by Alleyn's coat of arms, the central portion is the chapel, the left wing the almshouse, and the right wing the former school and now the estate office. The gardens in front were originally the village green. The layout is said to have been based on a similar institution in Amsterdam and there is talk of Inigo Jones having been the architect. He was certainly present at the foundation ceremonies on 21 June 1619, but there is no direct proof that he played any part in designing the college.

Dulwich Park

Carry on down College Road beside the College and turn left through the gate into Dulwich Park. When Dulwich Court, the manor farm and the closest farm to the centre of the village, was demolished and Court Lane laid out over the site, the College gave five of its former fields to the Metropolitan Board of Works. The Board then created this public park complete with boating lake and opened it to the public in 1895. When the road forks, bear left and then go straight on between the white bollards and over the riding track onto the tarmac path beside the boating lake. Go past the restaurant and carry straight on between the children's playground and the bowling green. At the crossroads in front of the rhododendrons, turn right and then fork left. Take the first right, join up with the outer, vehicle, road and exit from the park by the Rosebery Gate.

Across the main road is what was Dulwich Common, covering the northern slope of Sydenham Hill and now playing fields and golf links. On top of the hill (the southern boundary of the old manor of Dulwich), the slender Eiffel Tower-like TV mast is a landmark for miles around. Turn left on the busy road and walk for some way to the junction with Lordship Lane, the eastern boundary of the manor of Dulwich.

Dulwich Wells

The Harvester pub at the road junction was called the Green Man in 1704 when John Cox, the innkeeper, obtained permission to create a walk through the woods on the Common side of the road leading up to the local spa of Sydenham Wells. In 1739 Cox's son discovered a mineral spring in the grounds of the inn and developed the Green Man's own spa of Dulwich Wells, complete with bowling green and assembly room for breakfasts and dancing. Later a Dr Glennie opened a school here at which the poet Byron was a pupil for two years. Today's Grove Tavern opened in 1863, though the actual building dates from the 1920s.

Pissarro paints in Dulwich

Opposite the pub, turn right across the road and go through the gate into Cox's Walk, passing between Charles Barry's St Peter's Church and the Marlborough Cricket Club, founded in 1870. Follow the avenue up the hill and round the bend to the right. At the end, the footbridge crosses the railway line, now disused, that once carried passengers to Crystal Palace after it was re-erected on Sydenham Hill following the 1851 Great Exhibition. Art lovers might be interested to know that Camille Pissarro painted at least one picture from this bridge when he was living at Upper Norwood in 1870–71.

Instead of crossing the bridge go straight on through the gate into Dulwich Woods and keep to the high track on the left with the green posts (marking the boundary between the College's property and the London Wildlife Trust's Sydenham Hill Nature Reserve) on your right. After 50 yards (42 metres) or so, follow the path left down the embankment onto the old railway track (No. 6 marker post here) and turn right along the track. After a while you will come to the sealed entrance of the tunnel under Sydenham Hill. Take the path to the right and follow it up and over the tunnel entrance and out onto Crescent Wood Road. Turn immediately sharp right off the road into Peckarmans Wood and follow it round to the left in front of the houses in order to see the fine view, rather obscured by trees, of Canary Wharf, the East End and the City.

TV comes to Dulwich

At the end of Peckarmans Wood turn left, then right back onto the main road. The big houses up here were mostly built in the second half of the 19th century after the relocation of the Crystal Palace put the area on the map. An exception is the modern house on the left, an early (1933) work of the modernist architect Berthold Lubetkin. On the right the penultimate house has a blue plaque to the inventor of television, John Logie Baird. He lived here between 1934 and 1946 after moving his laboratories to Crystal Palace from Soho, where he had given the first public demonstration of his invention ten years earlier.

Dulwich Wood

Opposite the Dulwich Wood House pub, opened in 1858, turn right down Low Cross Wood Lane. It was somewhere near this lane that Samuel Mathews, the Dulwich Hermit buried in the village burial ground, was murdered in 1802. About 100 yards (90 metres) before the bottom of the lane, go right through the gate back into Dulwich Wood, a remnant of the ancient Great North Wood which once spread south from here to Croydon. Follow the path through the wood, bearing left at the central clearing where three paths branch off to the right. At the end of the path, exit through the gate and turn left on Grange Lane between the allotments and the golf club. Just beyond the golf club entrance there is a viewpoint cut in the hedge offering a fine panorama of the West End. The British Telecom Tower is the most conspicuous feature, but left of it the Houses of Parliament also stand out well in the right conditions.

The tollgate

Follow the lane down the hill. Where it bends left you pass what was Grange Farm, built in the early 19th century after the enclosure of the old common. The lane brings you out at one of Dulwich's most unusual features, the tollgate, the last one still operating in London. The gate was put up in 1787 when a neighbouring landowner built College Road as a short cut between his farm at Penge and fields he rented in Dulwich. He was not averse to other people using the road, but he was not going to let them use it for free. When his lease expired, the College kept both the road and the gate. A few years ago it was reported to be making about £17,000 a year.

Dulwich school

Turn right down College Road, passing between the tennis courts and buildings of Dulwich school, the modern incarnation of Alleyn's original foundation. Having made a lot of money out of selling land to the railway companies in the mid 19th century, the College commissioned Charles Barry to design these impressive new buildings in the 1860s. The school moved into them in 1870. The old manor house of Dulwich where Alleyn lived between 1613 and 1626 stood a few hundred yards behind the school buildings, roughly at the junction of Park Hall Road and Croxted Road. It was demolished in 1883.

Further on, on the right, you come to a pretty row of old cottages called Pond Cottages, with the Mill Pond, from which the cottages take their name, in front. In the 17th and 18th centuries this was a small industrial centre. The cottages belonged to a tile kiln where bricks and roof tiles were made. The pond was originally a clay pit from which the tile kiln obtained its main raw material until the pond naturally filled with water. The kiln seems to have ceased operating by the end of the 18th century and the pond subsequently acquired its name from the windmill that stood opposite on the other side of College Road. Following the enclosure of the Common, the mill was demolished in 1815.

When you reach the junction with Dulwich Common, cross straight over and continue along College Road. After some modern developments you come to Bell House, the finest Georgian house in the village. It dates from 1767 and was built for City stationer Thomas Wright. He later became Master of the Stationers' Company and then Lord Mayor of London before dying here in 1798. The house is now one of the School boarding houses.

Dulwich Picture Gallery

Beyond Bell House and its weatherboarded neighbour, you come, on the left, to Dulwich's main claim to fame apart from the school, the **Dulwich Picture Gallery**. This, the oldest public picture gallery in England, was designed by Sir John Soane in 1817 to house a superb collection of paintings bequeathed to the College by Sir Francis Bourgeois. Bourgeois, himself an artist, had in turn inherited the collection from the man who put it together, the dealer Noel Desenfans. Desenfans had originally intended to sell it to the King of Poland for a projected national gallery, but war prevented the deal from going through. Poland's loss was Dulwich's gain. Now a humble south London suburb is home to a collection of old masters that any national gallery would be proud to possess.

Now make your way back along Dulwich Village to North Dulwich Station, where the walk ends.

Greenwich

Location	5½ miles (8.8 kilometres) southeast of Charing Cross.
Transport	Greenwich Station (overground trains from Charing Cross and Cannon Street), Island Gardens Station (Docklands Light Railway and then Greenwich Foot Tunnel), Greenwich Pier (boats from **Charing Cross Pier**).
Features	**St Alfege's Church**; *Cutty Sark*; *Gypsy Moth IV*; **Royal Naval College**; **Trinity Hospital**; **National Maritime Museum**; **Queen's House**; **Old Royal Observatory**; **Ranger's House**; **Fan Museum**; Greenwich Park; Croom's Hill and elegant Georgian streets of West Greenwich; riverside walk; views of London; arts and crafts market (weekends).
Events	**Greenwich Festival**; **Tourist Information Centre**.
Refreshments	*in Greenwich centre* numerous cafés, bars, pubs and restaurants; *along the walk* various pubs plus café at Visitor Centre in Greenwich Park (near Circus Gate – see map page 113).

Greenwich was established as a little fishing port on the Thames long before the Norman Conquest. Its recorded history begins in the 9th century when King Alfred and his daughter granted it to the Abbey of St Peter in Ghent. Two hundred years later marauding Danes captured Archbishop Alfege at Canterbury and brought him hostage to their camp at Greenwich. In 1012 he was murdered following a drunken feast. The parish church, dedicated to his memory, was later built on the site of his martyrdom. In the early 1700s it was wrecked in a storm and replaced by the existing church, a monumental work by Nicholas Hawksmoor.

Greenwich's real history begins with its acquisition in 1427 by Henry VI's uncle, Humphrey, Duke of Gloucester. Humphrey transformed the old abbey buildings into a mansion called Bella Court, constructed a fortified tower on the hill behind and enclosed 200 acres (80 hectares) of wild Black Heath to form a deer park. Bella Court was subsequently enlarged by the Tudors into the great royal palace of Placentia, the birthplace and favourite residence of Henry VIII and Elizabeth I. Meanwhile, Greenwich village blossomed into an elegant court suburb and aristocratic playground.

England's first classical domestic building

In the 17th century Placentia was replaced by two new buildings: the early-17th-century Queen's House, the first classical domestic building in England, and the later 17th-century palace begun by Charles II after his restoration. The new palace, unfinished by Charles and lying in between the two royal dockyards of Woolwich and Deptford, was completed by his successors as the Royal Hospital for old sailors. From the early 1800s, the Queen's House, an exquisite building designed by Inigo Jones, housed the Royal Hospital School. Since the 1930s, when the school moved out of London, it has been part of the National Maritime Museum. The old Hospital, later a naval college and most recently a joint defence college, is currently in the process of being taken over by the Museum and by Greenwich University.

The old village centre of Greenwich stretched back from the riverside along Greenwich Church Street, with the church on one side and the Royal Hospital and Queen's House on the other. After Charles II began his new palace, the village began to expand, mainly around the park, which Charles had commissioned André Le Nôtre to landscape. The earliest developments were along Croom's (i.e. Crooked) Hill, the road that runs up the hill along the west side of the park. Later came Park Vista along the south side, and Maze Hill along the east side. Croom's Hill, the finest street in modern Greenwich, and Park Vista both feature on the walk.

Regency rebuilding

In the late 18th and early 19th centuries elegant streets were added to the west of the village below Point Hill, and in the 1830s the old congested village centre was rebuilt in Regency style. Following the building of the pier for steamboats in 1836 and the opening of the railway station in 1838 (the Greenwich–London Bridge line is the oldest railway in London), the village rapidly developed into a suburb and tourist centre.

Today its main attractions are concerned with its maritime past and its role in the development of the world's time zones. (The two are not, in fact, unrelated since the Old Royal Observatory in Greenwich Park, through which runs the Greenwich meridian line, was originally set up by Charles II to solve the longitude problem for sailors.) In the near future people will also come to Greenwich to see the Millennium Exhibition. This is being built on the Blackwall peninsula about 1 mile (1.6 kilometres) downstream and will be ready in time for the first day of the year 2000.

THE GREENWICH WALK

Start and finish Greenwich Station.
Distance 3½ miles (5.6 kilometres).

Come out of Greenwich Station onto the forecourt. Directly opposite across the High Road is Queen Elizabeth's College, the almshouse founded by historian and local landowner William Lambarde in 1574 and rebuilt by the Drapers' Company, who now run it, in 1817. Turn right on the High Road, go past the garage and take the first right into Straightsmouth. Follow this road under the railway bridge and then round to the right. As you approach the village centre, you get a fine view of the parish church of **St Alfege's**.

Go straight on into Churchfields. At the end look left along Roan Street and you will see the early 19th-century headmaster's house of the Roan School, one of Greenwich's old charity schools founded in the 1670s by John Roan, a local man and Yeoman of Harriers to Charles I. The original school building lay just to the

GREENWICH

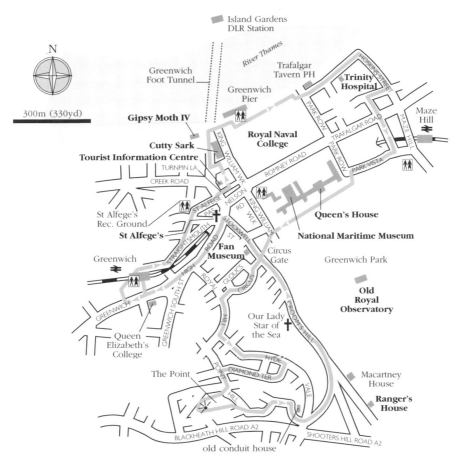

right of the schoolhouse and the site is marked by a plaque. Today the Roan School is situated in Maze Hill in East Greenwich.

Continue straight across Roan Street into St Alfege Passage. This takes you past the old burial ground on the left and the church and 1814 National School on the right, and brings you out in the centre of the village in Greenwich Church Street. Left is the river and right is the park. Crossing by the zebra (right), go straight over Church Street and through the arch into Turnpin Lane. This is one of the old lanes of medieval Greenwich, but the block it bisects was the part of Greenwich rebuilt around a new covered market between 1828 and 1831. Halfway along the lane, turn left into the market (originally for food, now arts and crafts at weekends) and walk straight through, noting the curious (and ungrammatical) traders' admonition above the arch as you pass out into College Approach (right are the gates of the old **Royal Naval College**).

Dockworkers' tunnel

Turn left into College Approach and then right, following Greenwich Church Street down onto the waterfront. Originally the street ran right down to the riverside past the Ship Hotel on the right. Having been bombed during World War II, the area was left open to form today's esplanade. In the middle is the domed entrance to the Greenwich Foot Tunnel, opened in 1902 to allow workers to reach the docks on the other side of the river (Canary Wharf Tower now dominates the newly redeveloped Docklands). From Island Gardens at the other end of the Foot Tunnel there is a famous view of Greenwich. To the left is *Gypsy Moth IV*, the first boat to be sailed round the world single-handed (by Sir Francis Chichester in 1966–67); and to the right is one of the great sights of maritime Greenwich, the *Cutty Sark*, a clipper ship that brought tea from China and wool from Australia in record times in the 1870s and '80s.

Walk down the side of the *Cutty Sark,* turn right under its bowsprit and continue past the pier entrance along the riverside walk. Ahead is a fine view of the Blackwall peninsula, the site of the Millennium exhibition and the new Port Greenwich. On the right you pass the pink granite monument put up in 1853 to the memory of Frenchman Joseph Bellot who lost his life attempting to discover the fate of Sir John Franklin's doomed Northwest Passage expedition.

Charles II's palace

Then you come to the old Greenwich Hospital, opened in 1705, closed in 1865 and replaced by the Royal Naval College and now set to become part of the National Maritime Museum and Greenwich University. The first block on the right was the one intended by Charles II to form part of a new palace. The other buildings were all completed later once the decision had been taken to build a seamen's home instead. From the centre there is a fine view of the Queen's House and behind it, up on the hill, the 17th-century **Royal Observatory**. The Observatory is both the home of GMT (Greenwich Mean Time) and the dividing point between the east and west hemispheres. The ball on top, originally installed in 1831, drops at 1pm precisely to signal the correct time for ships passing down the Thames.

Whitebait dinners

Beyond the College turn right by the Trafalgar Tavern (a favourite resort for dinners of Thames whitebait in the last century) and then immediately left into Crane Street behind it. Crane Street takes you into High Bridge and High Bridge brings you in turn to the Trinity Hospital almshouse. Courtier Lord Lumley had a house here in Tudor times. After the court left Greenwich in 1601, Lord Northampton acquired the house and in 1616 converted it into an almshouse for 21 local men. Rebuilt in Gothic style in 1812 and run by the Mercers' Company, it still fulfils that function today, though it looks somewhat incongruous in this rather industrial location.

Carry on under the power station gantry and turn right along Hoskins Street past the scrapyards. At Old Woolwich Road turn right behind the power station and then first left (the trees on the right belong to Trinity Hospital's garden) into

Greenwich Park Street. Cross Trafalgar Road (traffic lights on the left) and walk up to Park Vista and turn right. Here many of the houses – such as the Manor House at No. 13 – date from the expansion of the village in the late 1600s and 1700s.

Meridian

When you get to Feathers Place look left and you will see a plaque in the wall (and a metal strip in the pavement) marking the meridian, i.e. 0° longitude. The row of houses here – Nos. 36–33 incorporating The Chantry – was originally built for the Admiral Commissioner of the Naval Asylum (school). The westernmost section at the end of Park Vista now serves as St Alfege's vicarage.

The storming of Quebec

Beyond the vicarage, turn left into the park and then right along the walk beside the **Queen's House** and the **National Maritime Museum**. Up on the hill, where Duke Humphrey's Tower used to stand, is the Observatory and to the left of it the statue of General Wolfe. Wolfe's parents lived in Greenwich and Wolfe was buried in St Alfege's church after his death at the successful storming of Quebec in 1759.

Gloucester Circus

At the end of the tarmac walk, carry on past St Mary's Gate and then branch left past the Visitor Centre and the herb garden. Exit from the park at Circus Gate and go straight over Croom's Hill into Gloucester Circus, keeping to the left-hand side of the central garden. You are now in West Greenwich, the suburb adjacent to the old village developed from the late 18th century. The Circus was the work of Michael Scarles (he also designed The Paragon in Blackheath) and dates from the 1790s. Unfortunately, only the south crescent was built. The north side was completed as a square over 30 years later and then patched up after World War II, following bomb damage.

Leave the Circus at the far end and turn left up Royal Hill, named after its main developer, Robert Royal. Opposite the Prince Albert pub, turn left into Hyde Vale and walk up the hill past rather exclusive houses, particularly the villas on the right which date from the 1830s. Opposite No. 67 turn right into Diamond Terrace. Follow this round the side of the hill and then, at the end, turn left up steep Point Hill. Opposite West Grove Lane, turn right onto the tarmac path. From here there are wonderful views of east London and the City and the Northern Heights beyond. When you reach the steps climb up to the summit of the hill where there is a panel identifying some of the landmarks.

Lord Chesterfield's letters

Cross straight over the open space on top of Point Hill and continue on into West Grove. The busy road on the right is the main road across Blackheath to Dover. Stick close to the left-hand side of West Grove. At the junction with Hyde Vale there is a small 18th-century brick conduit house, once part of the water supply system for the Royal Hospital. Go straight over Hyde Vale, up the steps and left onto Cade Road. Away to the right now you can see **Ranger's House**, built in 1699 on the edge of the park and between 1748 and 1773 the home of the fourth Earl of Chesterfield. Chesterfield's letters to his son, published in 1774, became a standard guide to good manners, and many were originally written from here.

Croom's Hill begins at the junction of Cade Road and General Wolfe Road. Macartney House, on the right, was Wolfe's home after his father bought it in 1751. The Manor House on the left, behind the copper beech hedge, was built about 1690 for Rear Admiral Sir Robert Robinson and is one of the oldest surviving houses in the road. Below the Manor House is a green with a Catholic church and a fine presbytery next door. Downhill from the church is the oldest house in Croom's Hill, Heathgate House, built about 1635. Just further on you come to the second oldest building in the road, the roadside gazebo built in 1672 overlooking the park. The gazebo belongs to The Grange, a large 18th-century house standing behind the gazebo wall in its own grounds.

The Fan Museum

There are some late 18th-century houses in and around King George Street, but from Gloucester Circus the houses are older as you approach the foot of the hill. On the left near the bottom is a particularly fine early 18th-century terrace, with No. 12 and its neighbour now forming the **Fan Museum**, the only one of its kind in the world. On the right the Spread Eagle on the corner of Nevada Street is an old coaching inn and a relic of the days before the building of Nelson Road and College Approach when Nevada Street (then called Silver Street) was the main road through Greenwich. The increase of traffic along this road and the need for a more direct route through the town was one reason for the improvement scheme of 1830.

Carry on past the Spread Eagle down Stockwell Street. At the bottom turn left onto Greenwich High Road. After about 250 yards (128 metres) you will reach the station, where the walk ends.

Ham and Petersham

Location	9 miles (14.5 kilometres) southwest of Charing Cross.
Transport	Richmond Station (Underground District Line; overground trains from Waterloo or on North London Line), then either walk (1½ miles (2.4 kilometres) – directions given below) or bus 65 or 371 from station forecourt to The Dysarts bus stop in Petersham.
Features	**St Peter's Church**; **Ham House**; numerous historic houses of the 17th, 18th and 19th centuries; Petersham Meadows and farm; Ham Common; riverside walk and views of Thames and Richmond; **Ham Polo Club** (not on walk – see map page 119).
Refreshments	*Petersham* The Dysarts and Fox and Duck pubs; *Ham* various pubs, Chinese takeaway/fish and chip shop/café; *Ham House* tea room (closed Fri); *Richmond* cafés, sandwich bars, patisseries, pubs, restaurants and fast-food outlets.

Ham and Petersham lie side by side on the south bank of the Thames between Richmond and Kingston. In the Middle Ages Ham was part of the royal demesne of Kingston, whereas Petersham was monastic property belonging to the Abbey of Chertsey. In the 15th century the Abbey transferred its Petersham property to the Crown, so from that time on both villages were in royal hands and generally treated as a single place when it came to grants of land and other royal favours.

In the early 1600s both places had their big houses. Ham's was **Ham House**, territorially in Petersham but geographically in Ham. It was constructed in 1610 for Sir Thomas Vavasour, an adviser to James I's son, Prince Henry, who had recently been given his own household in nearby Richmond Palace. Petersham's manor house stood opposite the present Dysarts pub and was occupied by London lawyer George Cole and his family.

When King Charles I established his huge new deer park at Richmond, great changes came to Petersham and Ham, both of which lost much land to the new park. The Coles left Petersham Lodge, which became an official residence of one of the two deputy keepers of the new park. Meanwhile, the manors of both Ham and Petersham were granted to the King's childhood companion and whipping boy, William Murray, created Earl of Dysart in 1643. Dysart established himself in Ham House. The house was completely transformed in the 1670s when Dysart's daughter married, as her second husband, the Duke of Lauderdale. He was one of Charles II's ministers and member of an unofficial cabinet group called the Cabal, which often met at Ham House in a room now known as the Cabal Room. Ham House today is very much the creation of the Duke and Duchess.

The Dysarts of Ham

The Duchess's first husband was Sir Lionel Tollemache. It was a son of this marriage who inherited the Dysart title and with it Ham House and the lordship of the manors of Ham and Petersham. The Dysarts of Ham House remained the dominant family in the neighbourhood right down to 1948, when they finally gave up the house to the National Trust and decamped to pastures new. It was only 15 years before that that the village of Ham had finally been absorbed into the Borough of Richmond (Petersham was included in the borough when it was created in 1890).

Ham House may have been the 'big house' of the two villages, but it was not by any means the only mansion in the area. Attracted by the political importance of Ham House and New Park, by the royal presence in the palace and park of Richmond, and by the idyllic setting between park and Thames, many other wealthy and titled people built themselves suburban retreats in Petersham and Ham in the late 17th and 18th centuries. Most of these houses remain and feature on the walk.

England's most elegant village

The impressive houses in Ham are grouped around the large triangular common and spaced out down the long Ham Street leading from the common to the river. But in Petersham they are concentrated in a much smaller area around the junction of Petersham Road and River Lane. This concentration has led to Petersham's description in the past as the most elegant village in England. Today much of that elegance remains, but it is difficult to appreciate it with heavy traffic thundering along the dangerously narrow Petersham Road. Step off the road, however – into the churchyard next to Petersham Meadows or into River Lane where the farm is – and you quickly recover that feeling of rural tranquillity, as you will discover on the walk.

Ham, too, has its quiet places, thanks, ironically, to this same heavily used road. After leaving Petersham it crosses Ham Common in a southwesterly direction towards Kingston, so cutting off the village cradled in its great bend of the Thames. Standing close to the river, Ham House is at the farthest point from the road and it is here, surrounded by fields, parkland and the river, that you will probably feel yourself farthest away from the great city close by.

THE HAM AND PETERSHAM WALK

Start and finish Richmond Station or The Dysarts pub in Petersham (reached by buses 65 and 371 from Richmond Station).
Distance 2¾ miles (4.4 kilometres) starting and finishing at The Dysarts. (Richmond is another 1½ miles (2.4 kilometres) *each way*).

From Richmond Station to The Dysarts

Turn left out of Richmond Station and walk through the centre of the town, following the road round when it bends left. Go past the old town hall, now the library, on the right and at the roundabout (Richmond Bridge to the right) go

HAM AND PETERSHAM

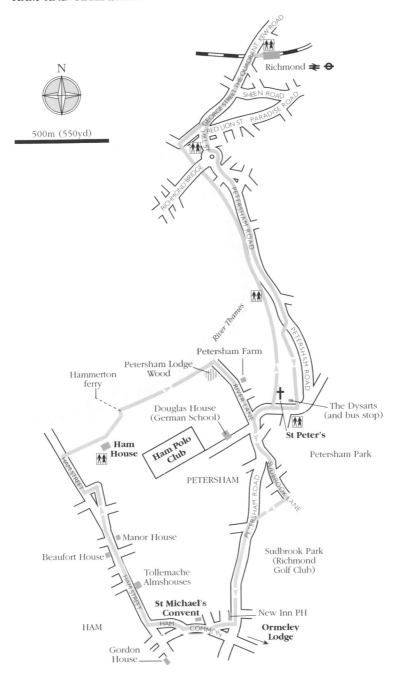

N

500m (550yd)

Richmond ≠ ⊖

GEORGE STREET · THE QUADRANT · KEW ROAD

SHEEN ROAD

RED LION ST · PARADISE ROAD

HILL ST

RICHMOND BRIDGE

PETERSHAM ROAD

River Thames

PETERSHAM ROAD

Petersham Farm

Petersham Lodge
Wood

Hammerton
ferry

RIVER LANE

Douglas House
(German School)

The Dysarts
(and bus stop)

St Peter's

**Ham
House**

**Ham Polo
Club**

Petersham Park

PETERSHAM

HAM STREET

PETERSHAM ROAD

SUDBROOK LANE

Manor House

Beaufort House

Sudbrook Park
(Richmond
Golf Club)

Tollemache
Almshouses

HAM STREET

**St Michael's
Convent**

New Inn PH

**Ormeley
Lodge**

HAM

HAM COMMON

Gordon
House

straight over, keeping right along the main road when a side road branches left up the hill. You are now on Petersham Road. Follow this for some way until, having reached relatively open country with Terrace Field on your left and Petersham Meadows on the right, you come to the Rose of York pub. Just beyond the pub, branch right along a woodland track. This takes you across what is actually part of Petersham Common, past the riding stables and brings you out on the main road once more at the entrance to the village. The Dysarts bus stop is just to the right.

The Dysarts and beyond

The section of Richmond Park opposite The Dysarts pub and accessed by Petersham Gate is the former Petersham Park where the Cole family lived in the early 1600s before Richmond Park was created. The house stood just off the road and the surrounding parkland covered both the flat ground around the house and the hillside to the east. When the Earl of Rochester was appointed Ranger of the new Richmond Park in 1687 he re-created Petersham Park, knocked down the Coles' old house and built himself a fine new mansion called New Park. This, in turn, was destroyed in 1721, when a fire broke out in the linen cupboard. William Stanhope then bought the estate and built a third house on the site, which – designed by the architect-Earl of Burlington – was one of the first Palladian houses in England. The Stanhopes, created Viscounts Petersham and then Earls of Harrington, lived on at Petersham Lodge until 1783. In 1834 when the property came into Crown hands, the house was knocked down and the grounds merged once more with Richmond Park.

From The Dysarts walk on into the village, taking care to keep well into the pavement, for the road is very narrow here and lorries sometimes have to mount the kerb in order to pass vehicles coming in the opposite direction. The fine houses start immediately with Parkgate and Church House on the right and then on the left, opposite the turning to the church, Reston Lodge. These houses date from the late 18th or early 19th century. The earliest houses come next, with Montrose House on the left, and Petersham House (with the round porch) and then Rutland Lodge on the right. These three houses all date from the late 17th century, when Petersham first became a fashionable suburb for the aristocracy. Montrose House takes its name from the Dowager Duchess of Montrose, who lived here between 1837 and 1847. Petersham House was built about 1674 for one of the keepers of the park. Rutland Lodge was built in the early 1660s for a Lord Mayor of London, subsequently disgraced for misappropriating funds intended for the rebuilding of the City following the Great Fire. It takes its name from a mid-18th-century resident, the Duchess of Rutland. In more recent times a serious fire destroyed the interior of the building and it was converted into flats.

Personal relationships

To some extent, personal relationships determined the occupancy, if not the building, of these houses in their early days. Montrose House, for example, was built for lawyer Sir Thomas Jenner. His daughter married another lawyer, Sir John Darnall, who lived in Rutland Lodge. Darnall's daughter married yet another lawyer,

Plate 19: The Terrace in Barnes is an attractive collection of 18th- and 19th-century houses overlooking the Thames (see page 81).

Plate 20: Topiary is one of the features of the immaculate gardens at picturesque Hall Place in Bexley (see page 90).

Plate 21: These houses in The Paragon, Blackheath's finest Georgian development, were converted into flats following bomb damage in the Second World War (see page 96).

Plate 22: Pagoda House in Blackheath was built as an aristocratic summer house in the 18th century (see page 95).

Plate 23: *Hare and Billet pond and All Saints Church on Black Heath (see page 94).*

Plate 24: *The centre of Carshalton village is graced by a large expanse of water (see page 101).*

Plate 25: *In Victorian times Dulwich College was rebuilt on a new site on Dulwich Common and surrounded by well-kept playing fields (see page 110).*

Plate 26: The Dulwich Picture Gallery, the oldest public art gallery in the country (see page 110).

Plate 27: The old tollgate on College Road, Dulwich, is the only one still operating in London (see page 109).

Robert Ord, Chief Baron of the Exchequer in Scotland, who built new Petersham Lodge halfway down River Lane. We pass this house on the way back from Ham.

The two houses facing you on the bend, one of which is now called the Manor House, were both built later than the three houses just mentioned, probably in the second half of the 18th century. Follow the road round to the left here. Beyond the garden walls where the road begins to widen out, you come to the east lodge of Ham House. This is also the main entrance to the **Ham Polo Club** and to Douglas House, another of Petersham's fine late-17th-century houses. This one takes its name from the eccentric Kitty Douglas, Duchess of Queensberry in the 18th century. She was a great patron of artists and writers, particularly of John Gay. She looked after his money, built him a summerhouse down by the river so that he could write in peace and allowed him to have his *The Beggar's Opera* rehearsed in her house. The house was bought by the German government in the 1960s and incorporated into a German school.

All Saints Church

Opposite the Ham House lodge, built in 1900, is a pair of much older cottages. These houses are, in fact, the original lodge houses for Ham House, constructed about the same time as the mansion itself. In those days the road from Richmond to Kingston passed behind Montrose House, rather than in front of it as now, and then joined up with the existing road about where the Fox and Duck is. Looking between the old lodges and the Fox and Duck you can see the campanile of All Saints Church. This has a curious history. The 18th-century Bute House (former home of George III's prime minister the Earl of Bute) used to stand on the site. In 1894 Mrs Loetitia Warde of Petersham House bought the empty house, knocked it down and built this extraordinary red brick church, partly as a memorial to her parents and partly because she expected Petersham's population to expand like Richmond's when the village was built up. But Petersham never was built up, so the church was never even consecrated, let alone used. It is now a recording studio.

Dickens writes *Nicholas Nickleby*

Cross the road at the traffic lights. When Petersham Road bears right past Cecil House, go straight on into Sudbrook Lane, Sudbrook (i.e. Southbrook) being an old hamlet to the south of Petersham. There are more handsome old houses down here, but they are far more modest in size than those in the centre of the village. One of them is the now-unidentifiable Elm Lodge where, in the summer of 1839, the 27-year-old Charles Dickens wrote the greater part of *Nicholas Nickleby*. Bute Avenue on the left leads to All Saints. Dickens Close on the right commemorates the writer's stay in the village. At the end of the road is the grand entrance to Sudbrook Park, home of Richmond Golf Club. The clubhouse, designed by James Gibbs and completed in 1728, was built for John Campbell, 2nd Duke of Argyll and Greenwich. Being the grandson of the Countess of Dysart who married the Duke of Lauderdale, and having been born in Ham House himself, Argyll had natural connections with Petersham.

In front of the gate, turn right into Hazel Lane. As you walk along you can glimpse the Campbell house through the trees. They had given it up by 1842.

Subsequently it was used as hydropathic treatment centre and hotel before coming into the possession of the seven-year-old golf club in 1898. At the end of the lane, turn left, cross at the traffic lights and continue walking along the road. You have now left Petersham and are on the way to Ham.

Ham Common

Ham starts with a row of cottages and the Fox and Goose pub on the right. The New Inn further on, and Sudbrook Lodge opposite, mark the beginning of Ham Common. Much of the Common was lost when Richmond Park was created, but substantial chunks remain. The area of Common on the left, crossed by Ham Gate Avenue, the entrance to which you can see up ahead, is mostly scrub and woodland. That on the right of the main road is mown grass and more like a large village green, with a cricket pitch in the middle and a pond over in the far right corner. One or two fine houses, notably **Ormeley Lodge**, were built in Ham Gate Avenue from the late 17th century, but the most popular sites for suburban retreats were around the triangular Common and down Ham Street, which we come to shortly.

St Michael's Convent

Turn right by the New Inn. Stafford Cottages here (now one house, but formerly a pair of cottages) is a comparatively rare survival from maybe the late 16th or possibly the early years of the 17th century when Ham House was built. Cross Bishops Close. South Lodge was built by Ham resident and wealthy philanthropist John Minter Morgan as a home for girls orphaned by the cholera epidemic of 1847–9. It has now been converted into flats. Morgan's own house on the other side of the Common has been a psychiatric hospital since 1948. More substantial houses follow – Hardwicke House and then Orford Hall, now **St Michael's Convent**. Beyond Avenue Lodge you come to another pair of lodges like the ones in Petersham. These flank the entrance to the southern drive of Ham House, which you can just make out at the far end. Across to your left, 18th-century Gordon House closes a fine view across the sunken pond in the corner of the Common.

Keep right, follow the road to the end and then turn right into Ham Street, the main thoroughfare of the old village. Well within living memory farms and cottages stood on the left side of the street, with a back lane behind (sections of which still survive) and farmland (and originally the common fields of the manor) beyond. Most of this land has now been filled up with housing estates. Unlike the farms, a few of Ham Street's big houses have survived. Beyond the 1892 Tollemache Almshouses and the Grey Court School is Grey Court, the boyhood home of Cardinal Newman, to whom there is a blue plaque on the front. Opposite the junction with Sandy Lane is Beaufort House and on the right another large house now called the Manor House.

Foot ferry

Carry on down Ham Street, past the allotments and games fields, until you come to the entrance to Ham House. Here turn right (if the gate is closed walk on down to the river and turn right along the towpath). Ahead is a fine view of the Star and Garter home for disabled soldiers on top of Richmond Hill. Just beyond the gates leading into the forecourt of the house, branch left along a track worn in the grass, aiming for the corner of the field. Go through the gate and out onto the towpath and turn right. Here Hammerton ferry, one of the last surviving foot ferries on the Thames, connects with Twickenham and its various attractions, including the Orleans House Gallery and Marble Hill. The latter, a beautiful white Palladian house, gradually comes into view as you walk back towards Petersham and Richmond.

When you reach the boats moored upstream of the island, you pass Petersham Lodge Wood on your right. Down the horse chestnut avenue in the middle is a vista of a bust on a pedestal in the grounds of Petersham Lodge. Once part of the Lodge's grounds, the wood is now owned by the local council and managed jointly with the London Wildlife Trust, assisted by local volunteers. Progress is slowly being made to turn the wood into a public nature reserve.

Eggs and honey

Beyond the wood turn right into River Lane. You re-enter the village between the council-owned farm on the left (where you can buy eggs and honey) and new Petersham Lodge on the right. This is the house built by Chief Baron Ord in 1740. Beyond you come to the Navigator's House and pink-painted Glen Cottage. Originally these two were one house and it was here that naval officer George Vancouver, the discoverer of the island that bears his name, lived from 1795 while writing up the official account of his 1791–94 Pacific voyage. Vancouver died in 1798 when he was only 40 and was buried in Petersham churchyard, the next stop on the walk.

At the top of River Lane turn left along Petersham Road once more and then left again into Church Lane, signposted to **St Peter's Church**. In most other London villages churches have been progressively enlarged over the years to accommodate increasing populations, but Petersham's, although a lot of work was done on it in 1840, has stayed more or less the same, reflecting the fact that as late as 1891 the population of the village was still only 629. Inside, the church still has its gallery and box pews, and there are memorials to many local people, including a fine effigy of George Cole (died 1624) of the original Petersham Lodge and a plaque to Sir Thomas Jenner (died 1707) of Montrose House. Outside, unusually for a London church, the churchyard is still being used for burials. One of the latest is that of Major-General Sir Humphrey Tollemache, sixth baronet, who died in 1990 aged 93. Vancouver's simple grave is halfway along the south wall, in between the wall and another Tollemache tomb.

From Church Lane a path leads off to the right along the north (Richmond) side of the churchyard. It comes out by The Dysarts bus stop, so go down it if you want to take the bus back to Richmond. If you would prefer to return on foot, go straight on down Church Lane and continue on into the path by the lampstand when the lane turns left to the nursery. Pass through the metal barrier and then go straight on (not right to the Rose of York) across the meadow, where from spring onwards cattle from the farm will probably be grazing. When you come to the riverside gardens carry straight on, go under the bridge across the river and then when you get to the White Cross Hotel turn right up Water Lane. Go straight on at the top and you will eventually reach the station and the end of the walk.

Kew

Location	7½ miles (12 kilometres) southwest of Charing Cross.
Transport	Kew Gardens Station (Underground District Line; overground North London Line trains), Kew Bridge Station (overground trains from Waterloo), Kew Gardens Pier (boats from **Westminster Pier**).
Features	**St Anne's Church**; **Royal Botanic Gardens and Kew Palace**; Kew Green and cricket ground; 18th-century houses, riverside walk and views of Strand on the Green; Maids of Honour tearooms (closed Sun).
Refreshments	*outside station* variety of cafés, bars, restaurants and takeaways; *between station and Kew Green* (see map page 126) Newens' Maids of Honour tearooms; *junction of Kew Road and Mortlake Road at entrance to Green* pubs, bars, restaurants; *north side of Green* pubs and Greek restaurant.

Kew is thought to derive its name from the old Anglo-Saxon word for quay or landing place. This is plausible since the village grew up at the south end of a ford across the River Thames. This ford – which gave its name to Brentford on the north bank – was the lowest on the Thames and therefore strategically significant in times of conflict. But commercially it was of little value and so Kew remained an unimportant place throughout its early existence. In the Middle Ages it was neither a manor nor a parish in its own right (it formed part of Richmond and Kingston respectively) and it was not even mentioned in any surviving documents until the early 14th century.

What really put Kew on the map was the development of Richmond as a royal residence by Henry VII and his Tudor successors in the late 15th and 16th centuries. With the court based at Richmond for extended periods, courtiers needed houses close by. Kew was a popular location because it was on the way to or from London, whether travelling by road or – as was more common in those days – by boat. Various royal children and more or less famous courtiers lived at Kew in the 16th century. One courtier was the unfortunate Henry Norris, executed for dallying with Henry VIII's second wife, Anne Boleyn.

Fishing village
In the early 1600s, Princess Elizabeth, sister of Prince Henry of Wales who resided at Richmond Palace, had her own little court at Kew. But despite this and other

royal connections, the village remained little more than a tiny fishing and farming hamlet with – in 1664 – only 29 houses. Three of these were, however, large.

In those days, the Green – then an empty common – extended all the way through what is now Kew Gardens to the ferry landing at Brentford Ferry Gate. The three large houses – Kew Farm, Kew House and the Dutch House – were all clustered near the ferry landing. The Dutch House – so called because of its Dutch style of architecture – was built in 1631 by Samuel Fortrey, a City merchant of Flemish extraction whose family had fled to England to escape Catholic persecution in the Spanish Netherlands. Kew House, about 100 yards (90 metres) to the south, was effectively the manor house of Kew. The Capel family lived here for half a century from the 1670s, and made a famous garden, full of rare trees and plants.

Royalty arrives

In the 18th century the Kew we know today began to emerge, particularly after the new Hanoverian royal family discovered its attractions as a country retreat. Prince George – later George II – moved into Richmond Lodge at the south end of what is now Kew Gardens. His son, Prince Frederick, succeeded the Capels in Kew House. The Dutch House and the other houses by the ferry were also acquired for use by royal children and courtiers. More courtiers' houses were built around the common, henceforward known as Kew Green. Over time all the royal residences, with the exception of the Dutch House – which is now **Kew Palace** – were demolished and their grounds combined to form one large garden. When George IV blocked off the road leading across the Green to the ferry and diverted the road beside the river, the **Kew Gardens** we know today were complete.

Botanic gardens

The botanic gardens were developed out of the Capels' old garden by Prince Frederick and Princess Augusta and much expanded during the reign of George III (who died in 1820). George's successors were not interested in Kew, so in 1840 the royal gardens were transformed into a publicly owned, professionally managed botanical institute. By 1865 the gardens were attracting 500,000 visitors a year. Within 20 years that figure had risen to 1.25 million. In 1869 Kew Gardens Station opened and, more than anything, changed Kew from a village to a suburb. Pollution had already killed off the fishing industry by mid-century. Now house-builders bought up the farmland and market gardens for city commuters. The old village remained relatively unchanged, however, and still looks today much as it must have done in the 18th century.

THE KEW WALK

Start and finish Kew Gardens Station.
Distance 2 miles (3.2 kilometres).

Come out of the station and take the right fork ahead (Station Approach). When you reach Kew Gardens Road, turn right and follow it as it winds down to the junction with Kew Road. Kew Gardens is behind the wall on the far side of the road. Turn

KEW

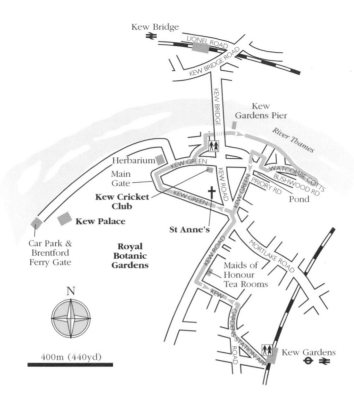

right on Kew Road and go past the famous Maids of Honour tea rooms run by the Newens family. The Newens make many kinds of delicious cakes and pies, but the star is the eponymous Maid of Honour, a little curd pastry that literally melts in the mouth. In 1887 Alfred Newens brought the recipe from Richmond – where the cakes had been made at least as far back as the early 18th century – and it remains a jealously guarded secret in the family to this day.

The old village of Kew starts just beyond the tea rooms with a row of early 19th-century houses and cottages facing the gardens. No. 300, for example, has a stone plaque on it saying 'Cumberland Place 1831'. Right at the end, the last two houses before the traffic lights (Nos 356 and 358) were originally one house and were the residence of Francis Bauer, Kew's chief botanical draughtsman and painter until his death in 1840.

Kew Green

At the traffic lights cross over to the left and follow the road round to the left into the main part of Kew Green. Not being a parish, Kew had no church of its own until a group of influential residents successfully petitioned Queen Anne for permission to build one on a disused gravel pit on the common. **St Anne's Church** on the right, completed in 1714, was the result. It was first extended in 1770 after

Kew had been made a parish in its own right, and thereafter several more times as the parish grew in population. Inside there are monuments to, among others, Lady Capel (died 1721), Francis Bauer and the 18th-century painter Thomas Gainsborough (1788). Gainsborough's grave is outside the church on the south side. Clearly visible nearby are the graves of several fellow artists: Jeremiah Meyer, miniature painter to George III; Joshua Kirby, Gainsborough's friend and the subject of the latter's *Joshua Kirby and His Wife* in the National Portrait Gallery; and Johann Zoffany. Zoffany did a painting for St Anne's, but it was rejected because he included one of the churchwardens as Judas! It can now be seen across the river in St Paul's Church in Brentford (see page 17).

Cambridge Cottage

The south side of the Green has perhaps the finest collection of period houses. No. 33, the one with the bow window over the garage, was owned in the 18th century by the Marquis of Bute, the man who helped Princess Augusta develop the botanical garden after Prince Frederick's death in 1751. Bute also owned the largest house on this side of the Green, No. 37 ahead with the porte-cochère protruding over the roadway. Later it became the residence of the royal Dukes of Cambridge and was renamed Cambridge Cottage. Edward VII donated it to the Gardens following the second duke's death in 1904. At this end of the Green many other buildings have been taken over by the Gardens, just as the court took them over in a previous phase in Kew's history. Note the plaque on the right of the gate into No. 47. This was the original main entrance to the gardens: at that time the road you are on went straight onto the ferry landing.

Follow the road round in front of the new main entrance (created after George IV blocked off the old road in 1824) and keep going past more of the Kew Gardens buildings, notably the Herbarium and the Library. Just beyond is the entrance to Ferry Lane, resited here when George IV blocked the original road. There is no ferry any more and the lane merely leads to a car park covering the lawn where Elizabeth I is said to have had secret assignations with her lover, Lord Leicester.

Beyond Ferry Lane is another row of exceedingly pretty houses, all different styles and sizes. In the 18th century, No. 77 (Beaconsfield) was the home of Mrs Papendiek, a minor court official whose memoirs are an important source for the history of court life at Kew during the time of George III. Over on the right is the **Kew Cricket Club**. Cricket has been played on Kew Green since at least Prince Frederick's time. He was a keen player himself and in 1737 captained a side against the Duke of Marlborough's eleven. The royal team won. Nowadays charity matches with show-business stars are a feature of the ground.

Kew's first bridge

Keep left when the road rises to join the bridge approach and turn left between Capel House (one of the finest houses on the Green) and the King's Arms. Walking down towards the river you see the modern developments in Old Brentford, and rising above them, the graceful campanile of the old waterworks, now the Kew Bridge Steam Museum. At the river turn right on the towpath and go under the bridge. Robert Tunstall, the owner of the ferry, built the first bridge across the Thames at Kew in 1759. A toll was charged until 1873, when the bridge was bought for the public and made free. The present bridge dates from 1903.

On the far side you pass Kew Gardens pier (boats to Hampton Court and central London) and the war memorial gardens. When you reach the steps leading down to Thetis Terrace/Willow Cottages, a good view of Strand on the Green, another former fishing hamlet, opens up on the far side of the river. As you walk along you are crossing what was the entrance to Kew dock, the main centre of the local fishing industry until it was wiped out by pollution around 1850. Looking across the river when you reach the modern flats you can see a large five-bay house to the right of the willow tree with a blue plaque on it. This is where the painter Johann Zoffany came to live in 1789 after making his fortune in India.

When you reach the end of the long low row of cottages, turn right into the passage next to the allotments, and then right again into the road (Watcombe Cottages). Go past the entrance to Old Dock Close and when you get to the pond turn right into Cambridge Cottages and then left again. When the creek leading to the pond and the old dock were filled in in the late 19th century, all the cottages here were built on the site. The area generally was known as the Westerly Ware, after the weir which the fishermen constructed across the river. There was an Easterly Ware further downstream. Take the first left, go past the entrance to Westerly Ware and Willow Cottages/Thetis Terrace on your right and pass through a narrow bottleneck to emerge on the Green by the pond again.

Painted by Gainsborough

Go straight on between the Green and the pond, passing the entrance to Priory Road (built on the site of a neo-Gothic house called Kew Priory). The biggest house on this side of the Green is No. 24, Haverfield House. John Haverfield managed the royal estates in Kew in the 18th century. His son was Robert Tunstall's partner in the building of the bridge. His granddaughter was the subject of the Gainsborough portrait *Miss Haverfield,* now in the Wallace Collection. (Gainsborough, incidentally, never lived in Kew. He generally stayed with his friends the Kirbys or with his daughter.)

Pissarro in Kew

On the far side of Haverfield House, No. 22 has a blue plaque to the Pre-Raphaelite painter Arthur Hughes, who came here in 1858 and stayed until his death in 1915. A little further on there is a blue plaque to the Impressionist Camille Pissarro in the entrance to Gloucester Road. In 1892 he stayed in a flat here for several months while trying to reassure the parents of a Jewish girl that it would be alright for their daughter to marry his son Lucien. He succeeded, and meanwhile painted several views in and around Kew.

From Gloucester Road carry on past the Coach and Horses (Kew's oldest inn) to the traffic lights. Go straight over and walk back along Kew Road, turning left at the Maids of Honour into Kew Gardens Road. From here make your way back to the station, where the walk ends.

Mitcham

Location	8½ miles (13.7 kilometres) south of Charing Cross.
Transport	Mitcham Station (overground trains from Waterloo – change at Wimbledon, and from Victoria – change at Mitcham Junction). On Sundays there is no service at Mitcham, so travel from Victoria, alight at Mitcham Junction and walk (approximately 1 mile or 1.6 kilometres).
Features	**St Peter and St Paul's Church**; Cricket Green and **Mitcham Cricket Club**; The Canons and **Merton Heritage Centre**; **Wandle Industrial Museum**; Ravensbury Park and River Wandle.
Events	**Mitcham Fair**.
Refreshments	*London Road* fish and chip shop, burger bar, Stagecoach café and Burn Bullock pub; *Ravensbury Park* Enzo's café (see map page 132); *Mitcham town centre in Upper Green area* variety of fast-food outlets.

Mitcham lies in the Wandle plain on the road connecting Tooting with Sutton. Spread out along the road over a considerable distance, it is centred on not one but two village greens, the Upper Green to the north and the Lower Green to the south. The Upper Green, which is not covered on the walk, is now the main shopping centre of the modern town of Mitcham. The Lower Green, which is covered by the walk, is the historic heart of the village and is a protected conservation area.

In the Middle Ages four separate manors emerged in Mitcham, all belonging originally to the church. The most important, lying to the east of the village centre, was Mitcham Canons, a property of the Priory of St Mary Overie in Southwark. The monastic estate was administered from the manor house just to the east of Lower Green. In its grounds it had a dovecote and a carp pond. Both these features survive and are seen on the walk. The manor house has disappeared, but a late-17th-century house called The Canons, now the home of the Merton Heritage Centre, stands on the site.

After the dissolution of the monasteries, the main secular owners of the manor of Mitcham were the Cranmer family. Robert Cranmer, descendant of the 16th-century Archbishop Cranmer and a wealthy East India merchant, bought the estate in 1656. It remained in his descendants' hands until shortly before World War II. The family lived not in The Canons, but in another large house called The Cranmers a few hundred yards to the south. This was demolished and a hospital built on the site when the estate was broken up and developed.

John Donne

Even before the dissolution of the monasteries, many merchants, lawyers, courtiers and government officials from London had discovered Mitcham as a pleasant and healthy rural retreat. The Ravensbury Manor on the River Wandle to the south of the village was acquired by a City vintner as early as the 14th century. Later, many country houses were built in and around the village, their amenities attracting Queen Elizabeth I here no fewer than five times in the 1590s. The poet and Dean of St Paul's, John Donne, lived in the village from 1605 to 1611. At about the same time, Sir Walter Raleigh acquired land in the village through his marriage into the Throgmorton family. Unfortunately, he had to sell it in 1616 to finance his disastrous expedition to the Orinoco. About a century later court physician Fernando Mendez built the magnificent Eagle House on the former Raleigh property. This and The Canons are the only two of Mitcham's historic mansions to survive. Unfortunately, Eagle House, recently restored as offices, is too far to the north of the village to be included in the walk.

Just at the time Eagle House was built, Mitcham was developing – for reasons that are not now clear – as one of the great early centres of cricket. The game was played on the Lower Green East, now renamed Cricket Green, from at least 1685, and in 1707 the villagers challenged an All-London team to a match on Lamb's Conduit Fields in Holborn which the rustics unfortunately lost. The first recorded match in Mitcham was played in 1711, and the game has thrived here ever since, making the village a shrine for devotees.

Mitcham 'shag'

Apart from cricket, Mitcham was also known in the 18th and 19th centuries for its industries on the Wandle and for its herbs. The Wandle mills turned out flour, paper, colourful printed calico cloth and tobacco products, particularly snuff and Mitcham 'shag'. The herb fields and distilleries produced lavender, camomile, wormwood, aniseed, liquorice and damask rose, and associated essential oils and waters. In 1805, the firm of Potter and Moore, pioneers of lavender water distillation on an industrial scale in 1749, had at least 500 acres (200 hectares) of medicinal and aromatic herbs under cultivation. No trace of the herb industry remains in Mitcham today, but the Ravensbury snuff mill and the Mitcham flour and paper mill still stand on the Wandle.

Public railway

Industrial development in the early 19th century in the Wandle area south of the village was helped by the arrival of the Surrey Iron Railway. Opened between Wandsworth and Croydon in 1803, this was the first public railway in the world. Horses pulled waggons along the tracks and users paid tolls at various gates as on a turnpike road. The steam railways killed it off quickly, but the Mitcham section of the track was incorporated into the Wimbledon–Croydon line, opened through Mitcham Station in 1855. When the main line from Victoria arrived at Mitcham Junction a few years later, Mitcham's transition from country village to urban suburb was set in full motion.

THE MITCHAM WALK
Start and finish Mitcham Station.
Distance 3 miles (4.8 kilometres).

Come out of Mitcham Station onto the London Road and turn right past the old station house with the arch in the middle. Built in the early 1800s as a private house, this was taken over by the railways in the 1850s and used until the 1980s. It has now been converted into offices.

Cricket Green
Carry on up London Road towards the village centre. After a while you come to Cricket Green, formerly Lower Green East and the larger of the two open spaces that together make up the Lower Green. All the historical landmarks in Mitcham are illustrated and described on the information panel across the road at the corner of the green. The green itself, of course, is the Mitcham cricket pitch and one of the oldest such pitches in the country. To the left is the White Hart, a former coaching inn dating from at least 1603 and given a handsome Georgian facelift around 1750. The Burn Bullock to the right is similarly a Georgian coaching inn with earlier origins (the fact that both were modernized and enlarged about the same time is clear evidence of the growth of road traffic). Originally it was called the King's Head, but it was renamed in 1975. Burn Bullock was a famous Mitcham cricketer, a member of the local club from the age of 17 and landlord of the pub from 1941 until his death in 1954. His wife Lil ran it until her retirement in 1975. Inside, the walls are covered with cricketing photographs.

Turn right by the pub. Behind the Georgian section you can clearly see the inn's original half-timbered part, certainly more than 300 and possibly as much as 400 years old. Beyond the pub is the pavilion of the **Mitcham Cricket Club**, with its verandah for watching play. Crossing the road to the pitch was a relatively easy matter when the pavilion was built in 1904. Now, with the great increase of traffic, it is infinitely more hazardous. Maybe it is just as well that there is a clause in the lease forbidding the club to have its own bar!

Miraculous appearance of water
Carry on along Cricket Green and past Mary Tate's almshouses, put up in 1829 on the site of the Tates' Mitcham house. The Tates were a wealthy family and had other property elsewhere. Miss Tate was the last surviving member of the Mitcham Tates and lived out in Northamptonshire at a large place called Burleigh Park, so she could afford to be generous. Just beyond the Queen's Head pub, cross the road to the obelisk on the north side. Mitcham went through a few years of drought in the early 1820s. When an artesian spring suddenly appeared here, locals took it for a miracle and the lord of the manor's son, the Reverend Richard Cranmer, decided to commemorate it with this monument, erected in September 1822. The Cranmer family lived in a large house to the right off what is now Cranmer Road.

Continue past the obelisk into Madeira Road and then after a short time turn left into the gates of The Canons. This is the house built in 1680 on the site of the

MITCHAM

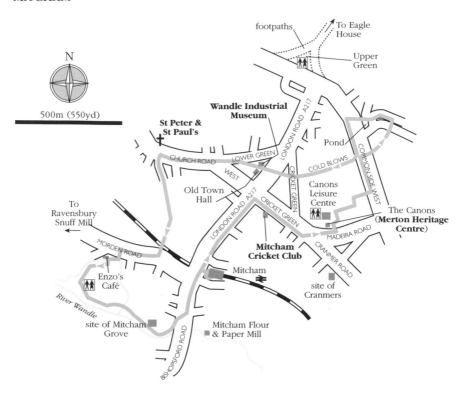

N

500m (550yd)

To Eagle House

footpaths

Upper Green

Wandle Industrial Museum

St Peter & St Paul's

LONDON ROAD A217

Pond

CHURCH ROAD   LOWER GREEN

COLD BLOWS

WEST

CRICKET GREEN

Canons Leisure Centre

COMMONSIDE WEST

Old Town Hall

To Ravensbury Snuff Mill

LONDON ROAD A217

CRICKET GREEN

CRICKET GREEN

MADEIRA ROAD

The Canons (Merton Heritage Centre)

CRANMER ROAD

MORDEN ROAD

Mitcham Cricket Club

Mitcham

Enzo's Café

site of Cranmers

River Wandle

site of Mitcham Grove

BISHOPSFORD ROAD

Mitcham Flour & Paper Mill

original monastic manor house. Now it is owned by the local council and used as the **Merton Heritage Centre** and local history museum. Turn right down the side of the house to the back garden. Here you can see the monks' carp pond and beside it the stone dovecote, dated 1511. Turn left along the back of the house, and then right, along the garden wall. When you reach the car park you can see dead ahead of you a stone let into the wall in 1816 by Mrs E. M. Cranmer to mark the eastern boundary of her property. Turn left along this wall and then right when you reach the playing fields.

The handsome Georgian mansion on the right now is Park House, built in 1780 for City lawyer Francis Gregg. Gregg was also manager of the Earl of Carlisle's extensive estates in the north, and served a s MP for one of the Earl's pocket boroughs in the 1790s. When you reach Mitcham Common, turn left along Commonside West and walk past the Windmill pub, which dates from about 1870 and recalls a former windmill. When you reach the lights, cross the road and walk along the path across the Common. This section of the Common is known as Three Kings Piece (after the pub of that name which you pass in a minute) and it is here that the annual **Mitcham Fair** is held every August.

Five generations of Charts

At Commonside East, turn left past the row of cottages and the Three Kings pub. In front is a duck pond, at least 300 years old, fed by a covered-in stream running alongside Commonside. At the junction with the main road, the weatherboarded Clarendon House was at one time the home of the Chart family, noted local builders and administrators. John Chart built the parish church in 1821. Five generations of Charts served in the local vestry and its successors. William Chart was appointed vestry clerk in 1761. His descendant, Colonel Stephen Chart, retired as town clerk in 1946.

At the traffic lights just beyond Clarendon House, cross the main road and turn left back along Commonside West. When you get to the lights where you turned onto the Common, turn right along Cold Blows, an aptly named footpath that once connected the village with the common fields on the far side of Commonside East. The path brings you back to Cricket Green and to some of the elegant houses overlooking it from the northeast side. Carry straight on across the Green towards the Victorian vestry hall, Mitcham's first town hall, designed by a Chart and built in 1887 on the site of the village lockup.

Cross London Road and pass between the vestry hall and the **Wandle Industrial Museum** on the right. Go straight across Lower Green West, passing on your left the old village school topped with a cupola and clock tower. Built as a Sunday school for 150 children in 1788, it became a National day school in 1812 and then one of the new elementary schools in 1870. From 1897 until 1987, when the church sold it, it served as the parish rooms. It has now been converted into flats and artists' studios.

14th-century chapel

As you continue into Church Road you pass a newer school on the left. At the entrance behind the fence you might just be able to make out a ruined arch. This is the only surviving portion of Hall Place, the manor house of Vauxhall, one of medieval Mitcham's three other manors besides Mitcham Canons. The now lonely arch was the entrance to the house's private chapel, constructed in 1349. Further along noisy Church Road you come to the vicarage on the left and then the parish church of **St Peter and St Paul** on the right. Mitcham once had its traditional medieval parish church, but in 1821 it was demolished and a larger one built in its place.

Cross the road by the church into Church Path (to be on the safe side use the zebra crossing round the corner ahead). At the end of the row of cottages, continue on along the footpath, called Baron Path because it once led to Baron House, named after an 18th-century barrister occupant, Oliver Baron. Two centuries before Baron lived here Queen Elizabeth I stayed in the house on two of her five visits to Mitcham.

Ravensbury Park

Having crossed the railway line and reached the end of the path, turn right onto Morden Road and then, just beyond Morden Gardens, left into Ravensbury Park. Follow the path round to the right past Enzo's café and across one of the channels of the Wandle. At the toilets the path forks. The right one leads to the Ravensbury snuff mill, in production until 1925 but now converted into flats. The walk takes the left fork, passing on the right the site of the old manor house of Ravensbury Manor acquired by a City wine merchant in the 1300s. At the bridge an information panel recounts the history of the area and tells how the last owners of the estate before it was developed and part preserved as a public park were the Bidder family, descendants of an engineering associate of George Stephenson of Stephenson's Rocket fame.

Private bank

Carry on along the path beside the Wandle. Having crossed two small bridges you pass houses on your left. Here, until 1846, stood Mitcham Grove, generally reckoned to have been the most beautiful of Mitcham's many secluded and gracious country houses. Between 1786 and his death in 1828, it was the home of Henry Hoare, senior partner of the private bank still flourishing in Fleet Street in the City and one of Mitcham's most public-spirited and generous residents. Hoare bought the house from Alexander Wedderburn, the lawyer and later Lord Chancellor, who in turn had been presented with it by Clive of India after successfully defending him against charges of corruption in the early 1770s.

The path brings you out on the London Road again. From the bridge on the right, the white Mitcham mill can be glimpsed a short distance upstream. The route of the walk, however, is to the left and Mitcham Station, where the walk ends, is up ahead by the traffic lights.

Rotherhithe and Bermondsey

Location	3¾ miles (6 kilometres) east of Charing Cross.
Transport	*Rotherhithe* Rotherhithe Underground Station (East London Line);
	Bermondsey London Bridge Station (Northern Underground Line and overground lines to the southeast).
Features	**St Mary's Church, Rotherhithe**; **St Mary Magdalen Church, Bermondsey**; **Bermondsey Street**, **New Caledonian Antiques Market**, remains of Bermondsey Abbey; Thames-side walk with views upriver to City and downstream to Canary Wharf; Rotherhithe wharves and warehouses; **Brunel's Engine House**.
Refreshments	*London Bridge Station and Tooley Street* numerous bars, cafés, takeaways and fast-food outlets;
	Bermondsey Street cafés and pubs;
	on the riverside between Bermondsey and Rotherhithe Angel pub:
	Rotherhithe Mayflower pub in village centre, Chinese restaurant near station, fish and chips/kebab/burger bar in Albion Street.

If its name is anything to go by, the little Docklands village of Rotherhithe on the south side of the River Thames started out as a landing place (hithe) for cattle (rother). No doubt the beasts were brought here by boat from south Essex and north Kent, were grazed in the fertile meadows behind the village and were then herded up to market at Smithfield on the northeastern flank of the City of London.

The village and its hinterland were low-lying and subject to frequent inundations by the Thames, so as more people settled in the area a great river wall (which may originally have been begun by the Romans) was built extending west to Bermondsey and east all the way around the peninsula opposite the Isle of Dogs to Deptford. Rotherhithe Street then emerged on top of the embankment, with houses, wharves and shipyards strung out along its 2-mile (3-kilometre) length. Here were built, repaired and berthed many of the ships that made London from very early times the busiest port in the world. Here also lived many of the seamen and ships' captains who sailed those ships to the four corners of the earth in search of maritime trade.

Greenland dock

As the number of ships using the port of London increased, more and more vessels were forced to anchor downriver in less sheltered reaches. To counter this problem the Howland family of Rotherhithe built on their property in the east of the parish

London's first major wet dock, surrounded by a windbreak of trees and capable of accommodating 120 sailing ships. Completed in 1700 and known originally as the Howland Wet Dock, it was later leased by the South Sea Company for their Greenland whaling fleet and re-christened the Greenland Dock.

Throughout the 18th century the Greenland Dock was surrounded by the meadows and market gardens of rural Rotherhithe, by this time criss-crossed with a complex, Dutch-style network of drainage ditches and dykes. In the 19th century, as the British trading empire got into full swing, these meadows were gobbled up by more and more docks on the Greenland model until virtually the whole Rotherhithe peninsula was one vast sheet of water. The four companies that built the docks amalgamated in 1864 to form the Surrey Commercial Dock Company. The Surrey docks subsequently became the main centre of London's imported timber trade.

The growth of the great docks on the peninsula mirrored Rotherhithe's decline as a shipbuilding centre. In place of the old shipyards, wharves, warehouses and mills came to dominate the waterfront. These in turn became redundant in the 1960s and 1970s when London's historic docks were closed. Eight out of the 11 Surrey docks were subsequently filled in and many of the warehouses demolished. But the Greenland Dock, not seen on the walk because it is too far away from the village centre, survives at the heart of a modern housing and leisure development and a number of warehouses have been converted into homes or workshops. The empty warehouses that remain in the heart of Rotherhithe serve as an evocative reminder of the village's maritime past and add a kind of Gothic atmosphere to the walk, which passes right by them.

Bermondsey Abbey

The connection between Rotherhithe and Bermondsey is based on more than geography: in the Middle Ages a large part of the manor of Rotherhithe was owned by Bermondsey Abbey. Founded in 1082 by Aylwin Child of London and endowed with the manor of Bermondsey by King William Rufus, the Cluniac priory of St Saviour's was built in open countryside between Southwark and Rotherhithe about 1 mile (1.5 kilometres) inland from the river. Servants and tenants of the priory (which converted into a Benedictine abbey in the 1390s) lived in houses around it and formed the nucleus of the village, worshipping in St Mary Magdalen Church just outside the abbey's north gate. The lane connecting the north gate with London Bridge gradually became Bermondsey Street and the high street of the village. In the vicinity of modern Tanner Street, Bermondsey Street crossed the River Neckinger. Where the Neckinger joined the Thames the abbey built a mill and a dock. The latter still survives as St Saviour's Dock.

The leather industry

In the Middle Ages, drawn by the water supply and the availability of oak bark for tanning, leatherworkers settled at Bermondsey and made it the centre not only of London's, but the country's, leather industry. Skins came from the Smithfield slaughterhouses to be processed at Bermondsey before being marketed at Leadenhall Market in the City. When Leadenhall became too small in the 19th century, the

Plate 28: The main entrance of the Trinity Hospital almshouse in Greenwich (see page 114).

Plate 29: A pretty cottage tucked away in Diamond Terrace, Greenwich (see page 115).

Plate 30: Cows from Petersham Farm graze contentedly in the lush meadows between the village and the Thames (see page 123).

Plate 31: One of the finest 17th-century houses in England and now the property of the National Trust, Ham House was formerly the ancestral home of the Earls of Dysart (see page 117).

Plate 32: The pond on the east side of Kew Green originated in Tudor times as a riverside dock for the royal barge (see page 128).

Plate 33: Mitcham's immaculately maintained Cricket Green has witnessed matches ever since the game began 300-odd years ago (see page 131).

Plate 34: Ducks and swans cohabit peacefully on a quiet backwater of the Wandle in Ravensbury Park, Mitcham (see page 133).

Plate 35: *The hollow-post windmill on Wimbledon Common dates from 1817 and now houses a fascinating windmill museum (see page 146).*

leather market was brought to Bermondsey, so making the area the centre of the leather trade as well as the leather industry. Both have departed now and been replaced by the New Caledonian Antiques Market.

After the closure of Bermondsey Abbey, the first and greatest secular owner of the manor was the courtier and administrator Sir Thomas Pope, the builder of Bermondsey House on the site of the abbey, and founder of Trinity College in Oxford. Rotherhithe, meanwhile, passed through various hands until the early 19th century when it came into the possession of Court governess Jane Gomm and then her brother, Field Marshal Sir William Gomm. The Gomms married into the Carrs, becoming the Carr-Gomms. The Carr-Gomms were the last lords of the manor of Rotherhithe and their name lives on in the area in various local charitable institutions.

THE ROTHERHITHE AND BERMONDSEY WALK
Start London Bridge Station.
Finish Rotherhithe Station.
Distance 3½ miles (5.6 kilometres)

Turn right out of London Bridge Station onto Tooley Street. Opposite the entrance to Hay's Galleria, turn right into Weston Street and walk underneath the station overhead. Turn left onto St Thomas Street and then right into Bermondsey Street. Apart from some warehouses and factories at this top end, Bermondsey Street retains – unusually for this part of London – much of its original character as a community high street, and also many of its original houses, particularly the little row on the right, of which No. 78, with its oriel window and weatherboarded attic workroom, is the highlight. Restoration will no doubt reach these houses before long, for Bermondsey Street is now a conservation area and much refurbishment work has already been done in the lower half of the street.

St Mary Magdalen
Further on, the street names of Tanner Street and Morocco Street, where Bermondsey Street crossed the River Neckinger, flag the site of the former leather market. The market building, now converted into offices, stands on the far side of the market area at the end of Morocco Street. The parish church of **St Mary Magdalen**, built around 1680 on the site of an earlier church which had become unsafe, is at the bottom of the street, with the old Georgian rectory on one side and the modern rectory on the other. All around are warehouses full of antiques, spilling over from the Friday morning **New Caledonian Antiques Market** which moved here from north London after World War II. It is mainly a market for dealers, but collectors come here too. You have to be here early to get the best bargains though: like most wholesale markets, most of the day's business is done while ordinary folk are still tucked up in bed.

Resurrection men
Carry on the past the church and the disused graveyard. The building on the corner is the old parish watch-house where the parish constables reported for duty and

ROTHERHITHE AND BERMONDSEY

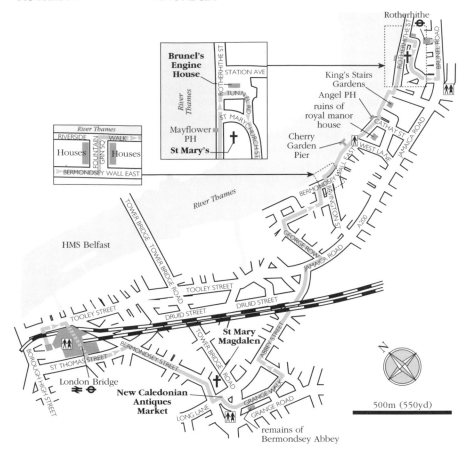

where a watch was kept on the graveyard to prevent resurrection men stealing fresh corpses to sell to nearby hospitals for dissection. At this point you are standing on the site of the north gate of Bermondsey Abbey. Bermondsey Square ahead represents the main quadrangle of the abbey. The abbey church lay along Abbey Road to your left. After acquiring the dissolved abbey in the 1540s, Sir Thomas Pope knocked the church down and used the stone to build Bermondsey House on the eastern side of the old abbey quadrangle. As you can see, nothing substantial is left of the abbey now, or indeed of Pope's house. Even Georgian Bermondsey Square has almost entirely disappeared: only a rather forlorn group of houses from the southwestern corner is left. On Friday mornings the open space in the middle of the square is filled with antiques stalls.

Cross the square diagonally to its southeastern corner and turn into Grange Walk. Grange Walk ran from the abbey's eastern gatehouse to the abbey grange or farm. Several very old houses survive on the right-hand side of the street. No. 7, one of the oldest, must have been part of the gatehouse, for the gate hinges still protrude from its pink-coloured façade. Having passed the disused 1830 girls' charity school building on the right, you come to No. 67 on the left, the most handsome house in the street, currently being restored with the assistance of English Heritage.

Now you are at the eastern extremity of the Bermondsey village area. Open fields originally stretched from this point to Rotherhithe. Today housing estates, industrial buildings and main roads are more in evidence. We now have to make our way through all these developments until we reach the docklands strip beside the Thames.

London's first railway line

Turn left into The Grange and then right into Abbey Street. Ahead Canary Wharf Tower rises above the bridge carrying the railway line to London Bridge Station. Opened in 1836 and extending as far as Greenwich, this was the first railway line in the capital. As you pass beneath the bridge, note the handsome fluted columns and fine brickwork of the original structure and the way it has been widened over the years to accommodate more tracks.

At Jamaica Road turn right and then first left into George Row. Jacob Street at the far end marks both the beginning of the riverside warehouse area and the site of Jacob's Island, a notorious Victorian slum surrounded by polluted mill streams. This is where Dickens set the death of Bill Sikes in *Oliver Twist*. Turn right into Chambers Street, where there are still many vacant warehouses and mills, and then left into Loftie Street. Here film studios and scenery makers have put some of the empty spaces to productive use. At the end of Loftie Street turn right into Bermondsey Wall East and then left through modern Fountain Green Square to reach the riverside directly opposite Wapping Pier Head, the former entrance to the London Docks. Turning right along the riverside there are fine views of the great terraces of warehouses on both sides of the river. On the left, the modern building painted white and blue is the base of the river police. On the right, in front of Canary Wharf Tower, are the warehouses and church spire of Rotherhithe, your ultimate destination.

Turner's *Téméraire*

At Cherry Garden Pier, named after a 17th-century resort visited by Samuel Pepys and the spot where Turner stood to paint his National Gallery picture of the warship *Téméraire* on its way to the Rotherhithe breaker's yard, you have to leave the riverside walk and return to the road. As you pass the entrance to West Lane on your right you cross from the ancient parish of Bermondsey into Rotherhithe. The first feature you come to is an open area with the Angel pub on the riverside and, in the centre, the partially excavated remains of Edward III's 14th-century moated manor house. Three panels around the site tell the story of the house, which was probably the manor house for that part of Rotherhithe not granted to Bermondsey Abbey. Originally in the hands of the noble Clare family, the house and land seem to have passed into royal control in or shortly before Edward III's time. A successor, Henry IV, is said to have lived here in 1412 while recovering from leprosy.

Royal landing stage
Carrying on, you come to the solitary office of Braithwaite and Dean, one of the few surviving firms of Thames lightermen. For centuries, lightermen have conveyed cargoes from ships out in the middle of the river to the warehouses ion the riverside quays. Beyond Braithwaite and Dean are the King's Stairs Gardens, the King's Stairs being the landing stage for the royal manor house. In the gardens you rejoin the riverside and walk through an arcade under a modern apartment block before coming back onto the road at the start of Rotherhithe Street. At this point it is hemmed in by tall warehouses and so narrow that it seems amazing that it should go on for almost 2 miles (3 kilometres) and be one of London's longest streets.

From this narrow section of the street you emerge in the centre of the old village of Rotherhithe. On the left beyond the Thames Tunnel Mills, one of the first industrial buildings in docklands to be converted into residential use, the Mayflower pub provides a clue to Rotherhithe's main claim to fame: the *Mayflower,* the ship that carried the Pilgrim Fathers over to America in 1620, was berthed here. Its master and part-owner, Captain Christopher Jones, moved to Rotherhithe from Harwich in 1611. He is buried in the churchyard, as are his three co-owners of the ship.

Continue on under the gantry. The late 18th-century warehouses left and right were formerly a granary belonging to the Grice family. Now they are home to Sands Studios, where the film *Little Dorrit* was made, and the Rotherhithe picture library. Behind the granary you come to **Brunel's Engine House**. This is the original pump house used during construction of the Wapping–Rotherhithe tunnel between 1824 and 1843. Inside, an exhibition tells the story of the tunnel – the first ever built under water – and the heroic struggle needed to complete it. Engineered by the Brunels, father and son, it is now used by the East London Underground line.

Prince Lee Boo
Turn right into Tunnel Road between the Engine House and the granary and then right again into St Marychurch Street. **St Mary's Church** was built by local people in 1715 and deliberately raised up high on a plinth to protect it from flooding. Inside there are many memorials to local ships' captains and some pieces of furniture made by wood salvaged from the *Téméraire.* The pillars look like stone, but are in fact tree trunks encased in plaster. The roof, resembling an upturned boat, must have been a doddle for the local boatbuilders who fashioned it. Outside the west end of the church are two interesting memorials: a modern one to the captain of the *Mayflower* and an original commemorating two people linked together by a fascinating story. In 1783 Captain Henry Wilson's ship was wrecked and he and his crew were cast away on the Pacific island of Cooroora, east of the Philippines. They got on so well with the islanders that, when they had built themselves a new ship and were about to return to England, the king of the island asked them to take his son with them to be educated in an English school. Wilson gladly brought Prince Lee Boo to his home in Rotherhithe and sent him to the local school. Although

much older than the other pupils he was a great favourite, but unfortunately had no defences against western diseases. After only six months he succumbed to smallpox.

You come out of the churchyard directly opposite the rectory and the former village school with its little figures of a boy and a girl above the door. The charity school was founded in 1612 by Robert Bell and Peter Hills, a seaman, to whom there is a brass memorial in the church. In Prince Lee Boo's day the school house was at the east end of the church, but in 1797 it moved to this house, where the master also lived. It still survives today as a modern primary school in Beatson Walk.

Sufferance Wharf

Turn right past the school. On the left now are the village watch-house and fire-engine house, both built in 1821, and on the right Hope Sufferance Wharf. From Tudor times onwards goods could only be unloaded in the port of London at 'legal' quays. When these became congested, other quays were licensed or 'suffered' to admit goods bearing low customs duties. Hope Wharf at Rotherhithe, stretching back from the riverside to this point, was one of these sufferance wharves. Follow the road round to the left, and at the end turn left into Brunel Road. Rotherhithe Underground Station, where the walk ends, is about 100 yards (90 metres) ahead on the left.

Wimbledon

Location	7½ miles (12 kilometres) southwest of Charing Cross.
Transport	Wimbledon Station (Underground District Line; overground trains from Waterloo and London Bridge stations).
Features	**St Mary's Church**; High Street and Eagle House; Wimbledon Common and Georgian mansions; **Southside House**; **Wimbledon Society Museum**; views of London; **Wimbledon Windmill Museum** and **Wimbledon Lawn Tennis Museum** (not on walk – see map page 144).
Refreshments	*Station and adjoining streets and shopping centre* variety of fast-food outlets, pubs, takeaways and cafés; *High Street* pubs, restaurants and coffee houses; *Crooked Billet and Camp Road* (halfway through walk) pubs; *Wimbledon Windmill Museum* (not on walk) café (and toilets).

Wimbledon has been one of London's most select suburbs for over two centurie snow, but its history goes right back to prehistoric times. Ridgway is presumed to be a relic of an ancient track leading to a ford over the Thames at Kingston, and the so-called Caesar's Camp on the Common – a circular space surrounded by a nearly levelled ditch and rampart – is actually an Iron Age hill fort. The village grew up to the east of the Common, on the edge of the high ground overlooking the valley of the River Wandle. The church and rectory stood, as they still do, on the lip of the plateau, enjoying fine views to the north and east now obscured by trees and buildings. The manor house joined them later. The two main roads of the village, Church Road and High Street, lay further back between the church and the common land where the villagers grazed their animals and gathered turf and firewood.

The manor of Mortlake

In the Middle Ages, Wimbledon was merely an outlying part of the Archbishops of Canterbury's great manor of Mortlake, which also included Putney, Roehampton and East Sheen. But whereas the manor house of the archbishops was at Mortlake, the parish church of the district was at Wimbledon. **St Mary's Church**, therefore, has been an important religious centre for the best part of a thousand years. This perhaps accounts for the substantial size of the new rectory built beside the church around 1500. Though much altered, the house still survives and is, by a margin of a century or so, the oldest building in Wimbledon – older even than the church which, having been rebuilt to provide more space in 1789, was again rebuilt for much the same reason in 1841.

Forced to surrender

In 1536 the then Archbishop of Canterbury was forced to surrender his Wimbledon property to Henry VIII and, shortly after, the virtually new rectory was leased out as a country retreat to politician and courtier Sir Thomas Cecil. The Cecils took to Wimbledon and, having risen to become one of the most powerful dynasties in Tudor England, moved out of the old rectory into a huge new country house completed in 1588 a few hundred yards/metres to the east. Sir Edward Cecil, third son of the builder of the house and a professional soldier, inherited the estate and was created Viscount Wimbledon in 1625.

The Cecils' house was pretty much in ruins by 1700, so when Huguenot merchant and financier Sir Theodore Janssen bought the estate, he demolished the old house and used the bricks to build a brand new one on the opposite side of the church. He did not enjoy his new property for long, however, for the South Sea Bubble ruined him and he had to sell up to the Duchess of Marlborough in 1724. The Duchess then built yet another house, but her descendant, Earl Spencer, had to replace it in 1799 after it had been destroyed by fire. This century has seen the destruction of both Lord Spencer's and Sir Theodore Janssen's houses, so although Wimbledon has had no fewer than four great manor houses over the centuries, not one has survived the vicissitudes of time to grace the village today.

The Spencer family finally left Wimbledon in 1846. After their departure the park, landscaped by Capability Brown, was mostly sold off for development. Later the local council was able to acquire one part, including the lake, and open it to the public. Another part was bought in 1920 by the All England Lawn Tennis Club and subsequently developed as the home of the Wimbledon tennis championships.

Healthy position

Wimbledon's healthy position at 150 feet (45 metres) above sea level and its proximity to London combined to make it a desirable retreat for wealthy merchants and professional men from the time of the Cecils onwards. In the beginning, the big houses these successful individuals built for themselves were, like the manor house, close to the centre of the village. Eagle House, built in 1613 by a founder of the East India Company, survives at the north end of the High Street and is seen on the walk. Later houses tended to be built outside the village, facing the common around Rushmere Pond. Those in Parkside on the east side have all disappeared, but several on the south and particularly the west sides have survived and are also seen on the walk.

Since the village was not on a main road and lacked any industry except for a few mills down on the river, Wimbledon's shopkeepers and tradesmen relied on the custom from these big houses for their living until well into the 19th century. Then came the railway and with it the tide of building that eventually filled in all the open land between the once-isolated village and central London. Luckily, however, the railway had to be built in the valley bottom, about half a mile from the centre of the village, so, as the following walk shows, Wimbledon was able to preserve much of its individual identity in a way that many of the other old village centres in and around London were not.

THE WIMBLEDON WALK

Start and finish Wimbledon Station.
Distance 3¼ miles (6 kilometres).

From the station forecourt turn right along the main road. Cross at the traffic lights and go straight on, passing the library on your right. At the end of the shops and just before the main road starts to climb the hill, turn right into Woodside. Walk along here and then take the first left into St Mary's Road. Follow this road – once called Hothouse Lane because it connected Lord Spencer's house at the top of the hill with his kitchen garden at the bottom – as it winds its way uphill to the top of the plateau on which the old village of Wimbledon and its Common sit.

Eventually you reach the junction with Arthur Road in front of the church. The edge of the plateau is to your right. Here stood three of the four manor houses: the Cecils', the Duchess of Marlborough's and Lord Spencer's. The last, Lord Spencer's, was demolished in 1948 and replaced in the 1970s with a school. All that is left of it is a well house across the road from the school entrance, built in 1798 to cover the earl's private artesian well and converted into a private house about the time the school was built. The fourth manor house – the one built by Sir Theodore Janssen about 1720 and demolished in 1900 – lay to your left in the vicinity of Alan Road. Nothing remains of this except a length of kitchen garden wall in one of the roads built over the site.

WIMBLEDON

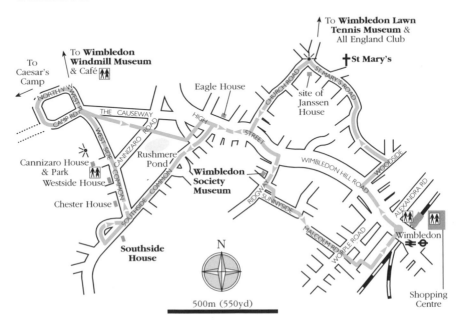

Memorials in the church

In the days of Wimbledon Park, Arthur Road did not exist. But when the estate was sold to John Beaumont for development in 1846, he built the lodge house in front of you to provide an entrance to the grounds. In 1872, when Arthur Road was constructed, Stag Lodge, as it is called, became redundant and was subsequently converted into a private house. Behind the lodge, the church, though relatively modern, contains many old memorials, particularly the large black marble tomb of Lord Wimbledon in the 17th-century Cecil Chapel and the fine memorial to James Perry in the entrance lobby. Perry, a Wimbledon resident, owned and edited the *Morning Chronicle* newspaper in the early years of the 19th century and had a large flour mill down on the Wandle. Round the back of the church you can see the tomb of Sir Joseph Bazalgette, one of the greatest British engineers of the 19th century and the builder of London's remarkable sewer system. Looking over the churchyard wall, the upper parts of Wimbledon's historic Old Rectory are also visible. The present rectory is a more modern house close by.

Fine view of London

Turn left at the junction with Arthur Road and continue along St Mary's Road. From the roundabout junction with Church Road there is a fine view to the north towards central London: if you cross over to the entrance to Burghley Road the British Telecom Tower in the West End stands out prominently. Turn left now into Church Road. Large houses line both sides of the road, those on the left being built on the site of Janssen's house, originally called Wimbledon House to distinguish it from Wimbledon Park and later renamed Belvedere House, not because of its hilltop site but because that was the name of the road in Lambeth where the then owner of the house – a wealthy timber merchant – had his yard.

Beyond Belvedere Avenue you come to Old House Close, a modern development laid out on the site of a late-17th-century merchant's house pulled down in the 1960s. Beyond the close the little houses and shops of the village start. This next section of Church Road, together with the short High Street, was really – apart from the large mansions – all there was to Wimbledon for centuries until the railway brought commuters, particularly from the 1860s onwards. At the junction with the High Street, the nucleus of the village, turn right along the oldest section of the street and cross to the other side at the lights. Continue and then turn left when you get to Southside Common. This soon brings you to the beginning of the Common behind the village.

What you see here is only the southeastern tip of Wimbledon Common, perhaps one-twentieth of it at most. People started building houses here during the late 17th century after all the best plots in the village had been taken. By the end of the 18th century the south, west and east sides of this little section of the Common – more a large village green really – had been almost completely built up. On the west side (opposite you now) most of the mansions remain. Here on the south side, survivors are less frequent. Claremont House on the left is one of the originals; it was built in 1650 by Thomas Hilliard, a retired merchant from the City of London. Beyond it, the crescent at the entrance to Murray Road is the old entrance drive of

Wimbledon Lodge, home of the Murray family from 1812 to 1905 when the house was pulled down. On the corner of Lauriston Road the former coach house of Lauriston House still stands, bearing a plaque to William Wilberforce. He inherited the house from his uncle in 1777 and lived here until he started his anti-slavery campaign nine years later.

King's College School
At the junction with West Side Common you come to King's College School, founded in 1829 under the auspices of King's College, part of London University. The school moved here from central London in 1897 – taking over an existing house and its 8-acre (3-hectare) grounds – and is now a well-known and highly successful boys' public school with associated junior school. On the far side of the school you pass the entrance to Wright's Alley, an ancient right of way between the common and the village fields below the Ridgway. Next is the late 17th-century **Southside House**, one of Wimbledon's finest houses and the ancestral home of the Pennington-Mellor family who still occupy it.

The Crooked Billet
A little further down the hill, turn right by the green-painted Gothic House (1763) and cross over into Crooked Billet, a collection of workmen's houses carved out of the Common when the big houses were being built. A 'billet' is a piece of wood cut to the right length for fuel, but the curious name presumably comes from the eponymous pub. Go past the rebuilt Cinque Cottages (originally built in 1872 for poor men over the age of 55) and turn right, passing in front of the Crooked Billet pub and the Hand in Hand. At the end of Crooked Billet turn left along the west side of the Common.

The first mansion is Chester House, dating from the 1690s and a century later the home for 20 years of the radical John Horne Tooke, one-time rector of Brentford. Next, where the tarmac gives way to the unsurfaced path, is Westside House, built in the time of Queen Anne by London merchant William Bourne. Continuing on, the pink and white house set well back from the road is Cannizaro House, also built by Bourne and in the 19th century the home of an impoverished Sicilian nobleman called the Duke of Cannizaro. Though the house is now a hotel and restaurant, its magnificent grounds – reached by a gate just beyond the hotel entrance – are public property and are well worth a look, both for themselves and for the views to the west across the valley of the Beverley Brook.

Wimbledon Windmill Museum
At the end of West Side, cross straight over into West Place, like Crooked Billet another collection of mainly workmen's cottages built on a patch of common in the 18th century. When you reach the corner, paths lead on into the main part of Wimbledon Common. The one marked as a cycle track and going straight on from the road is the way to the **Wimbledon Windmill Museum** in the centre of the Common. It takes about ten minutes to reach it, and it is well worth visiting as there is a café (and a public toilet) there too.

Caesar's Camp

Meanwhile the walk turns left, following the road round the houses to the junction with Camp Road. The Iron Age hill fort known as Caesar's Camp is about ten minutes' walk down the road to the right, in the middle of a golf course. On the left just here is the old village school, established in 1758 and used as such up until after World War II. It is now a private girls' school, but the original school building with its central octagon is still standing. Turn left past the school and then past the village's modern almshouses, former site of the old parish workhouse. When you get to the Common again, take the path between the roads heading back across the Common towards the village and passing the Rushmere Pond on the way.

Instead of re-entering the village by means of Southside Common, take the unsurfaced road called The Green to the left of it. This brings you back to the High Street opposite the entrance to Marryat Road, the site of Wimbledon House Parkside, one-time home of the novelist Captain Frederick Marryat's parents. Turn right along the High Street, passing first the Rose and Crown pub and then Eagle House, Wimbledon's oldest house apart from the Old Rectory. Built by an East India merchant, it became a school at the end of the 18th century and was extended forward to the High Street at that time in order to create extra space. It was fortunately saved from demolition at the end of the 19th century when the school moved out, and is now the office of the Islamic Heritage Foundation.

Prehistoric track

Keep going along the High Street and carry on when you get to the Church Road junction. This next section of the High Street was only created from the mid-19th century onwards when the village started to expand – the shops on the left where the Belvedere House garden had been were not built until 1924. Just before the road sets off down the hill, turn right into Ridgway, the former prehistoric track running along the southern edge of the plateau to the ford over the Thames at Kingston. On the corner of Lingfield Road is the **Wimbledon Society Museum**, a local history museum housed in the premises of the original village club and hall which were opened in 1859.

Cross over Ridgway here and turn left down Oldfield Road, a row of labourers' cottages built about 1820. Near the bottom go right into the passageway. This brings you out on Sunnyside Place. Here turn left and then, when the road comes to an end, carry on downhill via Sunnyside Passage. Both this and the previous passageway represent former footpaths leading from Wimbledon to the neighbouring village of Merton down in the valley. Sunnyside Passage brings you into Malcolm Road and Malcolm Road brings you to Worple Road. In a field a few hundred yards to the right of this point the original Wimbledon croquet and tennis club was founded in 1868 and the first croquet championship was held at the club two years later. Tennis was added in 1877, when the club was renamed the All England Croquet and Lawn Tennis Club. Cross straight over Worple Road and continue on into the next passage (lampstand at entrance). At the end, turn left, then right into Alt Grove. At the end of Alt Grove turn left along the path by the railway line and carry on until you reach the main road and station opposite, where the walk ends.

147

Further Information

Opening times

Opening times are constantly changing, so telephone before a visit to avoid disappointment. Churches are open at service times as well as at times indicated. Church phone numbers are for the vicarage/rectory unless otherwise indicated. Brief descriptions are given for places that are not otherwise described in the text.

National Gardens Scheme
Various private houses throughout London open their gardens on selected summer days to raise money for this national charity. Those featuring on the walks appear on the maps and in the listings below. For opening times see the Scheme's yellow booklet distributed to public libraries, or call the Hon. County Organizer, Mrs Maurice Snell, on 01932 864532.

BARNES
Barn Elms Nature Reserve Tel: 0181 876 8995 (Wildfowl and Wetlands Trust) for update on progress of nature reserve and details of public access.
Barnes Village Fair Takes place second Sat in July. Tel: 0181 878 2359 (Barnes Community Association) for details.
St Mary's Church Church Road. Tel: 0181 741 5422 (parish office); 0181 878 6982 (rectory). *Open* daily 10.30–12.30.

BEXLEY
Bexley Cricket Club Manor Way. Tel: 01322 524159 for fixture list.
Hall Place and Bexley Local History Museum Bourne Road. Tel: 01322 526574. *Open* Apr–Oct: Mon–Sat 10.00–17.00, Sun 14.00–18.00; Nov–Mar: Mon–Sat 10.00–16.00. *Grounds open* daily through the year. *Admission:* free.
St Mary's Church High Street. Tel: 01322 523457. *Open* by appointment.

BLACKHEATH
All Saints Church All Saints Drive. Tel: 0181 852 4280 (parish office, *open* Mon-Fri 10.00–12.00); 0181 293 0023 (vicarage). *Open* by appointment.

BRENTFORD
Boston Manor House Boston Manor Road. Tel: 0181 570 0622. *Open* last Sun in May to last Sun in Sep 14.30–17.00. *Admission:* free. *What to see:* ground and first-floor rooms with fine fireplaces and notable plaster ceilings.
St Paul's Church St Paul's Road. Tel: 0181 568 7442. *Open* daily. *What to see:* award-winning modern church plus Zoffany's 18th-century painting, *The Last Supper,* which was originally intended for Kew church and supposedly incorporates portraits of local people and the artist (Zoffany was living in Strand on the Green when he painted the picture).

CARSHALTON
All Saints Church High Street. Tel: 0181 647 2366. *Open* May–Sep daily 14.00–16.00.
Carshalton House and Water Tower St Philomena's School, Pound Street. Tel: 0181 773 4555 (Sutton Heritage Centre). *Open* **House:** selected dates from Easter, telephone

for details. **Water Tower:** Easter Mon, Easter–Sep: Sun 14.30–17.00 (**Hermitage** also *open* first Sun every month). *Admission:* charge. *What to see:* Blue Room, Painted Room, other principal rooms in the house; and plunge bath and orangery in the Water Tower.
Little Holland House 40 Beeches Avenue. Tel: 0181 770 4781. *Open* first Sun every month plus Bank Hol Sun and Mon 13.30–17.30 *(closed* Jan). *Admission:* free. *What to see:* Arts and Crafts house and interior, designed and made by craftsman Frank Dickinson, whose home it was until his death in 1961.
Sutton Ecology Centre The Old Rectory, Festival Walk. Tel: 0181 773 4018. *Open* reception and shop: Mon–Fri 10.00–16.00; nature reserve: daily 09.00–dusk; information sessions: Tue and Thu 16.00–18.00. *Admission:* free.
Sutton Heritage Centre Honeywood, Honeywood Walk. Tel: 0181 773 4555. *Open* Wed–Fri 10.00–17.00; Sat, Sun and Bank Hol Mon 10.00–17.30; tearoom: Tue–Sun 10.00–17.00. *Admission:* charge.

CHIPPING BARNET and MONKEN HADLEY
Barnet Museum 31 Wood Street, Chipping Barnet. Tel: 0181 440 8066. *Open* Tue–Thu 14.30–16.30; Sat 10.00–12.00, 14.30–16.30. *Admission:* free.
St John's Church High Street, Chipping Barnet. Tel: 0181 449 3894. *Open* Sat mornings and occasional afternoons.
St Mary's Church Hadley Green Road, Monken Hadley. Tel: 0181 449 2414. *Open* Second Sun every month 14.00–16.00.

CHISWICK
Chiswick House Burlington Lane. Tel: 0181 995 0508. *Open* Apr–Sep: daily 10.00–13.00 and 14.00–18.00; Oct–Mar: Wed–Sun 10.00–13.00, 14.00–16.00. *Admission:* charge.
Hogarth's House Hogarth Lane, Great West Road. Tel: 0181 994 6757. *Open* Apr–Oct: Tue–Fri 13.00–17.00, Sat and Sun 13.00–18.00; Oct–Dec and Feb–Mar: Tue–Fri 13.00–16.00, Sat and Sun 13.00–17.00. *Admission:* free.
St Mary's Convent Burlington Lane. See note on National Gardens Scheme on page 148.
St Nicholas's Church Church Street. Tel: 0181 995 4717. *Open* Sun 14.30–17.00.
Walpole House Chiswick Mall. See note on National Gardens Scheme on page 148.

DULWICH
Dulwich Picture Gallery College Road. Tel: 0181 693 5254. *Open* Tue–Fri 10.00–17.00, Sat 11.00–17.00, Sun 14.00–17.00. *Admission:* charge. *What to see:* works by Claude, Poussin, Rembrandt, Rubens, Van Dyck, Gainsborough, Reynolds, Velázquez, Murillo, Canaletto and Tiepolo, plus collection of 18th-century furniture, and tombs of the Desenfans and Sir Francis Bourgeois in purpose-built mausoleum.

ENFIELD
Forty Hall Forty Hill. Tel: 0181 363 4046. *Open* Thu–Sun 11.00–17.00. *Admission:* free. *What to see:* the mansion and local history collections, plus early packaging and advertising material, and the designs, tools and products of Aesthetic Movement furniture-maker Ada Jacquin. *Access from Enfield on foot:* along Silver Street, continues as Baker Street, right at roundabout into Forty Hill, follow signs – about 1½ miles (2.5 kilometres).
St Andrew's Church Church Street. Tel: 0181 363 8676 (parish office). *Open* Mon–Fri 09.00–15.00, Sat 09.00–13.00.

GREENWICH
Charing Cross Pier Tel: 0171 987 1185 for sailing times.

Cutty Sark and Gypsy Moth IV King William Walk. Tel: 0181 858 3445. *Open Cutty Sark:* Mon–Sat 10.00–18.00 (10.00–17.00 Oct–Mar), Sun and Good Fri 12.00–18.00 (12.00–17.00 Oct–Mar). *Gypsy Moth IV:* Apr–Oct as for Cutty Sark; Nov–Mar closed. *Admission:* charge. *What to see:* built in 1869, the *Cutty Sark* is the only surviving 19th-century tea clipper; lower hold contains large collection of ships' figureheads. The *Gypsy Moth IV* is the yacht in which Sir Francis Chichester made the first single-handed navigation of the world in 1966–7.
Fan Museum 12 Croom's Hill. Tel: 0181 858 7879. *Open* Tue–Fri 11.00–17.00 (16.30 in winter), Sat and Sun 12.00–17.00 (16.30 in winter). *Admission:* charge.
Greenwich Festival Summer arts and cultural festival. Tel: 0181 305 1818 for dates and programme.
National Maritime Museum, Queen's House and Old Royal Observatory Romney Road. Tel: 0181 858 4422. *Open* daily 10.00–17.00. *Admission:* charge. *What to see:* the National Maritime Museum is one of the leading museums of its kind in the world; the Queen's House is a former royal palace with royal apartments furnished in the style of the 17th century – the Great Hall on the ground floor contains the Maritime Museum's collection of marine paintings; the Old Royal Observatory consists of Flamsteed House, containing the Astronomer Royal's 17th-century apartments and observatory, and the Meridian Building housing the historic telescope collection.
Ranger's House Chesterfield Walk. Tel: 0181 853 0035. *Open* Apr–Oct: daily 10.00–13.00, 14.00–18.00 (dusk in Oct); Nov–Mar: Wed–Sun 10.00–13.00, 14.00–16.00. *Admission:* charge. *What to see:* the mansion plus important collections of Jacobean portraits and historical musical instruments.
Royal Naval College King William Walk. Tel: 0181 858 2154. *Open* daily 14.30–16.30. *Admission:* charge. *What to see:* decorated chapel designed by 'Athenian' Stuart and painted hall completely covered in magnificent murals by Sir James Thornhill between 1708 and 1723.
St Alfege's Church Greenwich Church Street. Tel: 0181 853 0687. *Open* by appointment.
Tourist Information Centre 46 Greenwich Church Street. Tel: 0181 858 6376. *Open* daily 10.15–16.45.
Trinity Hospital High Bridge. Tel: 0181 858 1310. *Open* by appointment with the Warden. *Admission:* free. *What to see:* courtyard, chapel and courtroom of the 17th-century almshouse rebuilt in 1812.

HAM and PETERSHAM
Ham House Ham Street, Ham. Tel: 0181 940 1950. *Open* Apr–Oct: Mon–Wed 13.00–17.00, Sat 13.00–17.30, Sun 11.30–17.30; Nov–mid Dec: Sat and Sun 13.00–16.00. Gardens open throughout year daily (except Fri) 10.30–18.00 or dusk if earlier. *Admission:* charge to house. *What to see:* outstanding 17th-century mansion with contemporary interior and furnishings largely intact.
Ham Polo Club Between Petersham and Ham, near the River Thames. Tel: 0181 334 0000. Afternoon matches every Sun May–Sep, spectators welcome.
Ormeley Lodge Ham Gate Avenue, Ham. See note on National Gardens Scheme page 148.
St Michael's Convent 56 Ham Common. See note on National Gardens Scheme page 148.
St Peter's Church Church Lane, Petersham. Tel: 0181 549 8296. *Open* by appointment.

HAMPSTEAD
Burgh House and Hampstead Museum New End Square. Tel: 0171 431 0144. *Open* Wed–Sun 12.00–17.00, Bank Hols 14.00–17.00. *Admission:* free.
Fenton House Windmill Hill. Tel: 0171 435 3471. *Open* Mar: Sat and Sun 14.00–17.00; Apr–Oct: Sat, Sun and Bank Hol Mon 11.00–17.30, Wed, Thu and Fri 14.00–17.30. *Admission:* charge (free to National Trust members). *What to see:* the mansion, plus

outstanding collections of porcelain and early keyboard instruments, and large walled garden.
Antiques and Crafts Market Entrances in Perrin's Court and Heath Street. *Open* Tue–Fri 10.30–17.00, Sat 10.00–18.00, Sun 11.30–16.30.
Hampstead Scientific Society Lower Terrace. Tel: 0181 346 1056 (roster secretary). *Open* mid-Sep–mid-Apr if sky is clear: Fri and Sat 20.00–22.00, Sun (for sun spots) 11.00–13.00. *Admission:* free, but donations welcome.
Keats House Keats Grove. Tel: 0171 435 2062. *Open* Mon–Fri 14.00–18.00 (13.00–17.00 Nov–Mar), Sat 10.00–13.00 and 14.00–17.00, Sun 14.00–17.00. *Admission:* free.
St John's Church Church Row. Tel: 0171 794 5808 (parish office); 0171 435 0553 (rectory). *Open* all day Mon–Fri, Sun and most Sats.

HARROW–ON–THE–HILL
Cat Museum The Other Shop, 49 High Street. No phone. *Open* Thu–Sat 10.30–17.00. *Admission:* free.
Harrow Old Speech Room Gallery Old Schools, Church Hill. Tel: 0181 869 1205 or 0181 422 2196. *Open* daily except Wed 14.30–17.00 (other closures during school exeats and at half term – call before visiting). *Admission:* free. *What to see:* school treasures (mostly donated by Old Harrovians) include collections of watercolours (with works by Cotman and Turner), butterflies and Greek, Roman and Etruscan pottery.
Harrow School Guided Tours One 'turn up-and-go' tour a term; others are prearranged, any time in term or holidays. Details from Mrs. Jean Leaf, Harrow School, 15 London Road, Harrow-on-the-Hill, Middlesex HA1 3JJ. Tel: 0181 422 2303. *Admission:* charge. *What to see:* a selection or all of the following – Fourth Form Room (the original school room with carved names), Old Speech Room Art Gallery, Speech Room, Chapel, Shepherd Churchill Dining Room, Fitch Room and, by special arrangement, the Vaughan Library.
Harrow Museum and Heritage Centre See page 153 under Pinner.
St Mary's Church Church Hill. Tel: 0181 422 2652. *Open* daily except Fri.

HIGHGATE
The Grove Several houses in this road participate in the National Gardens Scheme. See note on page 148.
Highgate Cemetery Swains Lane. Tel: 0181 340 1834. *Open* **Eastern Cemetery:** Apr–Oct: Mon–Fri 10.00–17.00, Sat and Sun 11.00–17.00; Nov–Mar: Mon–Fri 10.00–16.00, Sat and Sun 11.00–16.00. **Western Cemetery:** guided tours only, Apr–Oct: Mon–Fri 12.00, 14.00 and 16.00, Sat and Sun on the hour every hour 11.00–16.00; Nov and Mar: same as for Apr–Oct except last tour is at 15.00; Dec–Feb: Sat and Sun on the hour every hour 11.00–15.00. Both cemeteries closed during funerals. *Admission:* charge.
Kenwood Hampstead Lane. Tel: 0181 348 1286. *Open* Good Fri/1 Apr (whichever is earlier)–Sep: Mon–Sun 10.00–18.00; Oct–Maundy Thursday/31 Mar (whichever is earlier) Mon–Sun 10.00–16.00. *Admission:* free. *What to see:* 18th-century mansion with superb Adam interiors and major collection of paintings, including works by Reynolds, Gainsborough, Romney, Snyders, Van Dyck, Vermeer, Rembrandt and Boucher.
Southwood Lodge 33 Kingsley Place, off Southwood Lane. See note on National Gardens Scheme page 148.
St Michael's Church South Grove. Tel: 0181 340 7279. *Open* Sat 10.00–12.00.

ISLEWORTH
All Saints Church Church Street. Tel: 0181 568 4645. *Open* ruins of old church visible through door.
Syon House Syon Park. Tel: 0181 560 0881. *Open* Apr–Sep: Wed–Sun 11.00–17.00; Oct–mid-Dec: Sun 11.00–17.00 or dusk if earlier. *Admission:* charge. *What to see:* Tudor

house remodelled and, inside, completely redesigned with magnificent neoclassical interiors by Robert Adam in the 18th century; grounds landscaped by Capability Brown.

KENSINGTON

Commonwealth Institute Kensington High Street. Tel: 0171 603 4535. *Open* Mon–Sat 10.00–17.00, Sun 14.00–17.00. *Admission:* free (but sometimes charge for special exhibitions). *What to see:* three levels of galleries illustrating the art, history and culture of the 50 nations that make up the British Commonwealth.

Kensington Palace Kensington Palace. Tel: 0171 937 9561. *Open* Mon–Sat 09.00–17.00, Sun 11.00–17.00. *Admission:* charge. *What to see:* King William's and Queen Mary's private apartments, the magnificently decorated early Georgian state rooms, the suite of rooms where Queen Victoria lived until she was 18, and the court dress collection with men's and women's costumes dating from 1750.

Kensington Roof Gardens 99 Kensington High Street (entrance in Derry Street). Tel: 0171 937 7994. *Open* daily 09.00–17.00 (unless booked for a function – telephone before visiting). *Admission:* free. *What to see:* Europe's largest roof garden, built in the 1930s as an attraction for the Derry and Toms department store (closed 1973) and divided into three different areas: English Woodland, Tudor and Spanish.

Leighton House Museum and Art Gallery 12 Holland Park Road. Tel: 0171 602 3316. *Open* Mon–Sat 11.00–17.30. *Admission:* free. *What to see:* former home and studio of the painter Lord Leighton (1830–96); interior is one of the finest examples of aesthetic styling in the country; good collection of High Victorian aesthetic art, plus changing exhibitions.

Linley Sambourne House 18 Stafford Terrace. Tel: 0181 742 3438. *Open* Mar 1–Oct 31: Wed 10.00–16.00, Sun 14.00–17.00. *Admission:* charge. *What to see:* former home of *Punch* cartoonist Edward Linley Sambourne (1844–1910); decorated and furnished by him in classic Victorian 'artistic' style and perfectly preserved by his descendants.

St Mary Abbots Church Kensington High Street. Tel: 0171 937 5136. *Open* daily.

KEW

Kew Cricket Club Kew Green. Matches most Sat and Sun afternoons May–Sept.

Royal Botanic Gardens and Kew Palace Kew Green. Tel: 0181 332 5000. *Open* **Gardens:** daily Apr–Sept 09.30–18.00 (approx); Oct–Mar: 09.30–16.00 (approx). **Palace:** daily Apr–Sep 11.00–17.30. *Admission:* charge. *What to see:* world-famous botanical gardens covering some 300 acres (120 hectares) with huge glass houses, picture gallery and various garden buildings such as pagoda, orangery and thatched cottage; Kew Palace was last used by King George III (reigned 1760–1820) and Queen Charlotte, and contains much of their furniture and personal possessions.

St Anne's Church Kew Green. Tel: 0181 940 4616. *Open* Easter–Sep: Sat 10.00–12.00 and most Sat afternoons, Sun afternoons (with afternoon tea); Oct–Easter: Sat 10.00–12.00.

Westminster Pier Tel: 0171 930 2062 for sailing times.

MITCHAM

Merton Heritage Centre The Canons, Madeira Road. Tel: 0181 640 9387. *Open* Fri and Sat 10.00–17.00. *Admission:* free.

Mitcham Cricket Club Cricket Green. Matches take place virtually every Sat and Sun afternoon late Apr–Sept.

Mitcham Fair Funfair on Three Kings Piece. Takes place 12–14 August (if one of these days is a Sun, fair is closed and held over till following day).

Wandle Industrial Museum Vestry Hall Annexe, London Road. Tel: 0181 648 0127. *Open* Wed 13.00–16.00, first Sun every month 14.00–17.00. *Admission:* charge. *What to see:* exhibitions on the snuff, tobacco and textile industries and special features on William

Morris and Arthur Liberty (of Liberty's in Regent Street).
St Peter and St Paul's Church Church Road. Tel: 0181 648 1566. *Open* by appointment.

PINNER
Harrow Museum and Heritage Centre Headstone Manor, Pinner View, Harrow. Tel:
0181 861 2626. *Open* Wed–Fri 12.30–17.00 (dusk in winter); Sat, Sun and Bank Hols
10.30–17.00 (dusk in winter). *Admission:* free. *Access on foot from Pinner:* from Nower Hill or
Marsh Road, straight on into Pinner Road, cross George V Avenue into Headstone Lane –
about 1¾ miles (2.8 kilometres). *Access on foot from Harrow-on-the-Hill Station:* take north exit
from station, left on College Road, right into Headstone Road, straight on into Harrow View,
left into Headstone Gardens, right into Pinner View – about 1½ miles (2.8 kilometres).
Pinner Fair Takes place Wed after the Spring Bank Hol.
St John's Church High Street. Tel: 0181 886 3869. *Open* daily.

ROTHERHITHE and BERMONDSEY
New Caledonian Antiques Market Bermondsey Square. *Open* Fri mornings (early).
Brunel's Engine House Railway Avenue. Tel: 0181 318 2489 or 0181 748 3545. *Open*
first Sun every month 12.00–16.00. *Admission:* charge.
St Mary's Church, Rotherhithe St Marychurch Street. Tel: 0171 231 2465. *Open*
vestibule daily; nave visible through locked glass doors.
St Mary Magdalen Church, Bermondsey Bermondsey Street. Tel: 0171 407 5273.
Open by appointment.

WALTHAMSTOW
St Mary's Church Church End. Tel: 0181 521 0290 (church administrator); 0181 520
4281 (rectory). *Open* by appointment.
Vestry House Museum Vestry Road. Tel: 0181 509 1917. *Open* Mon–Fri 10.00–13.00,
14.00–17.30; Sat 10.00–13.00, 14.00–17.00. *Admission:* free. *What to see:* star exhibit is the
Bremer car, built in Walthamstow and a candidate for the title of first car built in Britain.
Walthamstow Village Festival Takes place in July. Tel: 0181 521 3864 or 0181 521
7111 for exact date and other details.
William Morris Gallery Lloyd Park, Forest Road. Tel: 0181 527 3782. *Open* Tue–Sat
10.00–13.00, 14.00–17.00; first Sun every month 10.00–13.00, 14.00–17.00. *Admission:* free.

WIMBLEDON
Southside House 3 Woodhayes Road. Tel: 0181 946 7643 or 0181 947 2491. *Open*
guided tours, 1 Oct–31 May: Tue, Thu, Sat and Bank Hol Mon 14.00, 15.00, 16.00 and
17.00. *Admission:* charge. *What to see:* house is mainly noted for its eclectic collection of historical memorabilia, including Anne Boleyn's vanity case and Marie Antoinette's necklace.
St Mary's Church St Mary's Road. Tel: 0181 946 2605. *Open* church is usually open; if
closed, enquire at adjacent Fellowship Office Tue, Wed and Fri mornings, and Thu all day
(closed Mon, Wed and weekends).
Wimbledon Lawn Tennis Museum All England Club, Church Road. Tel: 0181 946
6131. *Open* Tue–Sat 10.30–17.00, Sun 14.00–17.00 (times change during championships).
Admission: charge.
Wimbledon Society Museum Ridgway SW19. No phone. *Open* Sat 14.30–17.00.
Admission: free.
Wimbledon Windmill Museum Windmill Road, Wimbledon Common. Tel: 0181 947
2825. *Open* Apr–Oct: Sat, Sun and Bank Hols 14.00–17.00. *Admission:* charge. *What to see:*
early 19th-century hollow-post windmill plus pictures, models, machinery and tools, and
the story of windmills and windmilling.

Libraries

For readers who wish to delve deeper into the history of the 25 London villages described in this book, I have compiled a list of relevant libraries, both general community libraries and libraries specializing in local history. The community libraries are usually in the villages themselves and are a good place to start because they often have a handful of local history books. For more comprehensive local history coverage – and to be sure of seeing the books cited in the Bibliography on page 156 – a visit to the local history library covering the village in question will probably be necessary. (These generally cover whole boroughs rather than just one district.) Sometimes this will be in the same building as the community library. Sometimes, however, it may be in a completely different part of London. If the latter, I recommend making an appointment before your visit. Where all available local history information on a village is to be found in the community library, one address only is given below.

BARNES
Castelnau Library, 75 Castelnau. Tel: 0181 748 3837.
Local History See below under **Ham and Petersham.**

BEXLEY
Bexley Village Library, Bourne Road. Tel: 01322 522168.
Local History Hall Place, Bourne Road, Bexley. Tel: 01311 526574.

BLACKHEATH
Blackheath Village Library, 3–4 Blackheath Grove. Tel: 0181 852 5309.
Local History See below under **Greenwich.**

BRENTFORD
Brentford Library, Boston Manor Road. Tel: 0181 560 8801.
Local History See below under **Chiswick.**

CARSHALTON
Carshalton Library, The Square. Tel: 0181 647 1151.
Local History Central Library, St Nicholas Way, Sutton. Tel: 0181 770 4700.

CHIPPING BARNET and MONKEN HADLEY
Chipping Barnet Library, 3 Stapylton Road, Barnet. Tel: 0181 449 0321.
Local History Hendon Library, The Burroughs, Hendon. Tel: 0181 202 5625.

CHISWICK
Chiswick Library, Duke's Avenue. Tel: 0181 994 1008.

DULWICH
Dulwich Library, 368 Lordship Lane. Tel: 0181 693 5171.
Local History Southwark Local Studies Library, 211 Borough High Street, Southwark. Tel: 0171 403 3507.

ENFIELD
Central Library, Cecil Road. Tel: 0181 366 2244.
Local History Local History Unit, Southgate Town Hall, Green Lanes, Palmers Green. Tel: 0181 982 7453.

GREENWICH
West Greenwich Library, Greenwich High Road. Tel: 0181 858 4289.
Local History Woodlands, 90 Mycenae Road, Blackheath. Tel: 0181 858 4631.

HAM and PETERSHAM.
Ham Library, Ham Street, Ham. Tel: 0181 940 8703.
Local History Central Reference Library, Old Town Hall, Whittaker Avenue, Richmond. Tel: 0181 940 5529.

HAMPSTEAD
Heath Library, Keats Grove. Tel: 0171 435 8002.
Local History Holborn Library, 32–38 Theobalds Road, Holborn. Tel: 0171 413 6342.

HARROW-ON-THE-HILL
Gayton Library, Gayton Road. Tel: 0181 427 8986.
Local History Civic Centre Library, Civic Centre, Station Road, Harrow. Tel: 0181 424 1055.

HIGHGATE
Highgate Library, Chester Road. Tel: 0171 272 3112.
Local History See above under **Hampstead.**

ISLEWORTH
Isleworth Library, Twickenham Road. Tel: 0181 560 2934.
Local History Hounslow Library, Treaty Centre, High Street, Hounslow. Tel: 0181 570 0622.

KENSINGTON
Central Library, Hornton Street. Tel: 0171 937 2542.

KEW
Kew Library, 106 North Road. Tel: 0181 876 8654.
Local History See above under **Ham and Petersham.**

MITCHAM
Mitcham Library, London Road. Tel: 0181 648 4070.

PINNER
Pinner Library, Marsh Road. Tel: 0181 866 7827.
Local History See above under **Harrow-on-the-Hill.**

ROTHERHITHE and BERMONDSEY
Rotherhithe Library, Albion Street, Rotherhithe. Tel: 0171 237 2010.
Local History See above under **Dulwich.**

WALTHAMSTOW
Central Library, High Street. Tel: 0181 520 3031.
Local History Vestry House Museum, Vestry Road. Tel: 0181 509 1917.

WIMBLEDON
Central Reference Library, Wimbledon Hill Road. Tel: 0181 946 1136.

Bibliography

Place of publication is London unless otherwise stated.

Arthure, Humphrey, *Life and Work in Old Chiswick* (Old Chiswick Protection Society, 1982)
Barker, Felix, *Greenwich and Blackheath Past* (Historical Publications, 1993)
Bate, G E, *And So Make a City Here* (Hounslow, Thomasons, 1948)
Batey, Mavis, et al, *Arcadian Thames* (Barn Elms, 1994)
Blomfield, David, *The Story of Kew* (Richmond, Leyborne, 1992)
Blomfield, David, *Kew Past* (Historical Publications, 1994)
Boast, Mary, *The Story of Dulwich* (London Borough of Southwark Neighbourhood Histories 2, 1990)
Boast, Mary, *The Story of Rotherhithe* (London Borough of Southwark Neighbourhood Histories 6, 1980)
Boast, Mary, *A Trail Walk Around Old Rotherhithe* (Time & Talents Association, 1994)
Cameron, A, *Hounslow, Isleworth, Heston and Cranford. A Pictorial History* (Chichester, Phillimore, 1995)
Canham, Roy, *2000 Years of Brentford* (HMSO, 1978)
Clegg, Gillian, *Chiswick Past* (Historical Publications, 1995)
Cloake, John, *Richmond Past* (Historical Publications, 1991)
Cluett, Douglas, *Discovering Sutton's Heritage: the Story of Five Parishes* (Sutton Heritage Service, 1995)
Courlander, Kathleen, *Richmond* (Batsford, 1953)
Druett, Walter, *Pinner through the Ages* (Uxbridge, King and Hutchings, 1965)
Druett, Walter, *Harrow through the Ages* (Wakefield, S. R. Publishers, 1971)
Faulkner, T, *The History and Antiquities of Brentford, Ealing and Chiswick* (Simpkin, Marshall & Co, 1845)
Gelder, W H, *Monken Hadley Church and Village* (The Author, 1986)
Green, Brian, *Dulwich Village* (Dulwich, Village Books, 1983)
Green Brian, *Around Dulwich* (Dulwich, Village Books, 1982)
Grimwade, Mary, & Hailstone, Charles, *Highways and Byways of Barnes* (Barnes, Barnes and Mortlake History Society, 1992)
Higgs, Tom, *300 Years of Mitcham Cricket* (The Author, 1985)
Hounslow, London Borough of, Department of Arts and Recreation, Libraries Division, *Isleworth As It Was* (Hendon, Nelson, 1982)
Jones, A E, *An Illustrated Directory of Old Carshalton* (Carshalton, The Author, 1973)
Law, A, *Walthamstow Village* (Walthamstow Antiquarian Society, 1984)
McEwan, Kate, *Ealing Walkabout* (Warrington, Pulse Publications, 1983)
Mercer, John, *Bexley, Bexleyheath and Welling. A Pictorial History* (Chichester, Phillimore, 1995)
Milward, Richard, *Historic Wimbledon* (Wimbledon, Windrush and Fielders, 1989)
Milward, Richard, *Wimbledon. A Pictorial History* (Chichester, Phillimore, 1994)
Montague, Eric, *Mitcham. A Pictorial History* (Chichester, Phillimore, 1991)
Norrie, Ian, *Hampstead, Highgate Village and Kenwood* (High Hill Press, 1983)
Pevsner, N, & Cherry, B, *The Buildings of England. London: South* (Harmondsworth, Penguin, 1983)
Rhind, Neil, *Blackheath Village and Environs* (Bookshop Blackheath, 2 vols, 1976 and 1983)
Rhind, Neil, *The Heath* (Bookshop Blackheath, 1987)
Richardson, John, *Highgate Past* (Historical Publications, 1989)
Spurgeon, Darrell, *Discover Bexley and Sidcup* (Greenwich Guidebooks, 1993)
Spurgeon, Darrell, *Discover Greenwich and Charlton* (Greenwich Guidebooks, 1991)
Taylor, Pamela, & Corden, Joanna, *Barnet, Edgware, Hadley and Totteridge. A Pictorial History* (Chichester, Phillimore, 1994)
Tester, P, *Bexley Village* (Bexley Libraries and Museums Department, 1987)
Verden, Joanne, *Ten Walks Around Pinner* (Pinner Association, 1991)
Victoria County History: volumes for *Essex, Hertfordshire, Middlesex* and *Surrey* (Oxford University Press, various dates)
Wade, Christopher, *Hampstead Past* (Historical Publications, 1989)
Wade, Christopher, *The Streets of Hampstead* (High Hill Press, 1984)
Weinreb, Ben & Hibbert, Christopher, eds, *The London Encyclopaedia* (Papermac, 1993)

Index

Numbers in **bold type** refer to plates.

Aberdeen Terrace, Blackheath 95
Abernethy House 42
Adam and Eve Mews, Kensington 62
All England Croquet and Lawn Tennis Club 149
All England Lawn Tennis Club 143
All Saints Church, Blackheath 94, 148; **23**
All Saints Church, Carshalton 102, 148
All Saints Church, Isleworth 59, 151
All Saints Church, Petersham 121
Alleyn, Edward 104
Almshouses: Eleanor Palmer's, Chipping Barnet 25; Garret, Barnet 25; Highgate 51–2; Ingram's, Isleworth 60; Jesus Hospital, Chipping Barnet, 26 Leathersellers' Company, Chipping Barnet 25; Mary Tate's, Mitcham 131; Monoux, Walthamstow 75–7; Squires, Walthamstow 75; Styleman's, Bexley 89; Tollemache's, Ham 122; Trinity Hospital, Greenwich 114, 150; **28**; Wilbraham's, Monken Hadley 23; **3**
Ancient House, Walthamstow 75–6
Anne Boleyn's Well 101
Antiques and Crafts Market, Hampstead 40, 151
Archway Road 52–3
Archway, Enfield 37
Arkley 20
Arthur Road, Wimbledon 144–5
Arundel House 54

Bank, The 53
Barker's of Kensington 66
Barn Elms Estate 81
Barn Elms Nature Reserve 83, 148
Barn Elms Playing Fields 83
Barnes 80–5
Barnes Bridge 81
Barnes Common 84
Barnes High Street 81
Barnes walk 81–5
Barnet Common 20
Barnet Grammar School 26

Barnet horse fair 20
Barnet Museum 26, 149
Baron House, Mitcham 133
Battle of Barnet 21–3
Bay House 71
Beaufort House 122
Bedford House 31
Bedford Lodge 65
Bella Court, Greenwich 111
Bermondsey 135–41
Bermondsey Abbey 136, 138
Bermondsey Square 138
Bermondsey Street 137
Bermondsey Wall 139
Beverley Brook 84
Bexley 86–91
Bexley Cricket Club 87, 148
Bexley Local History Museum 87
Bexley Manor 86
Bexley walk 87–91
Bexleyheath 87
Blackheath 92–7
Blackheath Park 96
Blackheath Rugby Club 97
Blackheath Vale 95
Blackheath village 92
Blackheath walk 93–7
Blenheim Road, Chipping Barnet 25
Blount's Hole 93
Blue School 60
Boston House 29, 32
Boston Manor 16; **1**
Boston Manor House 15–17, 148
Brent, River 40
Brentford 15–19
Brentford Ferry Gate 125
Brentford Lock 17–18
Brentford walk 16–19
Bridge Street, Pinner 68–9
Brookscroft, Walthamstow 75, 78
Brunel's Engine House 140, 153
Burgh House 43, 150
Burleigh House 35
Bush Hill Park 38
Bute House 121
Butter Hill 103
Butts, The 19

Cabal 117–18
Caesar's Camp 142, 147
Cambridge Cottage, Kew 127
Campden House 62, 65
Canary Wharf Tower 139
Cannizaro House 146
Cannon Hall 44
Canons, Mitcham 129–31

Capel House, Kew 127
Carshalton 98–103
Carshalton High Street 98
Carshalton House 99–100, 148–9
Carshalton Park 99, 102
Carshalton Place 99
Carshalton Ponds 101; **24**
Carshalton walk 99–103
Castelnau 83
Cat Museum 48, 151
Cator Estate 93, 96
Channing School 53
Chase Green, Enfield 36
Cherry Garden Pier 139
Chester House 146
Chestnuts, Walthamstow 76
Ching Valley 78
Chipping Barnet 20–6
Chipping Barnet and Monken Hadley walk 21–6
Chiswick 27–32
Chiswick House 27, 30–1, 149; **4**
Chiswick Mall 28
Chiswick Press 32
Chiswick Soap Company 28
Chiswick Square 29
Chiswick walk 28–32
Chiswick Wharf 30
Cholmeley's School 50, 52
Church Farm, Pinner 69
Church Road, Wimbledon 145
Church Row, Hampstead 40
Church Street, Chiswick 28, 30
Churchfields, Greenwich 112
Claremont House 145
Clarendon House, Mitcham 133
Cleveland Gardens, Barnes 81
College Estate, Dulwich 105
College of God's Gift, Dulwich 107–8
Commerce Row, Dulwich 105
Commonside, Mitcham 133
Commonwealth Institute 64, 152
Constable, John 40, 42, 44
Coppin's House 62
Corney House 27
Crane, River 56–7
Cray House 89
Cray, River 90
Cricket clubs: Bexley 87, 148; Kew 127, 152; Marlborough 108; Mitcham 131, 152
Cricket Green, Mitcham 130–1; **33**
Cromwell House 53
Crooked Billet 146
Croom's Hill, Greenwich 112, 116

Crystal Palace 108–9
Cutty Sark 114, 150

Dartmouth Row, Blackheath 92
de Toni Manor House 74
Derry and Toms 66
Diamond Terrace, Greenwich
 115; **29**
Distances from Central London 9
Dollis Brook 26
Donne, John 130
Douglas House 121
Dr Johnson's Lock 19
Duke of Northumberland's River
 57
Dulwich 104–10
Dulwich College 107–8; **25**
Dulwich Common 105, 108
Dulwich Court 108
Dulwich Hamlet School 106
Dulwich Park 108
Dulwich Picture Gallery 110, 149;
 26
Dulwich School 110
Dulwich Society 106
Dulwich tollgate 109; **27**
Dulwich village 107
Dulwich walk 105–10
Dulwich Wells 108
Dulwich Wood 109
Dutch House 125

Eagle House, Mitcham 130
Eagle House, Wimbledon 143
Earls Terrace, Kensington 63
East Barnet Gas and Water
 Company 25
East End Farm, Pinner 71; **17**
East End Farm Cottage 71–2
Edwardes Square 63
Eleanor Palmer's almshouses 25
Eliot Place, Blackheath 95
Eliot Vale, Blackheath 95
Elm Lodge 121
Elm Row, Hampstead 44
Elmdene 71
Enfield 33–8
Enfield Chase 33
Enfield market 35
Enfield Town 33
Enfield walk 34–8
Essex House 84

Fairholt 23
Fan Museum 116, 150
Fenton House 39, 43, 150
Festival Walk, Carshalton 101
Fisherman's Place 30
Fitzroy Farm 55
Fitzroy Park 54
Fives Court, The 71
Flambards 48
Flask pub, Highgate 55; **11**

Flask Walk, Hampstead 43
Fleet, River 40
Forty Hall 34, 149
Frognal Lane 41
Frognal Way 41
Fuller, Smith and Turner's Griffin
 Brewery 28, 30

Gallery Road, Dulwich 107
Garret Almshouse 25
Gentlemans Row, Enfield 34,
 36–7; **6**
Glebe, Barnes 83
Gloucester Circus, Greenwich 115
Golden Square, Hampstead 1
Gordon House 57
Gordon House 122
Grand Union Canal 16
Grandon 23
Grange Walk, Bermondsey 138
Grange, Greenwich 116
Grange, The 71
Great North Road 50, 53
Great West Road 16, 28
Greenland Dock 135–6
Greenwich 111–16
Greenwich Church Street 112
Greenwich Foot Tunnel 114
Greenwich Hospital 114
Greenwich meridian line 112, 114
Greenwich Palace 111–12
Greenwich Park 112
Greenwich University 112–13
Greenwich village 111
Greenwich walk 112–16
Grey Court 122
Grote's Buildings and Place,
 Blackheath 94
Grove, Carshalton 99, 103
Grove, Highgate 54, 151
Gumley House 57–8
Gumley House Convent School
 58
Gunnersbury House 17
Gypsy Moth IV 114, 150

Hadley Brewery 25
Hadley Green 20
Hadley Highstone 25
Hadley House 23
Hadley Hurst 24
Hadley Wood 24
Hall Place, Bexley 87, 90, 148; **20**
Hall Place, Dulwich 104
Hall Place, Mitcham 133
Hall's Farm 71
Ham 117–23
Ham and Petersham walk 118–23
Ham Common 122
Ham House 117–18, 122, 150; **31**
Ham House lodge 121
Ham Polo Club 121, 150
Ham Street 118, 122

Hammersmith Bridge Company 81
Hammerton ferry 123
Hampstead 39–44
Hampstead Heath 39, 51
Hampstead reservoir 42
Hampstead walk 40–4
Hampstead Waterworks Company
 54
Hanwell 15, 17
Harrow High Street 48; **9**
Harrow Museum and Heritage
 Centre 45, 69, 151, 153
Harrow School 46–9, 151; tuck
 shop 48; **10**
Harrow walk 46–9
Harrow workhouse 48
Harrow-on-the-Hill 45–9
Haverfield House 128
Headstone Manor Farm 69
Headstone Manor Recreation
 Ground 69
Heathfield House 95
Heaths and commons 10
High Street, Kensington 62
Highgate 39, 50–5
Highgate almshouses 51–2
Highgate Cemetery 53, 151
Highgate Literary and Scientific
 Institution 53
Highgate Ponds 54; **12**
Highgate School 52
Highgate walk 51–5
Highgate West Hill 55
Highgate Wood 55
Highstreet House 89
Hogarth's House 28, 149
Hogarth, William 28, 30
Holland House 64
Holland Park 64
Holland Street 65
Holly Bush Hill 42
Holly Terrace, Highgate 55
Holly Walk, Hampstead 42
Homestead House 83
Honeywood, Carshalton 101
Hope Sufferance Wharf 141
Hurst Road, Walthamstow 78

Ilchester Place, Kensington 64
Ingram's Almshouses 60
Island Gardens, Greenwich 114
Isleworth 56–61
Isleworth Ait and boatyard 59; **13**
Isleworth Brewery 61
Isleworth House 57
Isleworth walk 57–61

Jackson House, Bexley 89
Jackson's Lane 51
Jacob Street 139
Jamaica Road 139
James Allen Girls School 106
Jesus Hospital almshouse 26

John Lyon School 48
Keats House 43, 151; **8**
Keats, John 40, 43
Kensington 62–7; **15**
Kensington Chapel 62
Kensington Church Walk 65; **14**
Kensington High Street 66
Kensington Palace 64, 66, 152
Kensington Roof Gardens 66, 152
Kensington Square 66
Kensington walk 63–7
Kenwood 51, 54, 151
Kew 124–8
Kew Bridge Steam Museum 18, 127
Kew Cricket Club 127, 152
Kew dock 128
Kew Farm 125
Kew Gardens 125–6, 152
Kew Green 126; **32**
Kew House 125
Kew Palace 17, 125
Kew Priory 128
Kew walk 125–8
Kid Brook 92–3
Kidd's Mill 59
King Charles's Well 46
King's College School, Wimbledon 146
King's Stairs Garden 140
Kitson Road, Barnes 83

Lamb Brewery 30
Lauderdale House 53
Leadenhall Market 136
Leathersellers' Company almshouses 25
Lee 95
Lee, River 33
Leighton House Museum and Art Gallery 64, 152
Libraries 154–5
Limes, The 60
Lion Wharf 59
Little Holland House 101, 149
Little Park 35
Little Sutton 28
Livingstone Cottage 23
Livingstone, Dr David 23
Lloyd's Place, Blackheath 94
Local history collections 154–5
Loftie Street 139
Lordship Lane 108
Lower Green, Mitcham 129, 131
Lower Square, Isleworth 60

Macartney House, Greenwich 116
Maids of Honour tearooms 126
Manor House, Bexley 89
Manor House, Greenwich 114
Manor House, Ham 122
Manor House, Isleworth 59
Manor of Dulwich 104

Manor of Harrow 46
Maps 11–13
Marble Hill 123
Markets: Antiques and Crafts, Hampstead 40, 151; Barnet 20–1; Enfield 35; Leadenhall 136; New Caledonian Antiques 137, 153; Walthamstow 78
Marlborough Cricket Club 108
Mary Evans Picture Gallery 94
Mary Tate's Almshouses 131
Mascalls, Carshalton 99, 102–3
Meadway, Chipping Barnet 21
Melbury Road, Kensington 64
Merton Heritage Centre 129, 132, 152
Milbourne House 84
Millennium Exhibition 112
Millfield Lane, Highgate 54
Mitcham 129–34
Mitcham Canons 129
Mitcham Cricket Club 131, 152
Mitcham Fair 132, 152
Mitcham Grove 134
Mitcham walk 131–4
Monken Cottage 23
Monken Hadley 20–6
Monken Hadley Common 24; **2**
Monkenholt 23
Monoux Almshouses 75–7
Montagu House 95
Montpelier Row, Blackheath 97
Montpelier Vale 93
Montrose House 120–1
Morden College 93, 96
Morris, William 75, 78
Mortlake, Manor of 142
Moss Lane, Pinner 68, 71
Mount Vernon 42
Museums: Barnet 26, 149; Bexley Local History 87; Cat 48, 151; Fan 116, 150; Harrow Museum and Heritage Centre 45, 69, 151, 153; Kew Bridge Steam 18, 127; Leighton House Museum and Art Gallery 64, 152; National Maritime 112–13, 115, 150; Vestry House 77, 153; Wandle Industrial 133, 152; Wimbledon Society 147, 153; Wimbledon Windmill 146, 153

National Gardens Scheme 148
National Maritime Museum 112–13, 115, 150
National Schools, Bexley 91
New Caledonian Antiques Market 137, 153
New Grove House 43
New Park 118, 120
New River 33, 37
Northern Heights 39

Nower Hill Green 71
Old Ford Manor House 25
Old Grammar School, Dulwich 107
Old Hall, The 54
Old House Close, Wimbledon 145
Old Rectory, Carshalton 101
Old Royal Observatory 112, 114, 150
Old Speech Room Gallery, Harrow 48, 151
Orford House 75, 77
Orleans House Gallery 123
Ormeley Lodge 122, 150
Osterley Park 17
Oxhey Lane Farm 71

Pagoda House Blackheath 95; **22**
Paines Lane, Pinner 68
Palmer, Mrs Eleanor 25
Paragon, Blackheath 96; **21**
Park House, Mitcham 132
Park Vista, Greenwich 112
Parkhill Road, Bexley 88
Perrin's Court, Hampstead 40; **7**
Petersham 21
Petersham 117–23
Petersham Common 120
Petersham Gate 120
Petersham House 120
Petersham Lodge 117, 120–1, 123
Petersham Lodge Wood 123
Petersham Meadows 118; **30**
Petersham Park 120
Petersham Road 118, 10
Phillimore Gardens 65
Pinn, River 72
Pinner 68–73
Pinner Common 72–3
Pinner Green 73
Pinner High Street 68–9
Pinner Hill 70
Pinner House 70–1
Pinner Park 69, 71
Pinner Village Gardens 68
Pinner walk 69–73
Pinnerwood Farm 71
Placentia 111
Pond Cottages, Dulwich 110
Pond Road, Blackheath 97
Pond Square, Highgate 53
Pope, Sir Thomas 137
Port Greenwich 114
Putney Bridge 84
Pymmes Brook 20

Quaggy Valley 96
Quaggy, River 95
Queen Elizabeth's College, Greenwich 112
Queen's House, Greenwich 111–12, 115, 150

Railshead 56
Ranelagh Club 84
Ranger's House, Blackheath 95
Ranger's House, Greenwich 115–16, 150
Ravensbury Manor 130, 134
Ravensbury Park 133–4; **34**
Rayners Lane 68
Red Post Hill 105
Refell's Brewery 91
Reston Lodge 120
Richard Reynolds House 59
Richmond Bridge 118
Richmond Golf Club 121
Richmond Palace 117
Richmond Park 120
Rocks Lane 83
Rose House, Barnes 81
Rotherhithe 135–41
Rotherhithe and Bermondsey walk 137–41
Rotherhithe Street 135, 140
Royal Blackheath Golf Club 97
Royal Hill, Greenwich 115
Royal Hospital School 112
Royal Naval College, Greenwich 112, 150
Rutland Lodge 120

Silver Hall 60
Silverhall Neighbourhood Park 60
Sir Walter Cope's House 62
South Row, Blackheath 97
Southside House 146, 153
Southwood Lodge 51, 151
Speech Room, Harrow 46
Squire's Mount 44
Squires almshouses 75
St Alfege's Church, Greenwich 112, 150
St Andrew's Church, Enfield 36, 149
St Anne's Church, Kew 126–7, 152
St Barnabas's Church, Dulwich 107
St John's Church, Barnet 22, 149
St John's Church, Bexley 88
St John's Church, Hampstead 41, 151
St John's Church, Isleworth 61
St John's Church, Pinner 70, 153
St Lawrence's Church, Brentford 17–18
St Margaret's Church, Lee 95
St Mary Abbots, Kensington 62, 66, 152
St Mary Magdalen Church, Bermondsey 137, 153
St Mary's Catholic Church, Hampstead 42
St Mary's Church, Barnes 83, 148

St Mary's Church, Bexley 89, 148
St Mary's Church, Harrow 45, 151
St Mary's Church, Monken Hadley 23, 149
St Mary's Church, Rotherhithe 140, 153
St Mary's Church, Walthamstow 75, 153
St Mary's Church, Wimbledon 142
St Mary's Convent, Chiswick 31, 149
St Michael's Church, Highgate 54, 151
St Michael's Convent, Ham 122, 150
St Nicholas's Church, Chiswick 30, 149
St Paul's Church, Brentford 17, 148
St Peter and St Paul's Church, Mitcham 133, 153
St Peter's Church, Dulwich 108
St Peter's Church, Petersham 123, 150
St Philomena's School 100
Stag Lodge, Wimbledon 145
Star and Garter Home 122
Stone Court, Carshalton 99, 101
Strand on the Green 28, 128; **5**
Styleman's Almshouses 89
Sudbrook 121
Sudbrook Park 121
Surrey Commercial Dock Company 136
Surrey Iron Railway 130
Sutton Ecology Centre 101, 149
Sutton Heritage Centre 101, 149
Swains Lane, Highgate 53
Sydenham Hill Nature Reserve 109
Syon House 17–18, 60, 151

Terrace, Barnes 81; **19**
Thackeray, William 23, 32, 66
Thames Tunnel Mills 140
Thames, River 27; villages beside 9
Thornycroft shipbuilding yard 28, 30
Tollemache Almshouses 122
Tooke's Green 71
Tooley Street 137
Town Park, Enfield 37
Townsend Yard, Highgate 53
Tranquil Vale 93
Transport 8, 10
Trellick Tower 43
Trinity Hospital Almshouse, Greenwich 114, 150; **28**
Trollope, Anthony 23
Tudor Cottage 71

Turnham Green 28
Tyburn, River 40

University Boat Race 81
Upper Butts 19
Upper Green, Mitcham 129
Upper Square, Isleworth 59

Vale of Health 44
Vestry House Museum 77, 153
Vestry Road, Walthamstow 77
Vinegar Alley, Walthamstow 76

Wakehams Hill 71
Walpole House 32, 149
Walthamstow 74–8
Walthamstow Grammar School 75–7
Walthamstow High School 78
Walthamstow House 75
Walthamstow Market 78
Walthamstow Village 77
Walthamstow walk 75–8
Wandle Industrial Museum 133, 152
Wandle Mills 98–9, 130
Wandle, River 98, 142; **34**
Wapping Pier Head 139
Water House, Carshalton 100
Water House, Highgate 55
Water House, Walthamstow 75
Waverley House 60
Wax Well, Pinner 72; **16**
Waxwell Farm 68
Waxwell Lane, Pinner 72
West Greenwich 115
West Middlesex Water Works Company 81
Westbourne, River 40
Westfields, Barnes 85
Westminster School 27, 32
Westside House 146
Whaddon Ponds 101
Whitestone Pond 43
William Morris Gallery 78, 153; **18**
Wimbledon 142–7
Wimbledon Common 145
Wimbledon Lodge 146
Wimbledon Society Museum 147, 153
Wimbledon walk 144–7
Wimbledon Windmill Museum 146, 153
Windmill Hill 42
Wood Street, Barnet 20
Woodhall Farm 68, 72
Worple Road, Wimbledon 147
Wricklemarsh 93
Wright's Lane, Kensington 62

York House Place 66